About the author: Born August 29, 1937 in Montreal, Canada; studied at the University of Western Ontario (B.A., 1958, M.A., 1960) and at the University of Rochester (Ph. D. 1962); Instructor to Associate Professor at the Ohio State University from 1962 to 1970; Dean of Faculties and Professor of Philosophy, Roosevelt University, September 1, 1970.

THE MORAL PHILOSOPHY OF GEORGE BERKELEY

ARCHIVES INTERNATIONALES D'HISTOIRE DES IDÉES

INTERNATIONAL ARCHIVES OF THE HISTORY OF IDEAS

33

PAUL J. OLSCAMP

THE MORAL PHILOSOPHY OF GEORGE BERKELEY

THE MORAL PHILOSOPHY OF
GEORGE BERKELEY

by

PAUL J. OLSCAMP

MARTINUS NIJHOFF – THE HAGUE – 1970

B
1349
.E8
04

PRINTED IN THE NETHERLANDS

For Joyce, whom I love

TABLE OF CONTENTS

ABBREVIATIONS OF BERKELEY'S WORKS

All references to Berkeley's Works are to the Nelson and Sons standard edition, edited by Professors Jessop and Luce. The abbreviations given here are used, and all references to other works are also abbreviated. The abbreviations for the other works may be found after the corresponding full titles in the Bibliography.

C   – Correspondence
M   – A Discourse to the Magistrates
SE   – Sermons
GE   – Guardian Essays
Q   – the Querist
A   – Alciphron, or the Minute Philosopher
TV   – An Essay Towards a New Theory of Vision
D   – Three Dialogues Between Hylas and Philonous
I   – Introduction to the Principles
DI   – Draft Introduction to the Principles
P   – The Principles of Human Knowledge
PC   – Philosophical Commentaries
PO   – Passive Obedience
S   – Siris
TVVE – Theory of Vision Vindicated and Explained

INTRODUCTION

Upon the whole, I am inclined to think that the far greater part, if not all, of those difficulties which have hitherto amused philosophers, and blocked up the way to knowledge, are entirely owing to our selves. That we have first raised a dust, and then complain, we cannot see.[1]

... there are some passages that, taken by themselves, are very liable (nor could it be remedied) to gross misinterpretation, and to be charged with most absurd consequences, which, nevertheless, upon an entire perusal will appear not to follow from them.[2]

In an effort to comply with these excellent principles of Berkeley's, I have tried to avoid complex language throughout this book, and to give all of his works the careful scrutiny he urges in order to avoid misplaced emphasis and quoting out of context.

George Berkeley was born in Dysert Castle, Thomastown, Kilkenny, Ireland, in 1685. He is among the best known of Western philosophers, but a brief sketch of the highpoints of his life might nonetheless be of some interest. His father William Berkeley was related to Lord Berkeley of Stratton, who was the Lord Lieutenant of Ireland from 1670 to 1672. His mother was probably related to General Wolfe, the conqueror of Montcalm in Canada. He was educated at Kilkenny School, and at Trinity College, Dublin, where he received Bachelor's and Master's degrees in 1704 and 1707 respectively. For a time he was a fellow of Trinity College. In 1721 Berkeley received both Bachelor of Arts and Doctor of Arts degrees in Divinity, and in 1734 he became the Bishop of Cloyne, after a long period dating from the publication of *Passive Obedience* in 1712, during which he was denied preferment on the basis of a suspicion that he was sympathetic to the Jacobites.

Berkeley was well-travelled, even by present-day standards. In 1713

[1] P., 3
[2] Preface to P

he made his first trip to the Continent, serving as chaplain to Lord Peterborough, a position he secured through the influence of his friend Jonathan Swift. He intended to visit Sicily, but only got as far as Leghorn. Then in 1716, he went abroad with St. George Ashe and visited Rome, Paris, Napels, Ischia, Sicily and various other places. As we shall see, this was a disastrous trip for the rest of the philosophical world. In 1728, he came to the United States, though naturally it was not known by that name then. He intended to found a school for Indians on Bermuda, and while waiting for the funds to arrive from the British parliament, he lived in Rhode Island until 1731. The funds, although voted, never arrived. In the same year that he sailed for the new world, he married Anne Foster.

In 1752, in ill health, Berkeley decided to visit Oxford, and on January 14th, 1753, he died there. To avoid live burial, not uncommon in those days, he directed in his will that he be kept above ground until putrefaction had begun. This was done, and then he was buried.

Berkeley was a man of many and varied interests. Maynard Keynes ranks him among the most astute economists of his time, along with Adam Smith, Malthus, Paley, Fleetwood and Swift.[3] He was profoundly interested in mathematics, and his criticisms of Newtonian mathematics and physics, especially of the theories of the infinitesimal calculus and absolute space and time are acute and remarkably modern. In at least one article he has been called a precursor of Ernst Mach and Albert Einstein![4] His researches with tarwater, humorous as they now seem, witness his sincere interest in medicine, and his practical attempts to aid his parishoners by discovering a remedy for a serious and widespread illness of the times. He is still listed as the discoverer of tarwater, an extract from resin, which is known today as a patent medicine in England.

But his first and last love was philosophy. *The Dictionary of National Biography* claims that Berkeley's *Three Dialogues Between Hylas and Philonous* is the "finest specimen in our language of the conduct of argument by dialogue". If it has a rival, I think it is Berkeley's own *Alciphron, or The Minute Philosopher*, written on the beach at Rhode Island and first published in 1732. It was popular enough to warrant a second edition in that same year. His other works, especially *The*

---

[3] Q., P. 96

[4] Popper, Karl, "Berkeley as a Precursor to Einstein and Mach", forthcoming in a new edition of Berkeley's *The Principles of Human Knowledge*, edited by C. M. Turbayne and to be published by the Bobbs-Merrill Company, Indianapolis

Principles of Human Knowledge, published when he was but 25 years of age and generally acknowledged as his best work, and *The Theory of Vision Vindicated and Explained*, are models of what clear, concise philosophical analysis and synthesis ought to be.

II

In a letter to the American Samuel Johnson, first president of Columbia University, we find the following comment:

As to the second Part of my treatise concerning the Principles of Human Knowledge, the fact is that I had made a considerable progress in it; but the manuscript was lost about fourteen years ago, during my travels in Italy, and I never had the leisure since to do so disagreeable a thing as writing twice on the same subject.[5]

This is not the only reference which proves that the *Principles* was to be a book of at least two parts, and perhaps three or more.[6] It probably would have been rewritten after its loss in 1716, had Berkeley not had so modest a view of his own philosophical importance. In the second part he was apparently going to discuss moral philosophy, metaphysics and philosophy of mind, and it is of course my purpose to develop what I think this moral philosophy would have been. Such questions as the nature of God, free will, and further explorations into the relations of mind and body were to be examined, as well as normative ethics, and just possibly a "logic of demonstration" for systematic ethics. Professor Jessop notes that in place of the various proposed parts of the *Principles* we now have three distinct works; *De Motu, The Analyst,* and *Alciphron,* which discuss some of the questions which were to be raised. But the principles which bind all of his works together are clear, and they never vary. As Jessop states the themes of the *Principles:*

... to refute the scepticism that makes the existence of a corporeal world problematic, and to vindicate theism, and by these means to call knowledge back to the service of man, and man to the service of God.[7]

Referring to the lost Part Two, Berkeley lists the "two great principles of morality" as the "Being of a God and the Freedom of Man".[8] This list is by no means complete. If it was extended to include Berkeley's actual ethical studies and works in ethical analysis, it would

[5] C., p. 282
[6] Editor's Introduction, vol. 11, p. 5
[7] *Ibid.* p. 7
[8] PC, 508

have to include the following: the epistemological-ontological foundation of normative ethics in "the Language of the Author of Nature";
some of the major tenets of what we now call Utilitarianism and Rule-
Utilitarianism; and a defense and exposition of a meta-ethical position
similar to what we now might call theological definism. Berkeley would
naturally not have recognized any of this terminology. On the other
hand, these additional principles, or at least the analyses leading to
them, might well be construed as studies leading to the establishment
of the "two great principles", and there is some reason to think that
this is what Berkeley had in mind.

The most common view of Berkeley's ethics in the minute amount of
writing there is on the subject is summarized in the editor's introduction to *Passive Obedience* in the Nelson edition of Berkeley's works. The
key points in that summary may be stated as follows: Berkeley was a
utilitarian, but this claim must be carefully qualified; he has no written
ethical system; he was not a hedonist; he did not believe that happiness
was the "essence of the moral life" and he did not define the moral
value of acts in terms of the value of their consequences, as traditional
utilitarians do; a more accurate classification might entitle Berkeley a
theological utilitarian; conscience, as with Bishop Butler, is absolute
for Berkeley, and is opposed by Berkeley both to natural benevolence
and to the calculation of results; The moral ideals promulgated by
conscience are similar to the laws of geometry because like the latter
they cannot be perfectly realized in this life, and this fact makes room
for choice based upon empirical circumstances; but this is true only in
the case of "positive" moral laws: - there are also "negative" laws, and
these forbid evil so that, since evil is that which ought never to be done,
there is no exception to and no room for choice based upon circumstances in the case of these rules; they allow only the fundamental
choice of whether to be moral or immoral.[9]

With some of these points I agree, and with many I disagree, as the
sequel will demonstrate. But whatever Berkeley's moral theory was, it
is impossible to discover and analyze it without examining his entire
philosophical system in some detail. This is because his ethics is fundamentally connected to his analysis of the real world and man. In
addition, since we can often learn about the positive views of a man
from his remarks about the claims of others, I shall examine Berkeley's
arguments against some of the Deists, and others of his time.

Alciphron is probably the most important of Berkeley's works so far

[9] PO, Editor's introduction, p. 7

as ethics is concerned, and not *Passive Obedience* as is commonly supposed, or at least this is my opinion. *Alciphron* was immediately criticized upon its appearance in 1732, by Lord Hervey, Mandeville and Peter Browne, among others. Much of the work consists in arguments against the Deists and others often included in that omnibus category, such as Shaftesbury. In one sense, *Alciphron* is a work in Christian apologetics, very like Butler's *Analogy*, and indeed it foreshadows some of the points in that work. But its importance as a unique work in moral philosophy is most often overlooked, and I find this hard to understand because of the plenitude of moral problems discussed in it, problems which more often than not are the same ones which modern moral philosophers worry themselves about. Among these issues are the following: probability as a sufficient ground for faith; determinism versus free will; the qualitative distinction among pleasures; the general good as a criterion for moral behavior; the nature of the general good; the way we learn what our individual good is, and the relation between private and public good; the claim that there is a "moral sense," and its relation, if there is such a sense, to our moral knowledge and behavior; the role of reason in ethics, and the emotive functions of ethical terms. This is by no means a complete list. On some of these topics, Berkeley proves to be the first philosopher to enunciate claims in ethics and meta-ethics now taken for granted, and the range of subjects discussed surely indicates its importance for moral philosophy. Even without its contemporary relevance, it would still be important as a source of careful criticisms of such people as Bernard de Mandeville, Anthony Collins, Mathew Tindal and John Toland, not to mention Shaftesbury and Peter Browne.

In *Alciphron*, as in all of Berkeley's works, the key to his theism, his philosophy of mind, epistemology and ontology, and to his moral philosophy, is discussed and examined in detail. This "key" is Berkeley's characterization of nature as a language, whose author is God. The metaphor is not unique with Berkeley (it is common among the works of the Deists for example) but his use of it, and his final acceptance of it as a literal truth, are to my knowledge unique, and his arguments about it are original and very provoking. Naturally, my claim that this is the key to his philosophy must be proven and this is one of my purposes.

As in the case of Berkeley's other major works, *Alciphron* was not unanimously cheered by its public. One adjective-monger called it:

... a tissue of libertine sophisms, gratuitously contrived in order to destroy the most sure and lofty principles of Morality, Politics, and even of Religion.[10]

And another critic, somewhat less acute and sophisticated than this one, understands Euphranor (Berkeley) to be saying

... that square things are round; and that vast, rough, opaque bodies, were little, smooth, luminous things, no bigger than sixpences.[11]

In those days, your reviewers were *really* your enemies!

Many of Berkeley's lesser known writings, such as his *Sermons* and the *Guardian Essays*, are also important for his moral philosophy, but they are almost never even mentioned. For example, the distinction between "natural" and "fantastical" pleasures, without which his so-called "hedonism" cannot be understood, and equally crucial for comprehension of what he means by "happiness," is discussed at length only in the *Guardian Essays*. And even in these lesser works, the language metaphor occurs again and again.

By this time it must be clear that although I am going to disagree with many of the claims in the "standard" interpretation of Berkeley's moral philosophy, I am also going to support one of the central ones, which is that if Berkeley was not a utilitarian, then at least there are several remarkable similarities, and in some cases identical views, shared by Berkeley and such later utilitarians as John Stuart Mill. But strangely enough, the few recent writers that there are on the subject have mostly doubted the utilitarian interpretation.[12] For example, one author, referring to Berkeley's discussion of moral rules in *Passive Obedience*, says this about it:

And so far are these laws from being the *a posteriori* conclusions of Utilitarian calculation, that "these propositions are called *laws of nature*, because they are universal, and do not derive their obligation from any civil sanction, but immediately from the Author of Nature Himself. They are said to be *stamped on the mind*, to be *engraven on the tables of the heart*, because they are well known to mankind, and suggested and inculcated by conscience. Lastly, they are termed *eternal rules of reason*, because they necessarily result from the nature of things, and may be demonstrated by the infallible deductions of reason.[13]

Certainly, such references to Berkeley are not *prima facie* the sort of

---

[10] Abbe Pierre Desfontaines, quoted in Harry M. Bracken, *The Early Reception of Berkeley's Immaterialism*, Martinus Nijhoff, the Hague (1965) p. 3
[11] Probably Lord Hervey
[12] Among the recent writers are John Wild, G. Dawes Hicks, G. A. Johnston, and C. R. Morris
[13] BM, p. 521

remarks that a utilitarian makes, and it is therefore incumbent upon me to explain them, which I shall do.

Secondly, many scholars have thought that Berkeley was more concerned with a logic of "moral demonstration" à la John Locke than with the substantive questions of ethics, such as the nature, use and content of moral rules. For Locke, mathematics and ethics both consisted of demonstrable truths, because the propositions of both disciplines dealt with complex ideas and those abstract ideas which Locke calls "mixed modes and relations." Just as the mathematician deals with the abstract general idea of a geometrical figure such as a triangle, and not with actual triangular things, so the ethicist deals with the abstract ideas of right and wrong and not with actual actions. The two sciences are both axiomatic systems, and thus the relations between the principles and the subsidiary rules of ethics, as of mathematics, are necessary.[14]

Berkeley disagreed profoundly with the doctrine of abstract general ideas, but the early entries in the *Philosophical Commentaries* can be construed as a hint that he thought Locke was on the right track in searching for a method of demonstration. This is what has led some scholars to think that with his own revisions of the theory, Berkeley too believed in moral demonstration. His remarks about a possible "algebraic" ethical demonstration, or a "mix't Mathematics" of ethics seem to lend credence to this view. But what the critics of the utilitarian position fail to see (for they are also the main supporters of this interpretation) is that although *deduction* is used in the systematization of ethics for Berkeley, it is trivial, because it succeeds only in virtue of the fact that the signs in ethics are arbitrary, as in mathematics. When we consider ethics aside from the logical aspects of its systematic expression however, we see that it is not at all trivial – it is a discipline involving reasoning about particulars, and practical action.[15] Berkeley thought that if ethics was demonstrable in a non-trivial sense, then there should be no widespread dissension about ethical principles – but there is.[16] Furthermore, not only does Berkeley disagree with the theory of abstract general ideas, but he also thought that geometry was an applied or practical rather than a pure science – his views of methematics as given in the *Principles, Alciphron, De Motu* and the *Analyst* are almost pragmatic or instrumentalist in the modern sense of those terms – and

[14] DB, p. 421
[15] DB, p. 423
[16] DB, p. 425

he rejects the theory of truth which was accepted by Locke and the Deists, the theory that truth is a function of the correspondence of ideas. Finally, there is a lot of evidence which suggests that the early interest in moral demonstration was temporary, and not renewed in the years of his mature philosophizing.

I believe that an excellent argument against the "moral demonstration" thesis has been given in an article entitled "Berkeley on Moral Demonstration," *Journal of the History of Ideas*, vol. XXII, number 2 (1961), by G. P. Conroy, and I shall discuss the matter along the lines raised in this paper. In addition, I shall examine certain related issues such as those raised by the claim that moral rules are *a priori* for Berkeley. I might say here that in the 17th century, one pretty well had to choose between two schools in ethics, the mathematical and the theological. This was because of the influence of Descartes and Spinoza on the one hand, and the revolt against authoritarian theories on the other, which was due to the advent of the Renaissance and the Reformation.[17] I believe that in this conflict, Berkeley is clearly on the side of the authoritarians, though I also think that his position is one which is compatible with a sort of utilitarianism – which is a claim I shall explain and clarify in the sequel.

Berkeley refers to Spinoza now and then in his writings, though not often. The latter's influence on Berkeley was slight, and came second-hand for the most part, through the Deists, particularly John Toland. Spinoza has no direct bearing on Berkeley's ethics, so far as I can see, except that there might be an indirect connection through Berkeley's criticisms of material substance, the theory of abstract general ideas, and his abandonment of moral demonstration. Berkeley's opinion of Spinoza was the then current ill-informed one – a hodgepodge of pejorative accusations designed to support the view that Spinoza was an infidel, an atheist, and a generally pernicious bounder. For all these reasons I shall not discuss Spinoza. In case some readers are interested in Spinoza's relations to the Deists, whom I shall discuss at some length, I recommend the works of Rosemary Colie, F. J. Heinemann and A. O. Lovejoy, especially those listed in my bibliography. John Toland's *Letters to Serena* are especially interesting in this connection.

---

[17] DB, p. 422

III

At some point in his mental ramblings before writing a book, every author asks himself why the book should be written, or at least, every author *should* ask himself this question. Here are my reasons for this book: 1. Important though George Berkeley is, there has never been a complete study of his moral philosophy. 2. The places where the subject is discussed are all excessively brief (they are all articles) often mistaken I think, and they concentrate on remarks in the *Philosophical Commentaries* and *Passive Obedience* for the most part, to the exclusion of the other equally or more important works. 3. The "key," as I have called it, to his philosophy, including ethics, is not so much as mentioned in any of the works, so far as I can recall. This key is the language metaphor. 4. Not only is this the first study of his moral philosophy of any detail, but it just might be important, because Berkeley either explicitly or implicitly stated or foreshadowed several crucial distinctions in ethics now largely accepted as sound. Of these I need only mention two here, which I shall discuss at length later: the distinction between the kinds of qualitative differences among pleasures, as well as quantitative ones, and the emotive as opposed to the cognitive uses of ethical terms. Mill is usually given credit for the first distinction, and A. J. Ayer and C. L. Stevenson, with a bow to Ogden and Richards, are usually considered to be the major authorities for the latter. But both claims are stated and carefully discussed by Berkeley.

I have many persons to thank, and I hope those not mentioned for reasons of space will understand and know of my gratitude. Professor C. M. Turbayne has been steadfast in his support, and readers of his own book, *The Myth of Metaphor*, will realize my debt to him. Professor Richard Garner gave me invaluable aid at the start of the project by patiently straightening my sometimes tortuous swerves around and through the confusing terminology and distinctions of modern ethics, and through many discussions of Berkeley. Professor Bernard Rosen read and commented on the MS in detail, and his remarks were also invaluable, and the same is true of Professors Alan Hausman and Wallace Anderson. The Ohio State University awarded me a grant of Assigned Research Leave which enabled me to travel in order to study Berkeley and the Deists, and it also provided some funds for secretarial help. Professor Robert Turnbull also worked hard for me, in ways too numerous, and sometimes too personal, to list here. The staff of the British Museum were uniformly patient and cordial, and I thank them heartily.   PJO, Columbus, Spring, 1969

CHAPTER I

THE LANGUAGE OF THE AUTHOR OF NATURE

A central feature of Berkeley's philosophy is his use of a certain metaphor, which he developed highly, and which he came in the end to accept as a literal truth. This metaphor is his characterization of the natural world as a language through which God speaks to man, instructing him in ways of caring for himself, enabling him to predict the future, or some of it, and teaching him how he ought to act. Berkeley was neither the first nor the last to use this metaphor (it is common in the works of the Deists for example) but so far as I know, no one else developed it to such a degree, and no one used it for such important purposes within a philosophical system. If I am correct, this metaphor, which is really a complete theory, is the keystone to George Berkeley's ontology, epistemology, and moral philosophy. In this chapter, I intend to do three things: 1. To show why Berkeley thought that nature was a language, and to demonstrate that the metaphor not only occurs constantly throughout his writings, but also that it undergoes a progressive development in them; 2. To show that he finally came to accept the metaphor as a literal truth, and 3. to demonstrate the importance of the language theory for the understanding of the foundations of his entire philosophy, including his moral thinking.

I. THE NATURE OF THE METAPHOR

In the *Essay Towards a New Theory of Vision,* Berkeley coins the phrase "Language of the Author of Nature"; in *Siris,* he speaks of natural laws as a "grammar" for understanding the "rational discourse" of nature.[1] In between these first and last works, in everything of philosophical relevance that he ever wrote, the metaphor recurs again and again. The first purpose of the metaphor was to serve as part of a proo

---

[1] S, 252-253; TV, 147

that God exists, and has certain attributes. Secondly (but closely related to the first purpose) Berkeley intended to disprove atheism and scepticism by demonstrating the trustworthiness of our perceptions, and the immediate involvement of God in our everyday lives.

The argument for the existence of God has two parts, and the language metaphor has little to do with the first part. This first part proceeds from his thesis that the existing things of the world are of two sorts, minds and bodies, and that perception is not an effect of bodies acting upon our minds.[2] The latter is true because there is no motion, in the sense of efficient causes, in the natural world:

... if we review singly those qualities of body, (impenetrability, extension and figure) and whatever other qualities there may be, we shall see that they are all in fact passive and that there is nothing active in them which can in any way be understood as the source or principle of motion.[3]

Examine your perceptions minutely, and you will find nothing in them which is motion – you will only find lights and colors, hardness, various odors, etc. The natural world therefore does not move for Berkeley, *if* by motion we understand what was once understood under the name "efficient cause," or what we now understand as "force." Such entities may indeed be posited as explanatory things, but this does not entail that they exist, and if we are to talk about existent bodies, then Berkeley believes that our experience informs us that they are inactive. What is this "experience" that so informs us? It is composed, with regard to its content, of what is given in sensation, which Berkeley calls "ideas of sense," and of our awareness of minds and relations, and finally of inferences which can be based upon these factors.[4] Minds, our experience again informs us, are active, and so they *are* causes. Moreover, *only* minds are active. Thus, if there are any causes, then they must be minds.[5] Since mental data are not given directly to sense, and all our knowledge of the real world, the natural world, is derived from this source, we have no immediate awareness of natural active causes.

But Berkeley also accepted the principle that nothing exists without a cause, and so our ideas of sense must also have a cause, which must therefore be a mind or minds. This is the heart of his famous (or infamous) dictum that the existence of ideas of sense, and thus of objects

[2] PC, 176A; P. 1; S. 290; DHP, p. 233
[3] DM, 22
[4] P. 1, 18, 19, 20, 25, 26, 27
[5] PC 712, 669

formed from them (more on this subject later on) consists in their being perceived by some mind. Clearly, I am not perceiving all things at all times, nor even any one thing at all times, nor is any other human mind. It is equally obvious that the top of Mount Everest does not disappear when no human is looking at it. Berkeley concludes that there must be a cosmic mind who *is* always perceiving all things, and he calls this cosmic mind "God".[6] In this deceptively simple way, Berkeley believes that he has achieved a brief and simple proof for God's existence. But hidden under the simple language is a mind-boggling set of ontological and epistemological principles, as startling as the "Copernican Revolution" of Kant – indeed, Kant's "revolution" probably owes a considerable debt to Berkeley.[7]

    For Berkeley's purposes, especially his moral ones, it would not do to rest with the simple proof of a cosmic mind, for such a being has no *prima facie* involvement in our personal lives. Berkeley was interested in proving the existence of the Christian God – a personal, wise, provident and benevolent god, immediately involved in the welfare of mankind. Thus, the second part of his proof for God is not strictly speaking a proof that God exists, but rather it is an argument which concludes that God has certain attributes. Neither of the two parts of the argument depends upon our actually perceiving God, for in Berkeley's view, we do not perceive even human beings this way. When I speak of men, I am not referring only to that which I see, but to that which I infer from what I see – the "thinking principle", the "individual thinking thing" which lies, so to speak, behind the appearances. Otherwise, corpses might be human beings. The thinking thing is inferred from signs and "tokens" which suggest it, such as the motions which are characteristic of those bundles of my perceptions which I call men. A particularly important set of these signs which serve as the ground for my inference to another mind is known as "language". When we perceive a man speaking or writing, what we perceive are "arbitrary, outward, sensible signs, having no resemblance or necessary connection with the things they stand for and suggest." Languages serve several purposes, and *if* nature is a language, then it should, through many and various combinations of signs, make known an indefinite number of things to us. It should teach us what to avoid and what to pursue for our own good, teach us the "natures" of the things we are

---

[6] DHP, p. 212
[7] Turbayne, Colin M. "Kant's Refutation of Dogmatic Idealism", *Philosophical Quarterly*, 5, 20 (July, 1955)

acquainted with, and tell us how to act with regard to both near and distant things, and this is just the beginning of a long list of functions which Berkeley thinks a natural language must have if it is to be a language. But if we can legitimately infer the existence of other human minds and their attributes from the language used by men, then if nature is a language "spoken" by a cosmic mind, we should also be able to infer the attributes of this mind from that language.[8] Among the attributes we infer of men's minds from their language, though not merely on this evidence, are their moral properties, and Berkeley thinks that if nature is a language, we ought to be able to make similar inferences about God. In particular, he thinks that we should be able to show that God is provident, wise, and good.[9]

Although the language metaphor is mentioned as early as Berkeley's *Philosophical Commentaries* (his private notebooks) its first careful development and formulation is in the *Essay Towards a New Theory of Vision*, and it arises in the context of Berkeley's efforts to solve a series of problems in vision, the most important of which is what we mean when we say that something is "at a distance" from us.

Berkeley's most important philosophical insight, the one which leads through him to Hume, is in my opinion his observation of the fact that the connections among the data of our various senses are contingent, not necessary.[10] He also noticed that in spite of this, we call what we see and what we touch by the same name,[11] and in fact as we shall see, we call related data of all these senses by the same name in most instances. There is a parallel phenomenon in language: there is no necessary connection between words and what they signify, whether the connection be taken to be one of resemblance or any other sort, and he found the similarity between this fact and the seeming lack of connection between, for example, what we see and what we feel, singularly informative.[12] To Berkeley it seemed that in both cases, the relation between the word and what it signifies, and the lights and colors and what we feel, is founded simply upon their previous constant conjunction.[13] Hence, so is the expectation we have of *future* events or sensations upon experiencing another set of events or sensations, and so is

[8] Alc. IV. 5-7
[9] *Ibid.*, 14
[10] TV, 127-130
[11] TV, 127
[12] TV, 128-129
[13] DHP, p. 202

the expectation which we have that words will retain the same meanings in the future.

The point seems simple enough, but the results of failing to realize it have been important, because they have involved our self-deception. We say that we hear a coach when not looking at it, but a coach is not only a set of auditory sensations; we say that we see a red-hot iron bar, but "the solidity and heat of the iron are not the objects of sight." If we were precise, we should say that we heard a sound which suggested the *visible* (or tangible, etc.) coach from experience, and that the heat and solidity of the iron bar, both tactile sensations, were suggested to us by the color and figure presented to sight.[14] We normally call a visible and a tangible cube by the same name, "cube". But again, if we are to speak accurately, we should say that we are talking about two quite different sets of data or sensations, even though we are using the same name to speak of both of them.

In the case of the analysis of distance, the same sort of considerations apply. There is no thing called distance. It is not a "line turned endwise to the eye", nor is it a function of the angles made by the imaginary lines connecting my eyes with a focal point. What does happen when I say that I see something at a distance is this: after the perception of certain visual sensations I come to expect certain tactile data, after there has been a sufficient period of association between the two sorts of data so that the expectation of the future data has been established. Other data are of course involved too, such as the sensation of eye strain and certain movements of the head.[15] Distance is therefore nothing in itself, but is rather a function of the measurement of the temporal interval between different sets of sensations. In Berkeley's words:

Looking at an object I perceive a certain visible figure and colour, with some degree of faintness and other circumstances, which from what I have already observed, determine me to think that if I advance forward so many paces or miles, I shall be affected with such and such ideas of touch: So that in truth and strictness of speech I neither see distance itself, nor anything that I take to be at a distance.[16]

The foundation of the suggestion causing me to expect certain sorts of sensations upon the occurrence of others is basic to his theory of the

---

[14] DHP, p. 204
[15] TV, 44, 45
[16] TV, 45

natural language. Either I know ideas of sense directly, or through suggestion established by the constant conjunction of sets of data. I can infer from my present data of sight that if I move my body for a certain length of time, I will experience different ideas or sensations, for example, the object will become more distinct, or I shall experience certain tactile data, which I am not now experiencing. But the suggestion which is the basis of this inference is not innate. It is learned, and this would not be the case if there was a necessary connection between the data of the various senses. It is learned in exactly the same way that the meanings of words in a language are learned. Very few people would want to quarrel with the claim that our knowledge of the meanings of words is not innate, but many disagree with the other claim. In Berkeley's view, there is a crucial experiment which we can use to test its truth. The experiment was first suggested in a letter from Dr. Molyneux to John Locke. If we could find a man born blind, who would therefore understand the meanings of words in terms of the data of senses other than sight, and if such a man could be made to see, then upon first gaining sight, one of the following two events should occur: (1) if there is a necessary connection between the data of touch and sight, then without learning, the man should recognize that what he now sees is the same thing as that which he feels. Or to put it another way, he should recognize that the word "cube", which he formerly understood to apply to what he touched, also applies to what he now sees. (2) If this does not happen, then it will be seen that he does not recognize that what he sees and touches are the same thing, and a period of learning will be necessary for him to associate the two kinds of data, and thereby learn the meanings of words which apply to both. If (1) happened, we could conclude that there was some sort of necessary connection between the data, whereas the connection would be contingent if (2) was the result. The advent of (2) would also support the thesis that the foundation of future expectations concerning data which normally occur after another set has been experienced is precisely the experience of their *common* association in the past.[17] Such cases have been found, and the evidence suggests that Berkeley is right, that is, (2) rather than (1) has been the result.

If Berkeley is correct, then we are left with the task of explaining the *continuity* of the natural world. The most important step in his particular solution, after the proof that God exists, is just this claim that the connection among the data of the senses is contingent, for it

[17] TV, 135

will turn out that as our expectation of the future is contingent upon regular constant conjunction, so those constant conjunctions are contingent upon the will of God. Before proceeding with the development of the metaphor however, I have still to discuss the other reasons Berkeley gives for believing that nature is a language.

As with the original insight concerning the mutual lack of necessary connection between words and what they signify and the data of one sense vis à vis those of another, so the rest of his evidence for the natural language thesis is also based upon a comparison between nature and actual languages. One of the first and most obvious facts about verbal and written signs is that they may suggest absent as well as present things. This seems to be true of my sense experiences as well, or at least, it is true of some of them. Certainly it is true if what we mean by "absent" is "not physically present", or "at a distance", as my remarks about the problem of distance in Berkeley prove. There is no reason to think that it is not true if what we mean by "absent" is temporally absent. For Berkeley, time consisted in the sequence of my ideas, and it is therefore safe to presume that to say that a significate was temporally absent would for him merely mean that there were other intervening data experienced between the idea of sense or the set of ideas taken as the sign or signs, and the ones taken as the significate. Whether signs signify what is present with them, or what is absent, they only make sense within a given context. It is easy to verify this in verbal languages, for examples of words which mean one thing in one context and another in a different one are too numerous to mention. It is also easy to discover *different* words which have the *same* meanings in some contexts. The reason the meanings of words can vary like this is simply that the nature of the associative relation changes with the introduction of new factors. Thus, the meaning of the word "help" is one thing when I hear or read it within the context of my home, as for example when my wife says "Help me with this vacuuming, will you?", and then walks out the door, and quite another thing when I hear it shouted by a man in the middle of a lake beside an overturned boat. In spite of our ability to change the meanings of signs by using different contexts however, we should not forget that the *ground* of the associative relation remains the same in any context, no matter what the nature of the sign is. For example, the ground of the relation between sounds and what they suggest is the same as that for the relation between characters and what *they* suggest: compare the grounds of these two signs and what they suggest: 'dòg and a dog, and "dog" and 'dòg. The ground in both cases is solely and simply constant conjunction. Notice that I am not denying, nor does Berkeley, that in some cases there are *other* grounds for the relation between two things, for example, there are inferences which we can make which are based upon the causal relation, and upon the relation of resemblance. But as we shall see, these relations are not sign-to-thing-signified relations for him. Effects do not *signify* their causes, though they can *imply* them. Furthermore, we shall see that inferences based on these two relations in particular are *necessary* for Berkeley, whereas those based upon the sign relation are not. For example, given that everything has a cause and that only minds are causal agents, it follows that my sense ideas have a cause which is a mind, and it would be contradictory to assert the opposite. The importance of this sort of inference for the first part of Berkeley's argument for the existence of God can scarcely be over-emphasized, but the inference does not depend upon the claim that nature is a language, so it should not be considered here.

We should also notice that there is clearly a difference between the relation of visual data to tactile ones, and the relation between two visual data of the same sort, say, two red spots. The latter sort of relation does not depend upon constant conjunction as the former does. Berkeley does not discuss the problem of resemblance anywhere at length, though it becomes crucially important for him, and the places where he does discuss it are inadequate. But the only point I wish to raise here is that there is a difference between the ground of this relation, and that between a sign and what it signifies, and it is only the latter relation which is involved in the establishment of the language metaphor at this stage.

Although the meanings of signs vary with their context, they must at any given time be used consistently to have meaning. That is to say, although a sign, say A, might mean X in context Y and Z in context W, it must retain similar meanings in similar contexts, for if it did not, there would be no basis upon which the association necessary for its understanding could be established. And this raises two other related points. The first is that a sign is always a sign to some user of the sign, and hence, all sign relationships are three-termed: a sign, its significate, and the user of the sign. Language is a tool, with many purposes; but words do not have purposes – their users do. Secondly, the decision to use a particular set of marks or sounds to be a sign, or the convention within which such usage arises, is arbitrary, in the sense that some other set of marks or sounds could have been used to perform the same function. But once the use is established, we must remain consistent with it at the penalty of not being understood. And it follows from these points that it is not *what* is used as a sign that defines it as a sign, nor a set of signs as a language, but rather it is the uses to which the signs are put, their scope, variety, etc. which provide the criteria for deciding whether this is a sign, and that set of signs a language. There are naturally many functions which language serves, among them the communication of ideas, for which many have thought it necessary that all words denote or name something. But this is not always so, as is shown by those uses of signs where the primary purpose is to cause or inhibit action, or to raise passions, etc. In such cases, ideas do not normally occur to us upon the use of the signs, and there is some doubt as to whether there are *any* ideas which correspond to some of the signs which may be used in these ways. In short, the communication of ideas is not the only role of languages.

In any language, there are certain basic signs which must be ostensively defined in order to tie the language to what it means, which is just one way of saying that the process whereby we may define the meanings of signs by giving other signs must come to an end with signs that are primitive, in the sense that they refer directly, and must be defined by giving that to which they refer. This is not to say that the things used as these basic signs, the marks or sounds, may not change, for the choice of these is arbitrary as I have already stated. It follows that even in the case of ostensively defined signs, inferences about future meanings will only be probable, and this is so even if it is also true, that at any given time we must be consistent in the use of signs in order to be understood and to understand the language. It is also important to note that for Berkeley, such inferences must be made by the understanding, for inference implies the possibility of error, and sense never errs.

Normally we are more interested in what is signified than we are in the sign. When I am reading a book, or typing this page, I am not particularly interested in the actual letters on the pages, but rather in what they mean. Because of this, we often overlook the sign and concentrate on the signified, and it is this fact which leads to the "telescoping" of our languages, as in the examples of hearing a coach and seeing a red-hot iron bar. When we come to talk about the meanings of words, and about the structures of our languages, this phenomena is often misleading.

Finally, it should be noted that signs can signify both backwards and forwards in time, as in the case of a footprint, or the orange light at the crossing.[18]

All of these points are for Berkeley factual claims about ordinary languages. But they are also claims which are true of nature, and if together they provide us with a definition of what a language is, then nature must be a language. He sincerely believed this, and set out to prove it. *The Essay Towards a New Theory of Vision* is an attempt to explain the relations between the data of sight and touch in terms of these very properties of language, and in the *Principles of Human Knowledge* the arguments are the same, except that they are now extended to the data of all the senses. The same principles are specifically ennunciated in *Alciphron, or the Minute Philosopher*. As with our own languages, so with the natural world. It is composed of

... arbitrary, outward, sensible signs, having no resemblance or necessary connection with the things they stand for and suggest ...

As words have no essential connection with what they mean, so colors have no necessary relation to the tangible data they may suggest. But as with words, natural signs make known "an endless variety of things", including the "natures" of things, what we ought to pursue and what we ought to avoid, and how to "regulate our motions" with respect to things which are both near and far, temporally and spatially, in order to achieve our ends.[19] How do they do this? The answer is once more, just as verbal signs do. Words do not cause their meanings, they *signify* them, and so,

... the connexion of ideas does not imply the relation of cause and effect, but only of a mark or sign with the thing signified. The fire which I see is not the cause of the pain I feel upon my approaching it, but the mark that forewarns me of it ...

Individual ideas, lights, colors, etc. are "formed into machines", that is, objects, among which there are also sign relationships, and the reason this occurs is identical with the reason that we combine letters and sounds into words, namely that

... a few original ideas may be made to signify a great number of effects and actions ...[20]

In both cases, individual data and objects, the ground of the signifi-

[18] PC, 221; DHP, p. 238; Alc. VII, 12; TVVE, 39, 40, 42; TV, 109, 140, 143, 147; Alc. IV, 5, 7, 12; Draft, pp. 137-139; P. 65
[19] Alc. IV, 7
[20] P. 65

cation is constant conjunction alone, and Berkeley is not speaking here about inferences made on the basis of resemblance or the cause-effect relation. On the lowest level our learning of sign relationships by constant conjunction of sign and significate is equivalent to learning by ostensive definition, though of course he does not call it that.[21] But on higher levels, any language must serve more extensive purposes than mere "pointing" or denotation, and Berkeley believes that nature meets this requirement too. To distinguish between our languages and God's, Berkeley calls those invented by men "artificial", and nature becomes the "natural language".[22]

2. SIGNS AND SYMBOLS, SUGGESTION AND JUDGMENT

It is regrettably necessary at this point to interrupt the continuity of my discussion of the language metaphor in order to discuss something essential to the understanding of Berkeley's theory, but which he himself does not examine in detail. He seldom discusses the nature of a sign itself, nor does he make distinctions among kinds of signs. Moreover, he makes an explicit distinction between "suggestion" on the level of sense perception, and judgments made by the understanding, but he does not seem to realize the enormous difficulties this distinction raises for his whole philosophy – it is a Pandora's box of nothing but trouble. It is, however, important to clarify these issues and their consequences before proceeding to the fuller exposition of the metaphor.

We might begin by distinguishing between a sign, and a sign-vehicle. A sign is a sign-vehicle with meaning, whereas a sign-vehicle, at this stage, might be anything – marks upon paper, noises, objects, etc. The point is that sign-vehicles, whether they be data of sense or objects or anything else, may *become* signs, if they are used for a consistent purpose within a linguistic framework, for which a necessary condition, with the exception of technical terms, is their constant conjunction with what is to be signified. This should not mislead us into thinking that all uses of signs are, or involve, conscious inferences, for Berkeley makes a clear distinction between mere perception and judgment, and between suggestion and inference. Suggestion and perception are functions of the senses, whereas inferences, judgments, are made by the understanding.[23] It follows, in the broad sense, that there are different *uses*

[21] TV, 147
[22] TVVE, 40
[23] TVVE, 42

of signs, some cognitive and others not, and in conjunction with this, there are different kinds of signs, notably, those which are symbols and those which are not. Some philosophers have held that all signs are symbols. Most would deny this, and H. H. Price is one who does.[24] Price's remarks are revealing when applied to Berkeley, for they expose the problems inherent in his views. Price is convinced that recognition is the most fundamental intellectual process. It is "the first stage towards the acquisition of a primary or basic concept", and hence thought and intelligent action depend upon it.[25] Recognition remains essential once we have basic concepts, for they would be useless unless we could recognize instances of them; in Price's words, unless the concepts were "cashable" in instances. There are two kinds of recognition, primary and secondary, and primary recognition is also called "noticing", which is "immediate", "direct", or "intuitive". Secondary recognition is "indirect, mediate, or inferential".[26] To say that secondary recognition is inferential is only to say that signs are involved in a way that they are not on the primary level, namely, they indicate something which is not noticed at the same time the sign is used.[27] Primary recognition is more involved with what I have called sign-vehicles; it is the "immediate awareness" of the "something given" in sensation.[28] In neither process is the complex sort of thought involving symbols found, for both kinds of recognition may be pre-verbal, and here Price seems to be presuming that symbols are all verbal, a point which will become important in a moment. Secondary recognition is dependent upon primary in two ways: we learn it by means of primary recognition, and we verify it the same way.[29] I cannot know that X is a sign of Y unless and until I have first become aware of X and Y, and I cannot recognize that the signification has or has not been fulfilled unless and until I can verify that X and Y have occurred, that is, notice them.

Secondary recognition can be mistaken, that is, illusions may occur, or at a much higher level, false inferences may be drawn. Primary recognition cannot be mistaken in Price's view, because the concept of being mistaken presupposes the use of signs or symbols within a developed syntactical framework, which mere "noticing" does not

[24] Price, H. H., *Thinking and Experience*, Hutchinson's University Library, London (1953), Chapter VI, *passim*. Hereinafter referred to as "Price, p.—"
[25] Price, p. 35
[26] Price, p. 45
[27] Price, p. 46
[28] Price, p. 47
[29] Price, p. 51

assume.[30] This is why primary recognition in Price's view does not involve signification, and *a fortiori*, symbolization. Obviously, the "syntactical" structure required at the lower levels of secondary recognition will be defined only in terms of conventional uses, since it might be pre-verbal. For example, clouds can signify that which is not present with them, rain, but this does not presuppose the use of symbols. Signification on this level is more practical than theoretical, tied to action more than to contemplation.[31] But nonetheless, the foundation from which "free" as opposed to "tied" thinking can develop, to use Price's terms, is present in secondary recognition. Some of the properties of "free" thought, thought occurring independently of perception, which are also properties of secondary recognition, are as follows: the sign relations are three-termed, involving a sign, an observer, and what is signified; the sign may signify both what is present and what is absent; the sign relation is established by constant conjunction; it may be falsified, or perhaps more appropriately on the lower levels, unfulfilled; the sign need not be a member of the class of objects to which the significate belongs (eg. visual sensations are not tactile ones) though it *may* be; there are both short and long range signs, and signs which point backwards in time as well as forward (eg. a footprint and a cloud); there are also strong and weak signs, and degrees of both.[32] The last point especially concerns a type of signification found in phenomena of "complication", an example of which is the seeming fact that ice *looks* cold. Here, what happens is that "The idea of coldness ... is 'complicated' (or 'blended') with the visual sensation, and does not just follow it or accompany it", which of course entails that complication may not be analyzed as common associative thinking. Interestingly, Price thinks that this is the sort of example which Berkeley is using in the *Essay Towards a New Theory of Vision*, which would, I think, come as a very considerable surprise to Berkeley.[33] In Price's view, this sort of sign is especially strong when it is short range. As he says, "one experiences a most disconcerting shock of surprise ... if the wall when touched feels quite soft."[34]

The analysis of weak signs reveals *negative* signs, for "if A signifies B and B fails to occur, I may recollect that in this case A was accompanied by something else X; and I may notice later that when A is thus

[30] Price, pp. 85-87
[31] Price, p. 91
[32] Price, pp. 106-107
[33] Price, p. 99
[34] Price, p. 109

accompanied, B regularly or fairly regularly fails to occur."[35] X therefore becomes a negative sign, which, like other signs, can be strong or weak, long range or short. It is a sign of the "non-occurrence of B". Negative signs must always be accompanied by positive ones, for the concept of what does not occur must be brought to mind by a sign *for* its occurrence, while at the same time I notice the stronger negative sign which indicates that it will *not* occur. Negative signs therefore arise only in situations of conflict, or as Price says: "p can only signify not-q when there is something else p_1 which weakly signifies q."[36]

Finally, for my purposes, there is even at the level of secondary recognition something which Price calls "chain-signification", where A, in the chain "A signifies B signifies C", can come to be taken as a sign of C after a long period of association. It is this sort of telescoping which I believe Berkeley to be talking about in his analysis of such examples as the hearing of the coach and the seeing of the red-hot iron bar, as opposed to Price, whom I presume would classify these as examples of complication.[37] But since these examples of Berkeley's are verbal, it would seem that they presuppose the use of symbols.

The distinction between signs and signs which are symbols is unclear. Certainly many different sorts of sign can become symbols, for example, words, gestures, pictures, images etc., so I see no reason to restrict the class of signs which can become symbols to *verbal* signs. What is it then which makes a sign capable of becoming a symbol? This is a very complex topic, and one which I cannot examine in detail here. I shall therefore restrict my comments to those criteria which are of some relevance to Berkeley's theory.

There are clearly properties of the sign-vehicle itself which are relevant to the question of whether, after it has become a sign, it can then also become a symbol. As Price notes, black clouds, though a sign of rain, are certainly not a symbol of rain in the way in which "rain" is.[38] Some philosophers have discussed the difference in terms of two different kinds of meaning, clouds meaning rain in the sign sense, and "rain" in the symbol sense, but this seems to beg the questions at their source. Certainly the question of the *use* to which symbols can be put is relevant here though, since if it could be shown that some signs cannot be put to typically symbolic uses, this might provide a criterion to distin-

[35] Price, p. 126
[36] Price, p. 127
[37] DHP, p. 204
[38] Price, p. 144

guish between the two. Two common sorts of symbolic uses are description, and various emotive functions. It is within the context of description that the concepts of truth and falsity seem to arise, and symbols so used are complex – usually sentences – and are always used within the framework of syntactical rules. Very few instances are to be found of symbols which have *only* emotive functions, but there are some: Prices' examples are intriguing – "faugh!", "pshaw!" and "boo!" Most symbols which can be used emotively are expressive as well. Description or reference is usually thought, in connection with the questions of truth and falsity, to involve a correspondence of some sort between some of the terms in the description, and what it is that is described, and if this is true, then it would be odd indeed to think of clouds as *descriptive* of rain, unless one were willing to equate the relation of "occurs before" with some sort of correspondence. It may be then that this typical use of symbols provides a criterion for distinguishing signs from symbols. But it is very important here to notice that the criterion depends upon a theory of meaning and a theory of truth – the correspondence theory – for Berkeley does *not* hold this theory, and the ramifications of this fact are fundamentally important for the natural language theory which he espouses.

There is another factor which must be considered, which is that it is usually thought that symbols must be *producible* by those who use them, whereas signs need not be. Thus, clouds (we shall presume) are not producible by man, whereas the word "cloud" is, and thus, the former may not be a symbol. Were this the case, it would seem to restrict Berkeley's natural language to a language of signs with no symbols.

But here again, Berkeley belongs to a unique class of which he is, I think, the only member. The signs in the natural language are certainly producible by God, who is their author, and therefore they may, on the above criterion, be symbols at least for God. But more importantly, he also believes, as we shall see, that humans can learn about God's intentions through nature because these are in some way expressed in the natural language. It would seem to follow that nature is in some way symbolic for us too. And strange though it might sound, truth and falsity are to be found in the natural language as well, because Berkeley thought these concepts had to do with the functions of the uses of signs and symbols alone, rather than some correspondence between the signs and "facts", be they ideas of sense, abstract general ideas, or things.

Certainly the general tenor of Price's remarks is informative when

Berkeley is considered through his schema. The distinction between primary and secondary recognition is parallel to that which Berkeley draws between perception and sensation on the one hand and judgments and inference on the other:

> To perceive is one thing; to judge is another. So likewise, to be suggested is one thing, and to be inferred is another. Things are suggested and perceived by sense. We make judgements and inferences by the understanding.[39]

Sensation is characterized, as is primary recognition, by immediate awareness, intuition, if you prefer, and its content is the given. It is also true for Berkeley that the ability to make inferences depends upon the given in sensation in just those ways specified by Price – to know that X is a sign of Y I must perceive both of them many times in constant conjunction, and to know whether or not the sign relationship is fulfilled or not, I must be able to verify that they have both occurred by perceiving them. Moreover, Berkeley seems to be saying that sensation cannot be mistaken, that the concepts of truth and falsity cannot be relevant to them because, to put it crudely, we see what we see. We are not mistaken when we see the "bent" oar in the water; the mistake occurs when we think it will *feel* that way, when we *judge* that *if* we touch it, then it will feel a certain way. Such judgments would only be "true" if negative signs were present which were stronger than the usual positive ones.

At the same time, the vagueness of Berkeley's claims appears when we press the comparison. Although inference-making at the level of understanding is compatible with the use of symbols in Price's category of secondary recognition, Berkeley's "suggestion" does not seem to fit well within primary recognition, because *some* sort of signification is present even on that level for him. I am, as it were, "set" for B upon the occurrence of A, provided they have occurred together in the past for Berkeley, and the question is how we are to interpret this "set". It seems to mean something close to unconscious expectation, almost akin to reflex action, and this would make it closer to Price's primary recognition, since "mistaken" reflexes would be strange. Nonetheless, it is clearly a more complex process than the simple atomic perception of which Price seems to be speaking, because there is no getting around the fact that for Berkeley, there are sign relations even among elementary data, as the *Essay on Vision* proves. Indeed, one can make a good case for the claim that the concept of falsehood for Berkeley, in spite of

---

[39] TVVE, 42

what he might *want* to say, *must* arise on the level of suggestion, for if he is correct, when we *do* come to make inferences on the level of the understanding, we can only be mistaken for one of two reasons: a) our inference may be justified because there was a previous constant conjunction supporting it, but the course of nature may have changed, or b) we may have mistaken the meaning of a sign, by failing to notice another contemporaneous sign or some such thing, as when I take A to be a sign of B, not noticing X, when X is a strong negative sign relative to B. *Had* I noticed X, A would have been a negative sign for B, of course.[40] The constant conjunction presupposed by a) and the consequent expectation which is established, is obviously a necessary condition for the making of inferences in Berkeley's philosophy.

I am of course speaking only of those sorts of inference which are probable in Berkeley's eyes – those we make about the course of nature – which comprise all of our knowledge of the real natural world with the exception of its causes, and the latter is not really an exception because it is the world of mind, which is not part of the natural world. These probable inferences are founded upon constant conjunctions of the data of sense, which constancy depends upon the free will of God. Since we cannot know God's intentions for the future, we cannot have certain knowledge of the future course of nature.[41]

When one pursues this distinction between the level of sense and that of understanding further in Berkeley, yet other problems arise. One fundamental issue arises in conjunction with one of his strangest and most astounding principles, enunciated in the *Essay on Vision* and carried consistently throughout his works. This is the assertion that in some sense, human perceivers make objects. Here is his clearest statement of this important theorem:

Whatever, therefore, the mind considers as one, that is an unit. Every combination of ideas is considered as one thing by the mind, and in token thereof is marked by one name. Now, this naming and combining together of ideas is perfectly arbitrary, and done by the mind in such sort as experience shows it to be most convenient: Without which our ideas had never been collected into such sundry distinct combinations as they now are.[42]

What this amounts to saying is that if there were no judgment, then there would be no objects. He is saying that objects "happen" much in

---

[40] PC, 221; DHP, p. 238
[41] PC, 794, 884, 885, cf. also chapter five
[42] TV, 109

the way that words do: – as the word "adultery" comes through convention to stand for the particular sounds ə-'dəl-t(ə-)rē (as well as for the practice adultery), so objects arise through the convention of considering one group or set of ideas of sense as one thing, and thence giving it one name. The set of ideas does not become a thing, as it were, until it is set off from other groups by being named. Of course, once the conventions are established, we must be consistent in their use.[43] Now this entails that the natural world is in fact arbitrary in two ways: first, it is dependent upon the free will of God, because the data occur in a sequence which is not dependent upon our minds (see chapter four). Secondly, so far as objects of *knowledge* are concerned, the world is arbitrary because these depend for their existence upon *our* organization of the world into named groups. Thus, the ontological question of what exists, and the epistemological question of the nature of the objects of knowledge, are intimately related for Berkeley, because what exists is what is known by some mind, and what is known by some mind is presumably a world of complexes of ideas standing in various sign-to-thing-signified relationships, each complex and set of complexes having an arbitrarily assigned name without which it is apparently not a possible object of knowledge.

There are glaring inconsistencies here, which cannot be reconciled. The simple statement of the contradictory position can be given in the form of two rhetorical questions: (1) How can the sign relations on the level of sense (where, so to speak, there are no objects) be the foundation of sign relations between objects and events on the level of understanding if this is true? (2) How can we be responsible for "making" the objects of knowledge if we are not responsible for the order of the presentation of data to sense, since the groups which are named are a function of this presentational order? The two questions both ultimately concern the same dilemma, which is what we are to make of the difference between the world perceived but not judged (what Kant was to call the phenomenal world) and the world resulting from the applications of our judgments to the world of perception. Let me use another metaphor to make the problem as clear as I can. Suppose you are given a picture puzzle. In the box, it is composed of a jumble of bits of cardboard without relation to one another. But as you place the bits in various positions to one another, they begin to take on what might in the broad sense be called meaning, at least in the sense that they stand in given relations to one another, and to you. Nature

[43] TV, 143

perceived but not understood is for Berkeley much like the bits in the box, provided that the elements for establishing suggestion and expectation (in nature, the succession of the "bits") is present in the box. Just as the picture does not emerge until the parts are placed in their proper relationships, so the meanings, the significations, in the language of nature, only become clear when nature is interpreted, that is judged, as a system of signs related to other signs. It is only *as* such a system of signs that nature is a possible object of knowledge, because nature *qua* object of knowledge implies the making of judgments, the subject matter of which is the complex of sign-relationships which are presented to sense.

We are all familiar with the phenomena of noticing something without interpreting it. But that is not knowing. To know, we must be able to tell what the sign or symbol signifies, that is, we must be able to *interpret* the sign, to "cash" it, in Price's terms. Just as noises are not words, but may become words when they attain meaning through convention, so a necessary condition for the advent of objects is that they, and the data of which they are composed, have become signs. Therefore, any language presupposes "readers", including the natural language. This is the central force of the "to be is to be perceived" maxim for the natural language – it may be sufficient for the existence of a datum that it be perceived, but to exist *qua* sign, and hence as a part of any language, it must be interpreted.

Upon such interpretation of nature, we see that it is

. . . a sort of rational discourse, and is therefore the immediate effect of an intelligent cause . . . Therefore, the phenomena of nature, which strike on the senses and are understood by the mind, form . . . a most coherent, entertaining, and instructive Discourse.[44]

It is clear to me that Berkeley has not made his case here, for reasons which are deeply embedded in the very purposes of his philosophy. The problem is, in terms of the puzzle metaphor, to explain the origin of the "elements of suggestion" in the box. Berkeley wants to do two incompatible things: he wants to make nature exhibit the intelligence of God independently of men, and secondly, he wants to hold a theory of meaning and language which will enable him to deny the theory of truth held by Locke and the Deists, and to accomplish certain other purposes which I shall discuss later on. The theory of language entails, among other things, that objects are formed by convention involving

[44] S., 254

the arbitrary grouping of data by assigning them a name. Only in this way do the objects of knowledge arise. But at the same time, he seems to say that some relation of signification, at least sufficient to establish "suggestion" at the level of sense and perception, is present in the given to sense *prior* to judgment. In short, the elements for suggestion must be present in the box. The conflict is roughly parallel with that which arises for Kant when he finds that he must attribute the irreversibility of the order of presentation of data to the senses to the noumenal world, while at the same time he wishes to explain the relations among data in terms of the forms of judgment, and to deny that the noumenal world is a possible object of knowledge. You cannot have it both ways. If the natural world is in any sense composed of sign relationships prior to the making of judgments about it by us, then since sign relations are three-termed for Berkeley, nature is intelligent and rational, i.e. interpreted, independently of our minds, that is, it is a system of signs to God. But if this is so, then two other problems must be solved: Since we have no ideas of relations for Berkeley, which presumably includes the sign relation, and since the ideas of sense are inactive, then how do we come to know the sign relations God knows? Relations, which are known notionally, seem to be posited by a mind.[45] If so, how does God posit them for us? If they are not given to sense, the only other alternative seems to be some sort of occasionalism, which Berkeley denied.[46] Secondly, if we "discover" rather than in some sense make sign relationships, then it seems that the existence of objects is not after all contingent upon convention, and that the only thing which is contingent is the particular artificial marks or words which we use to name things. True, artificial languages still remain essential for *propositional* knowledge in these conditions, but that is a far cry from the much stronger claim that there are no objects until they are "formed" by judgments of the given in sensation. These two problems arise no matter what type of relation we wish to consider in the language of nature: it may be a relation of resemblance, or a relation based upon co-existence, or the possession of special properties or a special likeness, but the same consequences are entailed.

Berkeley's theory of relations is not the only reason for these difficulties. His failure to distinguish between signs and symbols is probably another source of trouble. He could perhaps have ameliorated some of

[45] P., 89
[46] P. 49 (cf. also Jessop's note on the entry); P., 68-70 (cf. also the footnote about these entries); P. 82, 116 (and the footnote about them); DHP, pp. 213-215

the consequences of his views by defining the issue of propositional knowledge in terms of the use of symbols, and analyzed the language of the author of nature in terms of signs which are not symbols. For example, he could have argued that sign relations between or among *objects* are symbolic, whereas in the language of nature we are concerned only with the sign relations among data which are unnamed. But this would not unfortunately solve the central points, and it would be an embarrassing position for a philosopher who held that the Author of the natural language is the most rational being. Berkeley's failure to distinguish between signs and symbols and their functions is obvious in this passage, in which he is explaining why we more frequently confuse signs with their significates in the natural language than in artificial ones:

When we observe that signs are variable, and of human institution; when we remember there was a time they were not connected in our minds with those things they now so readily suggest; but that their signification was learned by the slow steps of experience: This preserves us from confounding them. But when we find the same signs suggest the same things all over the world; when we know they are not of human institution, and cannot remember that we ever learned their signification, but think that at first sight they would have suggested to us the same things they do now: All this persuades us they are of the same species as the things respectively represented by them, and that it is by a natural resemblance they suggest them to our minds.[47]

But in spite of these conflicts in his philosophy, I believe that I am correct in my interpretation of Berkeley's intentions and principles, and since it is not my primary purpose here to defend his theory but to expose it so far as it is relevant to his moral philosophy, I shall defer further criticisms for the time being.

3. FURTHER DEVELOPMENT, AND NATURAL LAWS

The position discussed in the *Essay Towards a New Theory of Vision* is an interim one. It analyzes only the relations between visual and tactile data, and in so doing it treats the sign relations between the two sorts of data as "one-way", that is, it makes the minimal claim that visual data are signs of tactile data, and says nothing about the function of tactile data as signs themselves. The *esse est percipi* conclusion is only extended in that work to visual data, though the premises of the argument, to

[47] TV, 144

an astute observer of the time, could be seen to extend to other data as well. Berkeley was a shrewd philosophical tactician! As one moves to the *Principles of Human Knowledge*, the *Three Dialogues Between Hylas and Philonous*, and especially *Alciphron, or the Minute Philosopher*, Berkeley's position is broadened to include the relations between data of all the senses, and these relations are treated as inter-significatory, rather than as "one-way". In addition, it is possible to argue, on the basis of the *Essay* alone, that he intended the "Language of the Author of Nature" merely as an explanatory *metaphor* and not as a truth. Finally, it is only in the later works, especially the dialectic *Alciphron*, that the application of his theory to moral philosophy begins to take place. This last development was foreshadowed even in the *Essay* however, so I do not mean to imply that the earlier works are irrelevant to moral philosophy. As he says in that book:

Upon the whole, I think we may fairly conclude that the proper objects of vision constitute "an universal language of the Author of nature", whereby we are instructed how to regulate our actions in order to attain those things that are necessary to the preservation and well-being of our bodies, as also to avoid whatever may be hurtful and destructive to them. It is by their information that we are principally guided in all the transactions and concerns of life.[48]

The extension of the sign theory to the data of all the senses is most evident in the *Three Dialogues*. There it is first agreed that "sensible things are those only which are immediately perceived by sense", and then the immediate objects of the various senses are listed as lights, colors, figures, sounds, odors, tastes, and tangible qualities. In addition, very importantly for my purposes, pain and pleasure are said to be nothing but intense sensations or ideas, and they thereby also become part of the natural language.[49] In what follows, it is made clear that *all* of the data of *all* of the senses exist only in a mind.[50] Furthermore, it is made plain that the sign relations between visual and tactile data are also to be found among the other data of sense. The regular and constant occurrence of groups of data is called "natural law", and Berkeley says:

. . . certain general laws . . . run through the whole chain of natural effects: these are learned by the observation and study of nature, and are by men applied as well to the framing artificial things for the use and ornament of life, as to the explaining the various phenomena: which explanation consists

[48] TV, 147
[49] DHP, p. 176
[50] DHP, p. 179

only in shewing the conformity any particular phenomena hath to the general Laws of Nature, or, which is the same thing, in discovering the uniformity there is in the production of natural effects;[51]

Now this is a very important remark. Natural effects, that is, those events which follow others, called their causes (but which are really signs for them), occur not at random, but regularly. These regularities are called natural laws, and one sort of scientific explanation of a particular event is to give the chain in which it occurs, that is, to give the natural law of which it and other things like it are a part. With such knowledge, we can make artifacts and so better our lives. But this is not the *only* function of natural law: that is, being able to tell what comes next in the great chain, or for that matter what came before, is not the only thing we learn from nature, even though learning this is important for our well-being. Each event in the sequences known as natural laws is not only a *natural* effect in the sense of that term used by Berkeley, but also a *causal* effect, the cause being the will of God. It is for this reason that through the study of natural law we should learn not only about nature, but about God, and specifically, we should be able to learn what it is that God wills. In so learning, we should also be able to discover what sort of a being God is. The connection between natural law and our well-being, and natural law and God's will, is therefore a central issue in Berkeley's moral philosophy, for as we shall see, we learn through these laws that God wills our well-being.

But problems also arise at the outset. Some of the difficulties are concerned with the relation between our ideas of sense and whatever their counterparts in God's mind are, for there is a difference. I shall postpone the discussion of this set of problems until the fourth chapter, where God's role is examined at length. Here, the more pressing issue is *how* natural laws indicate God's intentions, in addition to the performance of sign functions in the natural world. If it cannot be shown that his intentions are so revealed, then the whole point of the language metaphor is of course lost. Yet, the question has no easy, clear answer. Certainly, since intentions are not ideas, God's intentions cannot be *signified* by natural laws, for the latter is a relation confined to the realm of ideas of sense. It has been held that natural laws somehow "express" God's intentions, or more accurately, it has been held that they express his Ideas, but some knowledgeable Berkeley scholars believe that the Bishop of Cloyne denies this.[52] Moreover, even if it were true that

[51] P., 62
[52] PGB, pp. 26-27

God's *Ideas* were so "expressed", the moot point of whether his *intentions* are *a fortiori* expressed would still remain. This proposal is muddied by the fact that some sort of relation of resemblance seems to be presupposed between divine Ideas and our ideas, and the conundrum here involved will be one of the problems examined in the fourth chapter.

It has also been suggested that a *modus vivendi* might be achieved by distinguishing between what natural laws express, and what they "evince": thus, Mabbott says:

If I say 'there is the door', my words express a relation in space, but they evince anger. So God's words- our sense-data - express or suggest other sense-data, but evince His power and good will.[53]

But this suggestion, though it is possibly fruitful and certainly plausible, will not do, because I am interested here not just in God's attributes, but his *intentions* and desires for us in the prudential and moral fields, and when I know his attributes, I do not *a fortiori* know his intentions. What we must be able to do is show that the laws of the language of nature indicate in some way what God wants us to *do*, how he wants us to act.

As we have seen, there are at least two sorts of explanation for Berkeley: that which offers as the explanation of an event a natural law or a set of natural laws, and that which offers the *cause* of the event, which is a completely different sort of explanation. Constant conjunctions are the foundations of natural laws, those "analogies, harmonies, and agreements . . . discovered in the works of Nature" which, when reduced to "general rules", enable us to predict and explain events occurring at temporal and spatial distances.[54] When we "derive" phenomena from such rules or laws, we are really considering "signs rather than causes" because natural laws make no reference to minds, and minds are the only causes.[55] This "derivation" of phenomena consists either in predicting the circumstances, i.e. the sequence of events, in which they will occur because they have so occurred in the past, or in identifying the event as a part of a sequence now or in the past. But causal explanation is irrelevant to this except in so far as the sequence of events constituting natural law is an effect of a mind. A *complete* explanation of the universe involves the giving of both sorts of

[53] *Loc. cit.*
[54] P., 105
[55] P., 108

explanations, because natural laws *simpliciter* provide no purpose or *rationale* for the universe, and for Berkeley this was tantamount to a denial of the lawfulness of the universe itself. How could the natural world be sequential unless it was intentionally so?[56] And this provides the link between natural law and God. From the actions of a man we can tell quite a lot about his intentions, and so this is true of God, where "actions" in both cases really means the *effect* of actions, since acts are mental. Given that the past uniformities of nature are the effect of God's willing, and that willing is always purposeful, that is, directed towards the achievement of some end, as Berkeley thought, we should be able to learn what ends God is acting to achieve from the tendency of natural laws, and hence we ought to be able to infer his intentions. We can never attain *certain* knowledge of his intentions, since there is no necessary connection between what God willed in the past and what he might will in the future, but this is not a serious drawback, any more than is the fact that we can only judge a *man*'s future conduct probably.[57] For Berkeley then, to discover the ends to which natural laws lead *is* to discover why God acts, that is, the reasons for which he acts. Just as we can justifiably hypothesize about the intentions of a man from his conduct, so we can do so with God.

A study of the ends served by natural law *also* reveals God's goodness and wisdom, in just the ways that the ends for which men act reveal their moral character. There are unsolved (perhaps unsolvable) problems here. For example, the moral character of men is judged according to whether it meets certain criteria, whereas God is presumably good in himself, and, as we shall see, good itself is defined in reference to what is present to the mind of God. It follows that the cases of man and God are not parallel here, for it would seem that we learn what good *is* by learning what God wills, and by learning what man wills, we learn *whether* he is good. But for the moment it is sufficient to note that Berkeley believes that we can learn *what* God wills by learning the ends served by natural laws, since the latter are the effect of the will of God.

It might be argued that God's omnipotence is brought into question by this view, since he could have made his intentions known much more simply than he evidently has. However, this ignores the fact that we must not only know what those intentions are, but, assuming we too ought to act for the same ends, we must know *how* we can do this. We

56 P., 107
57 P., 107

must have foresight enabling us to predict, and to "regulate our actions for the benefit of life".[58] Merely knowing what God wants would not provide us with such knowledge, which is only possible for us through our actions about things in accordance with the multiplicity of natural signs. The issue of whether God could have made us differently, so that we would not have to have endured this disagreeable procedure, is not discussed by Berkeley. But he does argue that it is after all not all that difficult to learn from nature. Just as ideas are made into objects for the same reasons that sounds are combined into heard words and letters into written ones, so that from a few original sounds and/or letters we may signify a great deal, or, in the case of natural "words", "signify a great number of effects and actions", so natural laws which are sequences of these signs allow us to accomplish a still wider range of ends. In the case of artifical languages, the rules of combination are the rules of grammar; in the language of nature, they are the laws of nature.[59]

Even the physicist will eventually be led by his investigations to explanation in terms of final causes rather than efficient ones, for if he does not use such explanation, he will not be able to account for the regularity of the natural laws which are the immediate object of his study. This is because it is impossible to explain the train of events in nature when we consider signs as cooperating causes which conspire together to produce certain kinds of effects without becoming involved in "great absurdities". On the other hand, Berkeley thought, none of these absurdities are entailed if we consider natural events as complex signs whose purpose is "our information". So considered, the job of the natural philosopher is to discover what information the signs actually provide, and not to hypothesize about non-existent corporeal (efficient) causes and their mythical effects. The emphasis on this latter mistaken theory has

. . . too much estranged the minds of men from that active principle, that supreme and wise spirit, in whom we live, move, and have our being.[60]

But the considering of nature as a system of signs naturally leads us to God as the immediate cause, the Author, of the natural language.

The rules of the natural language testify to God's wisdom; his goodness is demonstrated by the fact that natural laws enable us to survive

[58] P., 30, 31
[59] P., 65
[60] P., 66

and prosper; and his preservation of the natural world shows us his power.[61] Mere observation of nature will not enable us to better the lot of humanity, because we may make mistakes through the misinterpretation of what is presented to our senses.[62] Moreover, God may change his mind and alter the course of nature at any time, though in fact he does not seem to do this often – so infrequently in fact that when he does, we call the change a miracle – and because of our carelessness, our knowledge of the laws of nature is inadequate, though the laws themselves, as presented to our senses, are clear enough.[63] For all of these reasons, our active participation, through the voluntary guidance of our conduct in accordance with what we are taught by the divine language, is required if we are to attain the ends we seek and ought to seek.

By the middle of the *Principles* it is evident that Berkeley is no longer considering the language metaphor as a metaphor. He says:

It is, I say, evident from what has been said in the foregoing parts of this treatise, and in Sect. 147, and elsewhere of the essay concerning vision, that visible ideas are the language whereby the governing spirit, on whom we depend, informs us what tangible ideas he is about to imprint upon us, in case we excite this or that motion in our own bodies.[64]

That Berkeley is now accepting nature as *really* a language is even more evident in *Alciphron*, which was written many years after the *Principles*. In the fourth dialogue of *Alciphron* the natural language theory is presented with particular emphasis on the "articulation, combination, variety, copiousness, extensive and general use and easy application of signs . . . that constitute the true nature of language." Finally, Alciphron puts the following question to Euphranor (Berkeley):

I propound it fairly to your own conscience, whether you really think that God Himself speaks every day and in every place to the eyes of all men.

Berkeley's reply could not be more emphatic:

That is really and in truth my opinion; and it should be yours too, if you are consistent with yourself, and abide by your own definition of language. Since you cannot deny that the great Mover and Author of Nature constantly explaineth Himself to the eyes of men by the sensible intervention of arbitrary signs, which have no similitude or connexion with the things

[61] P., 72
[62] DHP, p. 238
[63] PC, 221
[64] P, 44

signified; so as, by compounding and disposing them, to suggest and exhibit an endless variety of objects, differing in nature, time, and place; thereby informing and directing men how to act with respect to things distant and future, as well as near and present. In consequence, I say, of your own sentiments and concessions, you have as much reason to think the Universal Agent or God speaks to your eyes, as you can have for thinking any particular person speaks to your ears.[65]

The criteria used here to define a language had also been examined earlier on in the same dialogue.[66] Without much doubt then, Berkeley really believed that nature was as much a language as any set of signs invented by men. The particular passages I have chosen to prove this point emphasize that nature is a *visual* language, thereby conforming to the pattern of development begun in the *Essay Towards a New Theory of Vision*. But it is easy to provide evidence from other sources, and indeed from the *Principles* and *Alciphron* too, which show that the same premises which prove the data of vision to constitute a language are applicable to the data of other senses, and are in some places so applied by Berkeley.

Berkeley did not hold that nature and artificial languages had all or even most of their properties in common, for clearly this would be silly. What he did hold was that they both meet the *essential* criteria which define a language, as these are presented in *Alciphron*.[67] In addition to the contingent nature of the relation between signs and their significates, which is *the* essential property in both languages, there are at least these important similarities: the scope of natural and artificial languages are roughly similar; the meanings and natures of basic signs in both kinds of language are learned by ostensive definition; the laws of nature, like the rules of language, not only enable us to explain and interpret, but also to guide our actions.[68] In addition, just as we do not have ideas occurring to us each and every time that we use signs in artificial languages, so the occurrence of images and actual cognition does not happen every time we use the signs of the natural language.[69]

The assertion that we learn the meanings of signs in both languages by ostensive definition is implicit in Berkeley's examination of the contingent relation between signs and what they signify. Though he

---

[65] Alc. IV, 12
[66] Alc. IV, 7
[67] Alc. IV, 12
[68] PO, 7
[69] Alc. VII, 5-6

would not have known the meaning of the term "ostensive definition", a rose is a rose by any other name, and what we now understand by the words is just what is stated in this remark:

... there must be time and experience, by repeated acts, to acquire a habit of knowing the connexion between the signs and things signified; that is to say of understanding the language, whether of the eyes or of the ears.[70]

This statement is from *Alciphron*, but the principle is to be found much earlier in his writings, as this quotation from the *Essay Towards a New Theory of Vision* demonstrates:

... the manner wherein they (the proper objects of vision) signify and mark unto us the objects which are at a distance is the *same* with that of languages and signs of human appointment, which do not suggest the things signified by any likeness or identity of nature, but only by an habitual connexion that experience has made us to observe between them.[71]

This view is almost exactly the same as that put forward by Bertrand Russell in *An Inquiry Into Meaning and Truth* in his analysis of ostensive definition. With this fact about the natural and artificial languages established, together with the irrelevance of the nature of the particular sign vehicles used, it remains only to show that the scope of the uses of the natural signs is as wide as that of artificial ones, and we can conclude that nature is a true language. Berkeley believes that he has done this.[72]

Among the significant *differences* between the two languages are the facts that the signs of nature are created by God, and that they are the same in all nations and climes, and for all people.[73]

4. A THEORY OF TRUTH, AND NATURAL LAWS

Berkeley's famous attack on Locke's theory of abstract general ideas is more closely related to a later chapter than to the present one, but because the issue of the nature of truth is so central to the questions examined in this chapter, I must also analyze some of the implications of it here. The attack has three main purposes: (1) to show that the analysis of the possible objects of knowledge given at the start of the *Principles* is complete, and thereby (2) to refute the material substance

[70] Alc. IV, 11
[71] TV, 147
[72] Alc IV, 12; Note: It is interesting to compare Russell's *An Inquiry Concerning Meaning and Truth*, pp. 76 H. on this topic
[73] TV, 152

theory and the scepticism Berkeley thought attendant upon its acceptance, by showing that the concept of an inactive, unperceivable
material substance is contradictory, redundant, unknowable, and
lacks the explanatory power which its proponents claim; (3) to explode
the myth that every word has but one significate, which was, Berkeley
thought, the basis of the abstract-general-idea theory,[74] and to prove
that words become general for the same reason we combine several
ideas into one "machine", namely, to communicate more, and to do it
with greater ease. Thus, a general word is one which comes to signify
many particulars, and a general idea is one signifying many particular
ideas, but both the general word and the general idea are themselves
particulars.[75] It may be the case that the "great number of particular
ideas" which are signified by a general word are related by "some
likeness", and "are said to be of the same sort". But it is not the case
that "these sorts are . . . determined and set out by Nature", nor is it
true that classes or natural kinds of things are "limited by any precise,
abstract ideas settled in the mind, with the general name annexed to
them" as Locke had thought. Indeed, for Berkeley, "nor do they
(natural kinds) in truth . . . have any precise bounds or limits at all."[76]
The doctrine of natural kinds is therefore false. This subject is related
to my earlier examination of the Berkeleyan theory that we help create
objects by naming certain constantly recurring groups of sense data.
Given that objects of knowledge only arise in this way, and that the
concept of classes of objects is a result of inferences made by the understanding, it follows for Berkeley that we do not "discover" natural
kinds. Questions of all varieties come up here. If we don't discover
natural kinds, then why do people (not just philosophers) think that
they do? Is not Berkeley confusing two different issues here – the one
being the analysis of the uses of general terms, and the other the analysis
of the relation (resemblance) in virtue of which things are said to belong
to the same class or kind? To me, this seems to be true, and I think the
explanation of his confusion can be traced to his analysis of particular
objects, and the forms of the sentences in which their properties can be
given. The clearest example of his analysis of particular objects is this
famous passage:

As to what philosophers say of subject and mode, that seems very groundless
and unintelligible. For instance, in this proposition, a die is hard, extended

[74] Intro. to P., 18
[75] P., 65; Intro. to P., 12
[76] Draft, p. 128

and square, they will have it that the word die denotes a subject or substance, distinct from the hardness, extension and figure, which are predicated of it, and in which they exist. This I cannot comprehend: to me a die
seems to be nothing distinct from those things which are termed its modes or
accidents. And to say a die is hard, extended and square, is not to attribute
those qualities to a subject distinct from and supporting them, but only an
explication of the meaning of the word die.[77]

This quotation is part of a section of the *Principles* wherein Berkeley
has been defending his theory that the *esse* of objects consists in their
being perceived, and the specific objection being considered at this
point is that if one insists that qualities exist only "in the mind", i.e. if
their *esse* is *percipi*, then one is forced to the absurd conclusion that the
mind is colored, figured, etc. Berkeley's reply is that such qualities are
not modes or attributes of the mind, but that they are in the mind "by
way of idea", that is, "in the mind" means "perceived by the mind".
Modes and properties are attributes of something not identical with
them, as when Aristotle says that white can be in a man, but is not
identical with the man. Berkeley is denying this thesis, the thesis that
qualities are not identical with their subjects. If this is true, then what
becomes of the logical status of descriptions, for they now seem to be
trivially true. This criticism would certainly be well-founded, *if* one
held the idea-correspondence theory of truth of Locke and the Deists.
This is particularly obvious in the case of the die. What Berkeley is
saying here is that the predicate of a description is an "explication", to
use his word, of the subject term, by which I take him to mean that
once one has listed all the name's of the individual qualities on the
predicate side of the description, that is, all the names of the qualities
or properties which are in the collection named by the subject term,
then one has in fact given the complete extension of the name of the
collection. In short, "die" is identical in denotation and meaning with
the conjunction of the names of the individual qualities given on the
predicate side. There is nothing left over, as it were, once we have
given the conjunction of all of the properties, which is still to be included in an object's name. Now on the idea-correspondence theory
of truth, sentences such as "A die is hard, extended, and square", and
"Melampus is an animal" now become trivially true, because that
theory held that truth was a function of the correspondence of ideas.
Thus, in the case of the sentence about the die, the ideas named by
the subject and those named by the predicate are the *same*, and hence

[77] P., 49

the sentence is trivially true. In the case of the second example, the idea named by "Melampus" is related to that named by "animal" because the first is a member of the class named by the second.

But Berkeley's remarks about the "Melampus" example are a clear *rejection* of this theory of truth. There are not *two* ideas, one general the other particular, which are denoted in "Melampus is an animal", and any analysis which presupposes this is wrong-headed in the first place. He says:

But if a man may be allow'd to know his own meaning I do declare that in my thoughts the word animal is neither supposed to stand for an universal nature nor yet for an abstract idea ... Nor does it indeed in that proposition stand for any idea at all. All that I intend to signify thereby being only this, that the particular thing I call Melampus has a right to be called by the name animal.[78]

Exactly the same sort of analysis would apply to the example of the die. Earlier in the same place, he draws the distinction between particular and general words in these terms:

... a word becomes general by being made the sign, not of a general idea, but, of many particular ideas ... when I say the word Socrates is a proper or particular name, and the word Man an appellative or general name, I mean no more than this viz that the one is peculiar and appropriated to one particular person, the other common to a great many particular persons, each whereof has an equall right to be called by the name Man. This ... is the whole truth of the matter ...[79]

Types of words are therefore distinguished according to their *use*. But for Berkeley, the *meanings* of words are *also* a function of their use. There is no necessary connection between "die" and "hard, extended and square", any more than there is such a connection between either of these and the thing which is named by them both. We can, and sometimes do, change the names, whether simple (single) or complex (more than one word) which we apply to something, and one of the forms that change might take is to add something to the list of properties predicated in a sentence such as "A die is hard, extended and square", perhaps because we have noticed something that we did not notice before. Classes are simply tools, human inventions, which we use and change from time to time, their membership being open-ended because it depends upon what names of properties we wish to include in the meaning of the name we assign to the members of the class, in

---

[78] Draft, p. 136
[79] *Ibid.* p. 127

just the same way that the meaning of a proper name depends upon what names of what properties we wish to include on the predicate side of sentences such as "Socrates is 39, bald, with a large beard, etc. etc.".

Berkeley's analysis of the meanings of general words, and hence his analysis of classes or natural kinds, is in a sense a development of his analysis of the meanings of particular words – the difference is merely that general words may be used to name more things than one – but both types of word name in the *same way*, and the analysis of the way they name is the explication of ostensive definition, constant conjunction and the sign-relation which has already been examined. Perhaps then I am misstating the case when I say that Berkeley *confused* the problem of the uses of general terms with that of class inclusion because of resemblance: perhaps he just does not think that the latter is a problem, or that it is a pseudo-problem generated by the misuse of language. This might be an explanation of his cryptic remark:

. . . who sees not that all the dispute is about a word? to wit, whether what is perceived by different persons may yet have the term "same" applied to it?[80]

One thing, right or wrong, does seem to emerge from the discussion: Berkeley would emphatically deny the theory of truth held by the Lockeans and the Deists.

Some authors, such as C. M. Turbayne, have cast this problem in terms of definitions. The kinds of definition relevant to the issue are the denoting and the connoting. The first sort define a class of entities by reference to smaller classes, or to individuals, included in the class to be defined. For example, we might define the class or genus Dog by reference to the various breeds included in it, or at a lower level, by reference to the names of individual dogs such as Melampus. In the case of connoting definitions, the process is reversed, and we would define the meaning of the word "dog" by reference to the breed, and to properties of all the members of the class, such as being an animal, a quadruped, a carnivore, etc.[81] Connoting definitions have led us into some strange beliefs. Probably because they do not refer to particular entities or properties, they have seemed to some people such as Locke to name on the right hand side of a definition distinct and existing entities, sorts, classes, universals, abstract general ideas, defining

[80] DHP, p. 248
[81] Turbayne, C. M., *The Myth of Metaphor*, Yale University Press, New Haven (1962) pp. 80-81 (MM)

properties etc., and on the left hand side, to name a particular thing which "owns", "possesses", "exhibits" etc. these properties. They have also taken these definitions to posit a relation between what is named on both sides such that the sentence asserting the definition, for example, "Melampus is an animal", is true or false in virtue of this relation. This particular sentence hence presumably posits a relation between a particular, Melampus, and a universal, animality, such that if Melampus does indeed belong to the class of animals, then the sentence is true. It is this theory of truth which Berkeley denies, because among other things, there are not two ideas involved at all, only one. The sentence is, in Berkeley's view, an instruction, a rule of grammar, for using words in artificial languages, or in this case, an instruction for using the word "animal" in connection with Melampus. In the same way, in the case of the denoting kind of definition, sentences such as "Some dogs are dachshunds" instruct us in the use of less general rather than more general words or signs. This last procedure eventually comes to an end with some ostenisvely defined term, such as the name "Melampus". But whether we consider the issue as a matter of sorts of definitions, or as primarily the analysis of the meanings of general words vis à vis particular ones, it is clear that Berkeley rejects the idea-correspondence theory of truth.

There are additional reasons for this rejection which I have not yet mentioned, and which are not directly concerned with the attack on material substance or the theory of abstract general ideas. Three of these additional reasons are important here. The first is that Berkeley thought it impossible for us to have ideas of other minds. Instead, we have "notions" of them, as we also have notions of relations.

We comprehend our own existence by inward feeling or reflexion, and that of other spirits by reason. We may be said to have some knowledge or notion of our own minds, of spirits and active beings, whereof in a strict sense we have not ideas. In like manner we know and have a notion of relations between things or ideas, which relations are distinct from the ideas or things related, inasmuch as the latter may be perceived by us without our perceiving the former.[82]

Since this is true, then if the Deists and Locke were correct, it would follow that sentences about other minds, relations and God, could not be true, at least on their theory.

Secondly, there are a whole class of words which, though they *ultimately* involve reference to particulars, contexts, parables, metaphors

[82] P., 89

etc., have their primary importance in the practical guidance of human action. Examples of such terms are words such as "goodness", "justice", "virtuous", etc. These terms do not refer, as some have thought, to abstract general ideas:

> ... to frame an abstract idea of happiness, precinded from all particular pleasure, or of goodness, from every thing that is good, this is what few can pretend to. So likewise, a man may be just and virtuous, without having precise ideas of justice and virtue. The opinion that those and the like words stand for general notions abstracted from all particular persons and actions, seems to have rendered morality difficult, and the study thereof of less use to mankind.[83]

According to the traditional theory then, if Berkeley is right, we could make no decisions about the truth or falsity of sentences using these terms.

Finally, if nature is a language, then the concepts of truth and falsity presumably play some part in it for Berkeley. Strange though it may sound, natural laws must be true or false in some way. But this question becomes absurd if we have to pretend that the truth of natural laws is a function of the agreement of ideas, for even if resemblance were the foundation of this agreement or correspondance, resemblance is a relation and for Berkeley we have no ideas of relations.[84] But if Berkeley rejects this theory of truth, what is his substitute? I think it was very closely akin to the modern theories called Pragmatic and Instrumentalist. In the natural language, a law is a sequence of events, say a, b, c, which are followed by another event or complex of events, say Y. We often describe the actions of men in what are called dispositional terms, formulated in "law-like" statements of the form "If X is in circumstances a, b, c, then he will do Y." For Berkeley, the behavior of other beings, and indeed some of our own, is part of the language of nature, because for the observer it consists in a sequence of perceived ideas. We have no idea of the agent *per se* because he is of course a mind, and we can only perceive the effects of his mental acts.

> ... the passions which are in the mind of another are of themselves to me invisible. I may nevertheless perceive them by sight, though not immediately, yet be means of the colours they produce in the countenance. We often see shame or fear in the looks of a man, by perceiving the changes of his countenance to red or pale.[85]

---

[83] P., 100
[84] P., 89
[85] TV, 9

Similarly of course, we have no idea of God, but the "X" of all the laws of nature is God's mind, just as the "X" of dispositional statements about a man's behavior for Berkeley is a human mind. As observers, we use our knowledge of what usually follows upon X's being in circumstances a, b, c, to guide our own behavior. In the same way, and for the same reason, we use the laws of nature as "directions, rules of behavior, for the investigator to find his way about in reality".[86] This is close to the position I believe Berkeley held – that the truth of a natural law, as with the truth of a sentence such as "Melampus is an animal", is a function of its effects when interpreted and followed as a rule or direction. Laws and rules are only sensible within the context of some end which they serve. In the case of the "Melampus" example, the end is the correct use of the word "animal" and the achievement of the effects attendant upon its uses in various contexts.

But what end or ends are to be served by our use of the laws of nature, those steady, orderly, coherent trains or series found in nature, which are "the set rules or established methods, wherein the mind we depend on excites in us the ideas of sense"?[87] The answer is that an indefinitely large number of ends are to be served, because our knowledge and use of the language of nature

. . . gives us a sort of foresight, which enables us to regulate our actions for the benefit of life. And without this we should be eternally at a loss: we could not know how to act anything that might procure us the least pleasure, or remove the least pain of sense. That food nourishes, sleep refreshes, and fire warms us; that to sow in the seed-time is the way to reap in the harvest, and, in general, that to obtain such or such ends, such or such means are conducive, all this we know, not by discovering any necessary connexion between our ideas, but only by the observation of the settled laws of Nature, without which we should be all in uncertainty and confusion, and a grown man no more know how to manage himself in the affairs of life, than an infant just born.[88]

All of these particular laws and the ends they serve fall under a general end, if I might call it that. Near the end of his life, Berkeley said this:

All things are made for the supreme good, all things tend to that end: and we may be said to account for a thing when we shew that it is so best. In the Phaedon, Socrates declares it to be his opinion that he who supposed all

[86] S. Toulmin, *The Philosophy of Science*, Hutchinson University Library, London (1960); P., 91; cf. also *De Motu* and *The Analyst*
[87] P., 28
[88] P., 31

things to have been disposed and ordered by Mind (Sects. 154, 160) should not pretend to assign any other cause of them.[89]

I shall not attempt so ambitious a task as to prove that *every* natural law tends in Berkely's view to serve the "supreme good". But I shall try in the next chapters to show that among the natural laws of the divine language there are *moral* laws, and that the justification of these laws is that they serve a certain good which derives its value from God.

[89] S., 260

CHAPTER II

UTILITARIAN AND RULE-UTILITARIAN ELEMENTS IN BERKELEY'S NORMATIVE ETHICS

Among the signs in the natural language are those called pleasures and pains. For Berkeley, they are but intense sensations, or at least, pleasures and pains of *sense* are but intense sensations. These particular ideas of sense are deeply involved in the ways we learn the nature of our personal welfare, and together with other kinds of pleasures and pains, they also enable us to learn the nature of public welfare or well-being. In this chapter I shall discuss this matter, as well as the nature of private and public good and the rules we must follow to attain either. There are conflicting interpretations of the logical structure and roles of these rules, and this topic will be studied in conjunction with a discussion of *Passive Obedience*. In addition, there are other types of evidence which Berkeley adduces in favor of his conclusions, and I shall explain these.

I. KINDS OF PLEASURES AND PAINS, AND THE MORAL END OF MAN

Berkeley believed that we learn our personal well-being through the pleasures and pains which are signs in the natural language. In his view, no agent can be indifferent to pleasure or pain.[1] He believed that there was no viable distinction between our pleasure and our interest,[2] and he claimed that personal pleasure provides a perfectly good motive for action:

I'd never blame a Man for acting upon Interest. he's a fool that acts on any other Principle. the not understanding these things has been of ill consequence in Morality.[3]

[1] PC, 143
[2] PC, 541
[3] PC, 542

In considering my interest or pleasure however, I must also consider that of other people, for mine is bound up with theirs:

I am glad the People I converse with are not all richer, wiser etc. than I. This is agreeable to Reason, is no sin. Tis certain that if the Happyness of my Acquaintance encreases and mine not proportionably, mine must decrease.[4]

According to Berkeley, *what* we find pleasurable, at least on the level of sense, is not "strictly speaking" dependent upon our wills, but rather upon the will of God, who is the cause of the signs in the natural language, and hence of the natural laws which determine pleasurable and painful sensations.[5] So far, this sounds like simple hedonism, but in fact Berkeley does not hold such a theory. He claims that we are too prone to pay attention to our own good, and moreover, to our own *present* good.[6] He also makes careful distinctions among the different *kinds* of pleasures and among their relative values, and the differences in values are based upon qualitative as well as quantitative considerations.

The first clear distinction he makes is between pleasures which are valuable as a means and those which are valuable as ends in themselves. An example of the first sort is the pleasures of eating, and of the second, the pleasures of appreciating music.[7] This distinction alone would provide sufficient reason for a reconsideration of his apparently simple assertion that "Sensual Pleasure is the Summum Bonum. This the Great Principle of Morality. This once rightly understood all the Doctrines even the severest of the (Gospels) may cleerly be understood."[8] The emphasis must be on the phrase "rightly understood", and the remark must also be understood *not* to exclude other pleasures from the sphere of moral relevance. Just two entries later in the *Philosophical Commentaries*, he has begun to qualify this extravagant generalization:

Sensual Pleasure qua Pleasure is Good and desirable. by a Wise Man. but if it be Contemptible tis not qua pleasure but qua pain or Cause of pain. or (wch is the same thing) of loss of greater pleasure.[9]
Mem. to excite men to the pleasures of the Eye and the Ear wich surfeit not, nor bring those evils after them as others.[10]

---

[4] PC, 569
[5] PC, 144
[6] PC, 851
[7] PC, 852
[8] PC, 769
[9] PC, 773
[10] PC, 787

Hence, in addition to the distinction between value as means and value as end, the principle of moderation has also been introduced. Too much pleasure is no pleasure at all.

There are further distinctions among kinds of pleasures. For example, there are what he calls "natural" and "fantastical" pleasures. Natural pleasures are not dependent on

... the fashion and caprice of any particular age or nation, (and) are suited to human nature in general, and were intended by Providence as rewards for the using our faculties agreeably to the ends for which they were given us.

But fantastical pleasures "presuppose some particular whim or taste accidentally prevailing in a sett of people, to which it is owing that they please."[11] With this distinction Berkeley comes a step closer to the claim that true pleasure does not vary with time and place and custom, but rather depends upon the will of God. Then he proceeds to distinguish between our various "faculties", and to argue that each of these faculties is affected by different objects with regard to what it can enjoy. There is a "scale of pleasure" which is parallel to the division of our faculties, and in this scale, "the lowest are sensual delights". After the pleasures of sense come those of imagination, and finally, the pleasures of the imagination

... give way to the sublimer pleasures of reason, which discover the causes and designs, the frame, connexion, and symmetry of things, and fills (sic) the mind with the contemplation of intellectual beauty, order, and truth.[12]

There are then different kinds of pleasures, the kind being decided by reference to distinct faculties, and there are different values for each kind of pleasure, the criteria for their relative value being qualitative.

In his Eighth *Sermon* he enlarges upon the differences between pleasures of the imagination and those of reason. Profit and pleasure being the ends for which reasonable men strive through study, we find the pleasures of the imagination particularly attractive, because the study of such things as "eloquence and poetry" produces an "immediate pleasure" in the mind. When truths are conveyed in the forms of allegories, or by "beautiful images", a more lasting impression of them is gained, and when the understanding considers such truths, it too is "delighted and instructed."[13]

At this point then we can say that for Berkeley there are three sorts of

[11] GE IV, p. 193
[12] GE VI, p. 203
[13] GE VIII, p. 211

pleasure: of sense, imagination and reason, and there are various degrees of pleasure in each kind. They also differ in qualitative value, and the scale of this value runs from sensual pleasure as the lowest, to pleasures of the understanding as the highest.

In chapter one I mentioned Berkeley's statement in *Siris* that the language of nature will teach us the supreme good, and that the moral explanation of something consists in showing that it tends towards this end.[14] It has already been argued that God is the cause of all natural things,[15] and that the laws of the divine language give us foresight for the regulation and betterment of our lives.[16] Now Berkeley mentions another sort of evidence which leads us towards our own, and society's, well-being. He says that we have instincts "impressed on our minds by the Author of our nature" and that these instincts urge us toward the natural rather than the fantastical pleasures. If we follow these dispositions, the "least uneasiness" encountered in the pursuit of the pleasures they suggest will be overcome by the "greatest satisfaction in the enjoyment of them". "Nothing is made in vain", so we ought to believe that these instincts of ours have a purpose, and the purpose they seem to exhibit is to show us the way to true pleasure, i.e. those pleasures which the divine language teaches to be greatly rewarding. Natural pleasures are those which are "universally suited" to both our sensual and rational natures, which seems to imply that there are both fantastical and natural pleasures for all three faculties, sense, imagination, and reason. Then he claims that only those pleasures of sense which are "contained within the rules of reason" are to be called "natural", and this immediately rules out "excesses of any kind". As examples of irrational, fantastical pleasures Berkeley lists the following: desiring money for itself; the desire for outward distinctions "which bring no delight of sense, nor recommend us as useful to mankind"; the desire for things simply because of their novelty or strangeness. He believes that the pursuit of these pleasures carries its own penalties with it. Failure to exercize intelligence, and a permissive attitude to sense pleasures cause a "restlessness of mind", and force us into the pursuit of

... imaginary goods, in which there is nothing can raise desire, but the difficulty of obtaining them. Thus men become the contrivers of their own

---

[14] S., 258, 260
[15] PC, 433
[16] P., 31, 32

misery, as a punishment on themselves for departing from the measures of nature.[17]

All of this does not imply that men the world over have just the same desires and needs, any more than the fact of universal language implies that all men speak the same tongue. Things may be "natural to human kind" but at the same time not be found in all men, nor be exactly the same where they are found.[18] Nonetheless, what is agreeable to reason is what is natural, and what reason teaches us, through our examination of the natural language, is that the general good of mankind is "the rule or measure of moral truths."[19]

The first chapter demonstrated Berkeley's conviction that nature is a rational system, which proves God's existence, wisdom and goodness, and teaches us. Now I have shown that he claimed true pleasures of whatever kind to be rational, that is, natural, too. What is it then about these facts that is morally relevant? Or to put it another way, how are true pleasures and rationality related to what we ought to do?

The most important sources for information on this point are the first three dialogues of *Alciphron*, and the tract *Passive Obedience*. One of the facts we learn about the natural world is that throughout the plant and animal kingdoms, the mutual cooperation of the parts or members of a species is essential to the well-being of the whole. There is a "natural union and consent between animals of the same kind; ... even different kinds of animals have certain qualities and instincts whereby they contribute to the exercize, nourishment, and delight of each other."[20] In a vegetable, the "several parts ... are so connected and fitted to each other as to protect and nourish the whole, make the individual grow, and propagate the kind."[21] If we extend our perspective from individuals and from species to the entire universe, we will notice that without the sun, the earth would not exist, that water would be useless if it did not nourish plants and herbs, etc. Indeed, asks Berkeley;

... throughout the whole system of the visible and natural world, do you not perceive a mutual connexion and correspondance of parts? And is it not from hence that you frame an idea of the perfection, and order, and beauty of nature?[22]

[17] GE IV, p. 195
[18] Alc. I, 14
[19] Alc. I, 16
[20] Alc. I, 16
[21] Alc. I, 16
[22] Alc. I, 16

Now since nature is rational, and the effect of the will of God, there is a close relation between what is natural, rational, and moral. There is in fact "... the same union, order, and regularity in the moral world" that there is in the natural one. Men, being part of both worlds, were "made for one another".[23] We cannot consider our individual happiness apart from the well-being of the whole, because we are a part of it, and must, if we would be rational, try to achieve the common good of the whole.[24] In short, "a wise man should consider and pursue his private good, with regard to and in conjunction with that of other men."[25] This is why the general good is the "rule or measure of moral truths", a moral truth being one which "direct(s) or influence(s) the moral actions of men."[26] The general happiness must therefore be "a greater good than the private happiness of one man, or of certain men",[27] and so, taking all men's ends or goals into account, it must be the superior end. The wisest of men will consequently be those who serve this end by the best means. Virtuous conduct will be that which in fact tends toward the common good, and vice will be the opposite.

What sort of conduct *is* virtuous conduct? That is, what kind of actions do in fact serve the common good? Berkeley provides several examples, especially in the second dialogue of *Alciphron*. Speaking to Lysicles, who personifies Bernard de Mandeville (more about him later on) Berkeley argues against the thesis that vice is essential to the public well-being. Examples of vice are drunkenness and gluttony. According to this theory, vice creates "extravagant consumption" whereas frugality does not, and consequently in an evil society more money is circulated faster than in a moral one, making it in the long run better off. Berkeley asks whether a drunkard and a glutton are healthier and live longer than sober and healthy men, to which he receives the obvious answer, and then he asks whether one can eat and drink more in a long healthy life than in a short sick one. He again receives the obvious answer, namely that a healthy long-lived man will outstrip the reprobate and incontinent man in consumption. The conclusion is put to Lysicles in the from of a rhetorical question:

And you have granted that a long and healthy life consumes more than a short and sickly one; and you will not deny that many consume more than one? Upon the whole then, compute and say, which is most likely to pro-

23 Alc. I, 16
24 Alc. I, 16
25 Alc. I, 16
26 Alc. I, 16
27 Alc. I, 16

mote the industry of his countrymen, a virtuous married man with a healthy numerous offspring, and who feeds and clothes the orphans in his neighbourhood, or a fashionable rake about town? I would fain know whether money spent innocently doth not circulate as well as that spent upon vice? And, if so, whether by your own rule it doth not benefit the public as much?[28]

In addition, since societies are made up of individuals and families, Berkeley asks Lysicles another empirical question, which is whether he ever knew either any individuals or any families who thrived upon the vices he has described. Lysicles knows of none. Berkeley notes mildly that if vice benefits no individuals and no families who practice it, there is some reason to suspect the claim that it benefits society, which is after all a "great family".[29]

Berkeley has still to define exactly what the good of a man and a society is, and I am afraid that his answer is not very satisfactory, though I shall improve upon it later on:

. . . the good or happiness of a man consist(s) in having both soul and body sound and in good condition, enjoying those things which their respective natures require and free from those things which are odious or hurtful to them . . .[30]

Although it is one of the banes of philosophical ethics that the "good" or "Good" if you prefer has never been defined in a satisfactory manner, this answer is not particularly noteworthy even in this tradition. "Odious" and "hurtful" are themselves evaluative terms, and "good condition" is clearly question-begging. But for the moment, it will have to do. At least this much is clear: Berkeley conceives the state of happiness or good for an individual to consist in bodily and mental health, to which the fantastical pleasures will not lead. Money, for example, is a means to happiness, but useless unless one knows what happiness is.[31] Similarly, a wealthy nation is not necessarily a happy one, so even if vice did make society more wealthy, it would not thereby necessarily make it happier.[32] Indeed, having the means but not knowing how to use it can be quite harmful:

. . . for a people who neither know nor practice them (the means to happiness) to gain riches seems to me the same advantage that it would be for a sick man to come at plenty of meat and drink, which he could not use but to his hurt.[33]

[28] Alc. II, 5
[29] Alc. II, 5
[30] Alc. II, 9
[31] Alc. II, 9
[32] Alc. II, 9
[33] Alc. II, 9

Health depends upon the "bodily composition of a man" in the case of the physical, and upon "right notions", "true judgments", "regular will", and a state such that "the passions and appetites (are) directed to their proper objects, and confined within due bonds" in the case of mental health. These bonds are the bonds of reason according to which we must live if a state of happiness is to be achieved, and the man whose mind and body are in such conditions is properly called "virtuous".[34]

After his first discussion on this topic with Lysicles in *Alciphron* the subject of the qualitative difference among pleasures is raised again. Lysicles claims that he agrees in principle with Berkeley on the questions of health of mind and body and their relation to happiness and *a fortiori* to the state of virtue, but he insists that the true state of happiness results from the gratification of appetites of sense, and that such pleasure is enhanced by licence. For Lysicles, Berkeley's state of virtue would be one of deadly boredom, but on the contrary, "vice inspire(s) men with joy". If this is true of individuals, then according to Berkeley's own arguments, it should also be true of society in general. Moreover, if we are to take nature as our guide as Berkeley urges us, then we must admit that all other species seem to act in order to gratify their pleasures of sense, and that in fact men do too, whatever theory you might wish to hold. Thus, the *summum bonum* is indeed pleasure, but the pleasures of sense.[35]

In reply, Berkeley notes that if this view is sound, pleasures of sense are "at their highest when the appetites are satisfied", and in this event "the appetites must always be craving, to preserve pleasure alive", which of course suggests that Socrates was correct when he compared "the body of a man of pleasure" to a "leaky vessel, always filling and never full".[36] In addition, Berkeley thinks that Lysicles overlooks the fact, when he appeals to nature in support of his views, that so far as our observations of animals go, they have only the faculties of sense and appetite, whereas man has imagination and reason as well. These faculties differ in kind, and both in themselves and by their acts, they differ in value. It follows from this that "the pleasures perfective of those acts are also different." If reason is "higher" than sense and imagination, then it is reasonable to conclude that it is "attended with the highest pleasure". No one denies that the pleasures of sense are also

[34] Alc. II, 12
[35] Alc. II, 13
[36] Alc. II, 13

natural to man, but we must consider the *entire* nature of any species when we talk of its good, and for man to ignore his reason and depend solely upon his senses would therefore be irrational and simply inconsistent with nature, given that no other species is observed to "quit (its) own nature to imitate" another.[37] As Berkeley puts it in a graphic quotation:

Man and beast, having different natures, seem to have different faculties, different enjoyments, and different sorts of happiness. You can easily conceive that the sort of life which makes the happiness of a mole or a bat would be a very wretched one for an eagle. And may you not as well conceive that the happiness of a brute can never constitute the true happiness of a man?[38]

Sensual pleasure is nothing but a "short deliverance from long pain", and in a passage remarkably prescient of John Stuart Mill, Berkeley (Euphranor) again reasserts the qualitative difference among pleasures:

Do but look abroad into the world, and ask the common run of men whether pleasure of sense be not the only true, solid, substantial good of their kind.
Euphranor: But might not the same vulgar sort of men prefer a piece of sign-post painting to one of Raphael's, or a Grubstreet ballad to an ode of Horace? Is there not a real difference between good and bad writing?
Lysicles: There is.
Euphranor: And yet you will allow there must be a maturity and improvement of understanding to discern this difference, which doth not make it therefore less real?
Lysicles: I will.
Euphranor: In the same manner, what should hinder but there may be in nature a true difference between vice and virtue, although it require some degree of reflexion and judgement to observe it? In order to know whether a thing be agreeable to the rational nature of man, it seems one should rather observe and consult those who have most employed or improved their reason.[39]

(This passage also seems to assert the objective existence of vice and virtue, though if Berkeley had spoken accurately here, that is, consistently with his own principles, he would have said that the *effects* of virtuous acts, God's, are observable in nature.)

Berkeley thought that sense perceives only things which are present (further evidence that probable inferences about the future are made by understanding) and therefore cannot judge future pleasures, nor the pleasures of the understanding. Reasonable creatures take into account all the kinds of pleasures, present and future, and rate each pleasure according to its true value. To compute our long-run well-being only on the basis of present sense-pleasures is therefore simply to be guilty of "bad calculating", and in so far as the hedonist does this he shows himself to be of less intelligence than the prudent man. Even the Epicureans admitted that pleasure which leads to greater pain or hinders greater pleasure is really not pleasure, but pain. And conversely, they saw that pain which leads to greater pleasure or prevents greater pain is not really appropriately called pain. So we must consider pleasures of the intellect, imagination and sense, with regard to both "kind and quantity, the sincerity, the intenseness, and the duration of pleasures" in deliberating about our actions.

Let a free-thinker but bethink himself, how little of human pleasure consists in actual sensation, and how much in prospect! Then let him compare the prospect of a virtuous believer with that of an unbelieving rake.[40]

2. PASSIVE OBEDIENCE AND MORAL RULES

Passive Obedience is usually thought to be the most fruitful source of information about Berkeley's moral philosophy, but at the same time, it is paradoxically the source of diametrically opposed claims about it. In order to support my own conclusions, it is necessary to undertake an examination of these opposing claims, and solve the problems involved.

One of the central themes of the work is that in view of the nature of man, especially in view of the immortality of his soul (see chapters three and four) we cannot calculate our interests upon a merely temporal basis. Rather, we must take the view that our true well-being is related to eternal life. Obviously, virtuous lives are not always rewarded in the temporal world, but they will be, thought Berkeley, in the hereafter. So when we study the course of the language of nature, we must attempt to learn what we ought to do for our eternal as well as our temporal well-being. In order to explain how we can do this, he sets out to "make some inquiry into the origin, nature and obligation of moral duties in general, and the criteria whereby they are to be known."[41] This sounds as though Berkeley intends to investigate the *foundations* of morality, but in actual fact, he begins by *assuming*

[40] Alc. II, 18
[41] PO, 4

certain truths as axiomatic, investigates the criteria for recognizing them and studies their relations to our conduct. In addition, he examines some of the relations among moral rules themselves. I shall first provide a general outline of the complete argument of the tract, then the opposing theories about it will be presented together with the issues involved, and then I shall propose some solutions for these issues.

The general argument, though fairly long, can be simply summarized: a) Human beings are immortal; b) God exists and is perfectly good, and only God can ensure our happiness; c) Man, through his actions, can only effect other rational creatures and himself for moral good or evil, and only men are rational; d) Since God is perfectly good, then any end which he desires us to achieve must be some sort of good state of affairs somewhere, and since God is perfectly good, then in this finite world his end must be a state of good for finite created beings, i.e. men; e) Leaving out direct divine intervention, human actions in so far as they have consequences which are good must therefore cause a state of goodness for some men or many men, and again given God's goodness and justice, he must desire us to achieve as much good as possible, that is, a state of goodness for all men; f) It is clear (to Berkeley) that if everyone were to decide for himself the best ways to maximize human well-being, less good would be achieved than if everyone were to observe determinate laws set down by the ruling authority; g) The relationship between the creator and his creatures imposes a moral duty to abide by the will of the former, and it is evident that in the long-run it is in our interests to do so; h) If we can ascertain what God desires us to do, we are morally bound to do it; i) Given that nature is the language of God, and that he reveals his will to us through nature by teaching us that action in accordance with certain rules leads to the greater well-being of man, then we *can* ascertain what God wills us to do; j) What God wills us to do is to observe certain established laws which, when universally practiced, have an "essential fitness" to promote the general well-being, even if there seem to be particular exceptions; k) One of these rules is that we ought to obey the rightful ruler; l) But of course, no one can obey an unjust law actively; m) Therefore, although we cannot obey actively in all cases, we can abstain from disobeying and hence obey the "negative" moral rule of "passive obedience".

It is to be noted that the utility principle is not "discovered" in this argument, but rather is *deduced* from other premises. In fact, in *Passive Obedience*, three methods for discovering moral laws are rejected, though significantly their discovery through the natural language is not one of them. No evidence is offered for God's existence, nor are any arguments presented which support the claim that he has morally relevant attributes or properties. These are assumed. The specific deduction of the utility principle is stated in more detail than my general outline indicates, and can be easily given:

1. ". . . it is a truth evident by the light of nature, that there is a sovereign omniscient Spirit, who alone can make us forever happy . . . or miserable."[42]

2. " . . . a conformity to His will . . . is the sole rule whereby every man who acts up to the principles of reason must govern and square his actions."[43]

3. No man is entitled to more than another from God, except according to the criterion of moral goodness.[44]

4. The criterion of moral goodness presupposes that there was no morally relevant distinction among men prior to God's establishment of the moral end.[45]

5. God is perfect, so a) whatever end he proposes must be good, and b) it cannot be his own good, since God needs nothing. Therefore, it is the good of his creatures.[46]

6. Four and five imply that the general good of all men, for all times and places, is the moral end.[47]

Furthermore, once this deduction is performed, subsidiary deductions of "practical propositions" follow. An example of a practical proposition is "Thou shalt not commit adultery", and a simple deduction of this rule would be something like this:

One ought to obey rules justified by the utility principle.

The rule "Thou shalt not commit adultery" is so justified.

One ought to obey the rule "Thou shalt not commit adultery".

Such deductions are actually performed by Berkeley, the most notable examples appearing in section fifteen of *Passive Obedience*, and in the second dialogue of *Alciphron*. But the discovery *that* the practice of adultery is not conducive to the public well-being is *not* deduced from anything. It is discovered by "an impartial survey of the general

[42] PO, 6
[43] PO, 6
[44] PO, 7
[45] PO, 7
[46] PO, 7
[47] PO, 7

frame and circumstances of human nature";[48] it is "collected from observation".[49] It must therefore be noted at the outset that it is no contradiction to hold on the one hand that deductions of moral injunctions from rules and descriptions of practices can be performed, and on the other that the rules and practices are discoverable in the language of nature. It is furthermore no contradiction to hold on the one hand that the utility principle may be discovered from the language of nature, and on the other that it is deducible from propositions about God and his attributes. Berkeley performs the former sort of investigation in the works I have examined in detail aside from *Passive Obedience*; in the latter, he performs the deductions. Finally, it is no contradiction to hold that the existence of God, and the fact that he has certain attributes, is known by the "light of nature", and on the other hand to hold that his existence and his possession of these attributes may be inferred from the sorts of things we find in the real world and their natures (minds, bodies and relations). As we have seen, the inference from the natural world to God's morally relevant attributes presupposes that nature is a language.

It is certainly true that the structure of *Passive Obedience* is deductive, and it is this structure, together with several other misleading claims from the work, which have led some to espouse the view that Berkeley held a logic of demonstration, a "mix't mathematics" of ethics, something like Locke's theory. Taken by themselves, outside the context of his other works, some of the misleading statements do seem to place Berkeley in this tradition:

. . . the rational deduction of those laws is founded on the intrinsic tendency they have to promote the well-being of mankind. . .[50]

. . . whatsoever practical proposition doth to right reason evidently appear to have a necessary connection with the universal well being included in it is to be looked upon as enjoined by the will of God.[51]

In places, he seems to be equating the logical status of moral truths to that of mathematical propositions:

In morality the eternal rules of action have the same immutable universal truth with propositions in geometry. Neither of them depend upon circumstances or accidents, being at all times, and in all places, without limitation or exception, true. . .[52]

[48] PO, 15
[49] PO, 14
[50] PO, 31
[51] PO, 11
[52] PO, 53

He goes on to say that because a rule does not "reach a man's practice" in all cases is no more reason to deny its universality than it would be to deny it for the rule "multiply the height by half the base" for measuring triangles because the thing to be measured was not an exact triangle.

Because of remarks such as these, there are then two opposing schools of thought about Berkeley's moral philosophy. The issues upon which they differ can be stated precisely. The first point of disagreement is this: 1. One school holds that for Berkeley moral truths are *a priori*, while the other side thinks they are *a posteriori*. The case for the *a priori* side is well represented by the quotation from an article by H. W. Orange which I gave in the introduction, and which I shall repeat here for purposes of convenience:

> . . . so far are these laws from being the *a posteriori* conclusions of Utilitarian calculation, that 'these propositions are called *laws of nature*, because they are universal, and do not derive their obligation from any civil sanction, but immediately from the Author of nature Himself. They are said to be *stamped on the mind*, to be *engraven on the tables of the heart*, because they are known to mankind, and suggested and inculcated by conscience. Lastly, they are termed *eternal rules of reason*, because they necessarily result from the nature of things, and may be demonstrated by the infallible deductions of reason.'[53]

Upon first glance there is clearly no reconciling this claim, based upon something Berkeley actually says, with the view I have been defending. The position of this author seems to be further supported by Berkeley's assertion that the observance of moral laws has a "necessary connection" with our "universal well-being".[54]

The *a posteriori* side considers Berkeley's moral laws to be a species of natural law, and this position is represented by remarks such as these, from an article by G. A. Johnston:

> Now moral rules are natural laws, and all the characteristics of natural laws belong to moral laws. Hence the same order and regularity which we perceive in the natural world exists also in the moral realm. But the moral and natural spheres are only partly coincident. The moral realm is necessarily natural, but the natural world is not necessarily moral. Vegetable existence possesses all the attributes of the natural, but we cannot predicate morality of it. But the moral world, as we find it existing among self-conscious beings, is a realm of ends, in which man living according to nature considers himself not as an isolated and independent individual, but as "a part of a whole, to the common good of which he ought to conspire."[55]

[53] BM, p. 521
[54] PO 15
[55] DB, p. 426

My own theory is obviously more closely related to the Johnston side than to Orange's.

The second issue between the two interpretations concerns the method Berkeley uses in ethics, and it is closely related to the first problem, because the *a priori* claim seems to gain support from Berkeley's remarks about "moral demonstration" early in the *Philosophical Commentaries*. This is especially true, given the traditional meaning of "demonstration", i.e. deduction of propositions from self-evident or analytically true premises, resulting in conclusions as certain as the premises themselves. The second issue can therefore be stated this way:

2. Is Berkeley's method demonstrative in *Passive Obedience*, and if so, is this compatible with the thesis that moral truths are for him *a posteriori?* I shall discuss the second of the two issues first.

Demonstration is often confused with deduction, but the two are not the same. Deduction is merely the logical method used in demonstration. Demonstration is deduction of conclusions from immutable, self-evident, known-to-be-true premises, and the conclusions therefore have this same epistemological status, provided the moves in the deduction are intuited as are the premises. As a method for arriving at truths it is ancient, but it was prominent in the 17th and 18th centuries because of Descartes, and Spinoza used it impressively in ethics. Moreover, some philosophers saw it as the only way by which they could support a systematic ethics, while escaping from theological dogmatism at the same time. It was the system chosen by Locke. The word "knowledge" for Locke meant either demonstrative knowledge or intuitive knowledge, that is, either knowledge of the truth of propositions known to follow from others already known to be true, or direct knowledge itself. Locke thought that demonstration in ethics was possible because he thought that ethical terms were the names of nominal rather than real essences, just as the names of substances are in his view names of nominal rather than real essences, because the latter are unknowable for Locke. Ethics thereby became for Locke a science dealing with abstract ideas, and as such it was *a priori* because it was independent of actual experience. It is in this way that claims about demonstration and those about the logical structure of ethical propositions are related.

Early in Berkeley's writings, as I have mentioned, he makes statements which indicate that he was at least considering such a theory:

Morality may be Demonstrated as Mix't Mathematics.[56]

[56] PC, 755

Yet, at other times he seems to be saying that the whole enterprise of demonstration in ethics, though *deduction* is possible, is trifling:

> To demonstrate Morality it seems one need only make a Dictionary of Words and see which included which. at least. This is the greatest part and bulk of the Work.[57]
> Locke's instances of Demonstration in Morality are according to his own Rule triflng Propositions.[58]

Demonstrative ethics, he seems to be saying here, merely tells people how to use certain words. Moreover, he also seems to be saying that the propositions deduced will be trivial because they will be tautologous. This is G. P. Conroy's opinion in the article I mentioned in the introduction.[59] In addition, in so far as the Lockean view entails that ethical terms are the names of abstract general ideas, all of Berkeley's criticisms of that theory come into play. Finally, all of Berkeley's own philosophy of mind that we have is incompatible with the demonstration hypothesis. I shall discuss this philosophy in the next chapter, but here I should mention that for Berkeley, ethical acts are all of them acts of will. Volitions are acts of spirits or minds, of which we therefore have no ideas. We only have "notions" of minds and their acts. Conroy notes:

> If demonstration can be only of names which represent ideas and ideas of spiritual activity are systematically unknowable and impossible, then moral demonstration is impossible inasmuch as morality is a matter which primarily concerns the will, or volitions.[60]

No one denies that deduction is used in *Passive Obedience*, and indeed, in Berkeley's other works as well. But his method is clearly not demonstrative in the other works, and the amount of evidence I have accumulated in support of my theory surely indicates that *Passive Obedience* is an exception, if it (the method) *is* demonstrative there. I do not think it is, but at least for Conroy, the tract remains an enigma, for in his view, in spite of the inconsistencies with Berkeley's other works, the method of *Passive Obedience* is demonstration:

> This change of direction is puzzling. Yet if one realizes that Berkeley is here writing a treatise that is primarily political in nature and only secondarily ethical, one can better understand the particular problems. The ethical

---

[57] PC, 690
[58] PC, 691
[59] Conroy, G., "Berkeley on Moral Demonstration", *Journal of the History of Ideas*, vol. XXII, no. 2 (1961), p. 209 (BMD)
[60] BMD, p. 211

notions which Berkeley brings to bear on the question of loyalty are only extended and developed as far as his immediate purpose required. *Passive Obedience* is not an attempt to work out an ethical system in whole or in brief.[61]

He holds this view even though he says at the same time that the truths of *Passive Obedience* are not *a priori*:

His precepts on investigation illustrate themselves to be empirical generalizations upon experience or prudential maxims. He takes into account the feelings and inclinations of men. He starts from these and asks how they can be harmonized with God's purposes which cannot be demonstrated but which must come through revealed pronouncements to the common man, to the philosophical man through an induction of particulars, i.e. through seeing what courses of life, kinds of characters, and what types of acts lead to men's real happiness.[62]

This last set of remarks is of course consistent with my own view, and they are supported by much evidence, for example,

Reasoning there may be about things or Ideas or Actions but Demonstration can only be verbal.[63]

Quotations such as this also bring to mind Berkeley's view of mathematics, according to which mathematics is about signs or names, whose demonstrations, though practically useful, are trivial.

But if Conroy's views of Berkeley's precepts, even in *Passive Obedience*, are as the quote above indicates, then why does he think that the method of *Passive Obedience* is demonstrative? I certainly do not think it is, and in order to support the contention, I shall have to return to the first of the two issues, the logical status of the propositions involved in *Passive Obedience*, and to the explanation of those confusing remarks about "necessary connection", etc.

What does Berkeley mean when he speaks of a necessary connection between the moral laws of nature and our well-being? Whatever it is, it cannot be that he is thinking of a *necessary* connection if this means *logically* necessary, because if it was this sort of connection, then God could not be free. A necessary condition for the occurrence of any event, including consequences which follow upon our action in accordance with a rule, is God's concurrence. If it was a contradiction to assert that the law was obeyed but that the consequence did not follow, then

[61] BMD, p. 212
[62] BMD, p. 213
[63] PC, 804

God would not be free to intervene. Of course, consequences do in fact follow, but so long as God need not logically will any particular thing, the connection between the consequences of following rules and the rules must be contingent. Even in *Passive Obedience* Berkeley affirms that nature is nothing but "a series of *free* actions produced by the best and wisest Agent"[64] and since the effects of our acts of will are part of that natural language, God must freely concur in their advent. If God is free, omniscient and all powerful, as Berkeley thought, then the effects of obedience to natural moral laws cannot logically follow from them.[65]

Secondly, there are elements in Berkeley's theory of truth which prevent him from claiming *a priori* status for moral truths, *unless* by "a priori" we merely mean "independent of experience" in the sense that natural moral laws continue independently of their perception by individual human perceivers. This is a complex problem and I cannot discuss it at length here. Whatever else is true, this is: Berkeley's view of the nature of truth is not the traditional one, and certainly not Locke's. We have seen that Locke and the Deists believed that truth was a function of the agreement of ideas, such that the sentence "Melampus is an animal" would be true if the idea denoted by "Melampus" and that denoted by "animal" were related in given ways. But Berkeley thought there was only one idea involved, that of Melampus, and there is evidence to believe that he viewed the sentence, or its analysis, as an instruction telling us that we could also call Melampus by the name "animal".[66] Further, since we have no ideas of relations, minds, and several other things, propositions about them could not be true or false according to whether their names denoted ideas which stood in relations of whatever sort to one another.[67] In addition, if nature is a language then the laws of nature cannot be true or false on the idea-correspondence theory. This is because even if truth in the natural language was a function of resemblance among ideas, or class membership, or some other relation of correspondence, resemblance and class inclusion and the like are relations of which we can have no ideas for Berkeley, and he denies that there are natural classes.[68] Finally, natural moral laws are "rules directive of our actions"[69] and even if Berk-

[64] PO, 14
[65] P., 106
[66] Draft, pp. 136-137
[67] P., 89, 90, 100
[68] P. 89, 90
[69] PO, 7

eley did accept some sort of correspondence theory in the case of descriptions, which is doubtful in the light of such remarks as those in *Principles* 49, there is no reason to believe that rules would fall into the same category. He argues that the terms in the laws of arithmetic and geometry do not denote abstract general ideas as the Lockeans had held, and that the universality of geometrical signs, for example, a one inch line, and hence presumably of propositions formed from such terms, consists ". . . only in its signification, whereby it represents innumerable lines greater than itself".[70] Mathematical propositions are also concerned, though indirectly, with particulars; they "direct us how to act with relation to things, and dispose rightly of them".[71] The same themes are found throughout *De Motu* and the *Analyst*. In my view, Berkeley's theory of truth, both in mathematics and in general, is much like Pragmatism or Instrumentalism, and if this is true, then remarks such as those about "necessary connection", and claims such as ". . . the eternal rules of action have the same immutable truth with propositions in geometry" must be interpreted accordingly. If they are, then the "*a priori*" claim is, if true, sensible only in the sense I have mentioned, namely the sense in which I claim a truth is *a priori* because it is independent of the perception of any given human perceiver. But of course the proponents of this theory would not want to say this.

I conclude that the necessary connection of which Berkeley speaks when talking about moral laws and our well-being is not to be understood as referring to the logical structure of moral laws, nor to some sort of *synthetic a priori* connection between signs and significates in the natural language (though this is a theory for which some evidence could be mustered, and which has never been considered) but rather to the relations between minds, especially God's, and mental acts together with their effects. The effects are "necessary" because of God's goodness and benevolence and power, *if* he wills that they occur; but he need not.

Our knowledge of moral laws therefore remains probable – it depends upon the assumption that the future will resemble the past. The moral laws themselves are not logically true. Our knowledge that certain effects will occur if we obey moral laws is also probable, because this depends upon God's will, which we cannot know.

From these propositions if follows that demonstration cannot be Berkeley's method in ethics, and although I think that this is also true

[70] P., 126
[71] P., 122

of *Passive Obedience*, if I am mistaken in this point, I believe that I am still correct with regard to his other works. Given the political motive of *Passive Obedience*, and the evidence gathered from the other works, it therefore seems reasonable to assume that this tract is an exception to Berkeley's rule, and in line with his own recommendations, should be read as such. But again, if I am right, demonstration is not even the method there.

It remains to consider Berkeley's contentions that natural moral laws do not derive their sanction from civil sources, but from God, and that they are "stamped on the mind . . . engraven on the heart" because all of us know them well, and because they are "suggested and inculcated by conscience".[72] The question is what analysis we are to give this, and how that analysis affects the relation of God to the obligation accruing to moral laws. The answer is that the two claims – that moral laws are "stamped on the mind", and that they derive their obligation from God and not from any civil source – have nothing to do with one another at all. The first claim should be understood in a dispositional sense. Although he does assert that basic moral laws are "engraven on the heart", he qualifies this claim very carefully, even in *Passive Obedience*. In the words of C. D. Broad:

All that he will admit is that there are innate antipathies to *some* kinds of action which are in fact wrong. But antipathies to certain kinds of action are often due simply to early training, and it is difficult or impossible to distinguish these from genuinely innate antipathies. Berkeley's conclusion is as follows. It is a mistake to assume that, when a strong antipathy is felt towards an act, the act must therefore be a breach of a fundamental moral precept. It is equally a mistake to assume that, where no such antipathy is felt, the act is *not* a breach of such a precept. In all cases, he says, we must decide what is and what is not a fundamental precept 'not by any emotion in our blood and spirits, but by . . . sober and impartial reason.'[73]

At the very most then, innate antipathies are *prima facie* evidence of the status of acts *viz à viz* moral laws, and they are certainly not moral laws themselves, as the "*a priori*" theory would lead us to believe. There is no clash between the affirmation that we have dispositions to recognize certain acts as right, and the claim that the process by which we become aware of moral laws, and the subsequent formulation of those laws, is the result of *a posteriori* reasoning. And the entire matter seems irrelevant to the question of the source of obligation.

[72] PO, 12
[73] Broad, C. D. "Berkeley's Theory of Morals", *Revue Internationale de Philosophie*, (1953), p. 74 (BBTM)

If we claim that deduction and not demonstration is the method of *Passive Obedience*, and if we interpret remarks such as those just considered in a dispositional sense rather than within the *a priori* tradition, and finally if we take into account Berkeley's remarks about truth and his criticisms of the idea-correspondence theory, then *Passieve Obedience* becomes consistent with Berkeley's theories about natural moral law and our knowledge of it. Since God's will is arbitrary and thus undetermined, and since our knowledge of his will is probable, because based upon constant conjunction, it follows that verbal demonstration can only end up with probable conclusions, which is a claim consistent with Berkeley's remark that moral laws "result from the nature of things", i.e. from the divine language and God's will. Therefore, what was at first sight an insoluble dilemma in the interpretation of Berkeley turns out to be no dilemma at all.

With this interpretation in mind, I now return to the argument in *Passive Obedience* to consider it in more detail.

3. TWO KINDS OF MORAL RULES, AND SOME THEOLOGICAL IMPLICATIONS

Even in *Passive Obedience*, Berkeley affirms that moral behavior is learned. When we are young, we are most attracted by the impressions of sense, and it is only after long experience that we become aware that present good is often attended with greater evil in the long run, and that there are qualitative differences in the value of things.[74] For this reason, sound thinking dictates a consideration of the remote consequences of our actions. God, as the sole "maker and preserver of all things . . . is . . . with the most undoubted right, the great legislator of the world; and mankind are, by all the ties of duty, no less than interest, bound to obey His laws."[75] Morality therefore consists in conformity to God's will, and our first duty is to find out what his will is:

For laws being rules directive of our actions to the end intended by the legislator, in order to attain the knowledge of God's laws we ought first to enquire what that end is which He desires should be carried on by Human actions.[76]

The end which God desires was known by him from eternity, prior

[74] PO, 5
[75] PO, 6
[76] PO, 7

to any existing distinctions among men, and therefore the differences among men are not relevant to the discovery of what that end is. What we infer from this fact is that the end cannot be the private good of this or that man or group of men, but rather it must be "the general well-being of all men, of all nations, of all ages of the world, which God designs should be procrured by the concurring actions of each individual."[77] How is this end to be achieved? It will not do to leave it to the impulses of men, benevolent though they may be, because impulse varies among men, and like any passion it is subject to abuse.[78] Fortunately however, we do not have to rely upon impulse. God has so instituted natural law that the effects of obeying it are as sure to follow as are the laws themselves from God's will. This is not a logical necessity, as we have seen – it is simply to say that we will be better off for obeying the natural moral law because God so wills it.[79] Given that the general welfare is achieved by following natural moral law, we merely have to ascertain what these laws are, and follow them. The criterion of a subsidiary moral law or rule, that is, one which governs a particular class of actions specifically, is whether or not it meets the requirements of the utility principle. I shall say more on this point in the next section of this chapter.

Among the laws of nature and morality binding upon man which Berkeley was concerned to support was this one: "Thou shalt not resist the supreme power".[80] Obedience to government concerns the general well-being rather than that of individuals, and is "universal enough" to be considered as a case of natural law, that is, the constant conjunction between obedience to government and the consequent increase in the general well-being is universal enough to be so considered.[81] It is in his discussion of this issue that Berkeley draws the distinction between two kinds of natural moral law: positive and negative ones. First, he argues in support of his assertion that loyalty, or at least passive obedience, is a natural moral law. He points out that although civil polity is a result of human institution, so is all moral action, in the sense that it involves voluntary acts of will. Further, there is a tendency in all men, "a natural tendency or disposition to a social life . . . natural because it is universal, and because it necessarily results from the differences which distinguish man from beast", without which

[77] PO, 7
[78] PO, 13
[79] PO, 15
[80] PO, 15
[81] PO, 18

we could not live in a social state suitable to our natures. Without obedience under law, this societal life cannot be maintained, but the law enjoining obedience to civil law cannot itself be a civil law, so it is, for all these reasons, to be accounted a natural moral law.[82] Yet we must distinguish, because there are inevitable conflicts between moral rules in certain circumstances, and because a man can never do an unjust act morally, between positive and negative rules. The difference between the two sorts of rule is explicated as follows:

> Now, the ground of that distinction may be resolved into this, namely, that very often, either through the difficulty or number of moral actions, or their inconsistency with each other, it is not possible for one man to perform several of them at the same time; whereas it is plainly consistent and possible that any man should, at the same time, abstain from all manner of positive actions whatsoever. Hence it comes to pass that prohibitions or negative precepts must by every one, in all times and places, be all actually observed: whereas those which enjoin the doing of an action allow for human prudence and discretion in the execution of them, it for the most part depending on various accidental circumstances, all of which ought to be considered, and care taken that duties of less moment do not interfere with and hinder the fulfilling of those which are more important. And, for this reason, if not the positive laws themselves, at least the exercise of them, admits of suspension, limitation, and diversity of degrees.[83]

Negative laws are therefore absolutely binding, whereas positive ones may, due to particular circumstances, vary in the mode of our compliance with them, or application of them.

There is an important *logical* point in the distinction between the two sorts of law. There are situations in which one finds oneself where one cannot obey both of two competing positive moral rules. For example, "Keep your promises" and "Answer questions truthfully" cannot both be obeyed in a situation where one is asked a question after promising not to reveal the answer. In such cases, the agent has to consider the moral value involved in violating one of the rules rather than the other, since he must violate at least one of them. For Berkeley, such a situation never arises in the context of negative moral rules, because rules such as "Never break your promises" and "Never answer questions falsely" can both be obeyed at the same time simply by not answering at all. C. D. Broad has outlined the logical structure of the theory. He points out that if Berkeley is right, then if we are prohibited from performing some moral act, the prohibition is logically equivalent

[82] PO, 25
[83] PO, 26

to a moral obligation to do one of two things: if you cannot lie, then either you must tell the truth, or not answer at all. Following the example above, it would also be the case that if you cannot break a promise, then you must either give an answer which obeys the promise, or not say anything at all. Schematically, if X and Y are both morally obligatory, then the conjunction (X.Y) is morally obligatory. In the case of the "lying versus keeping your promises" example, both X and Y are disjunctions. X would be the disjunction "Either tell the truth or say nothing" and Y would be "Either keep your promises or say nothing". But the hypothesis here posits that it is impossible to both tell the truth and keep your promise. Let "Tell the truth" be T. and "Keep your promises" be P. Let "say nothing" be N. X is therefore (T v N) and Y is (P v N) and (X.Y) is [(T v N). (P v N)]. But by hypothesis both T and P are *impossible*. It follows in both cases that N is obligatory.[84] Broad also points out that we should not take the phrase "*negative* law" in a pejorative sense, since obviously it might take a tremendous positive effort of will to obey a negative law.

What Berkeley does not consider is the possibility that some moral decisions require a mechanism of precedence whereby we can decide to *break* some positive moral rule. One example which is often cited is the hypothetical case where a man has a choice of telling a lie and thereby preventing a war, or telling the truth and causing it. Given that silence would also cause the war, it would seem that one has an obligation to lie, odd though this might sound, because the obligation to prevent wars is greater. Berkeley's theory does not seem to be capable of handling such a case, or certainly the theory suggested by *Passive Obedience* alone cannot handle it.

It seems at times as though Berkeley is speaking of a dual criterion for moral law, especially when he says things like this:

... nothing is a law merely because it conduceth to the public good, but because it is decreed by the will of God, which alone can give the sanction of a law of nature to any precept.[85]

But in fact, Berkeley is doing nothing of the sort, since natural law is an immediate effect of the will of God, as is its *tendency*, when obeyed, to serve the general good. Or to put it another way, natural laws would not serve the general good unless God so willed it. It is misleading for Berkeley to speak this way, because it might delude the

[84] BBTM, p. 80
[85] PO, 31

reader into thinking that there were *two* factors a moral agent must discover, namely, the will of God, and the natural law, whereas in effect the one is the expression of the other. The distinction *is* relevant in discussions about the ground of moral obligation, as we shall see, but only so far as the distinction between a cause and its effect is concerned.

It might be objected to Berkeley's theory, or so he thought, that revolution, though evil, was sometimes necessary to overcome a still greater evil, malevolent tyranny. This objection is obviously related to the one I mentioned a moment ago, about having to make choices in which one moral rule must be violated. Berkeley's reply is that first of all, the end does not justify the means, even if the end is good.[86] Moreover, even if there are occasional exceptions to the general tendency of natural laws, it is still *generally* true that following them serves the common good: we must keep in mind that it is the well-being of all people in all ages in all climes which is the moral end, and thus we should adopt that course of action which is known to accomplish this more than any other.

It might be further charged that by holding this view Berkeley makes God the author of moral evil, but he thinks this is not so for two reasons: first, moral evil results from human failings and acts of will (more on this in the third and fourth chapters) and the second reason is that accidental circumstances leading to evil effects should be attributed to their proper cause, not to the law. Even though the negative moral rule enjoining passive obedience has a general tendency and "essential fitness" to promote the public good, a tyrant can always abuse it. But in this event the blame should be laid on the tyrant and *his* voluntary acts, not on the law, which is an effect of the will of God and which, *if* followed, will achieve its end.[87] We impute guilt to one another because we know that we will acts in virtue of our knowledge of the consequences we can expect to follow upon them, and which we know to be either good or bad.[88] In short, God cannot be blamed if the tyrant does not follow his laws, and because the tyrant doesn't is no good reason why we shouldn't, provided we know a) that the law is a moral law, and b) that it therefore tends, when obeyed, to further the general good. This, I think, is the import of another remark of Berkeley's which might be misconstrued as evidence in support of the *a priori* thesis:

[86] PO, 35
[87] PO, 41
[88] PC, 157

And as it would not be thought to detract from the universality of this mathematical rule (measure the height by half the base to determine the area of a triangle) that it did not exactly measure a field which was not an exact triangle, so ought it not to be thought an argument against the universality of the rule prescribing passive obedience that it does not reach a mans' practice in all cases where a government is unhinged, or the supreme power disputed.[89]

The authors of mathematical laws cannot be blamed if we misapply or misinterpret them.

Another reason why rules might not fit practices in some cases is that there is more than one rule operative in the mathematical and moral worlds, and they depend upon one another in basic ways. Given that all the moral rules of the universe tend when followed to the same end, they form what C. D. Broad calls a "coherent system" which Berkeley describes as "a system of rules or precepts, such that, if they be *all* of them at all times and places by all men observed, they will necessarily promote the well-being of mankind, so far as that is attainable by human action." Any given rule might therefore be a fundamental law, even if action in accordance with it did *not* in particular cases serve the general well-being, provided that the reason was that other fundamental rules were *not* observed. The entire system is necessary to achieve the end, not just one or two rules.[90]

We might also make non-culpable mistakes, which are not attributable to God. We might for example think that a given series of regular events in nature constitutes a natural law when it does not, or more accurately, we might think that given events do occur in a series when they do not, and hence draw unfounded inferences about what would happen if we acted according to the "law", thereby causing evil effects. No one is to blame for this. But because such mistakes are a possibility, those whose responsibility it is to teach morality have a further obligation to study and learn, and one result of such a study will be to confirm that order is essential to the state and thus to the well-being of man. Since this is so, the laws of the state maintaining order, one of which is passive obedience, cannot be divorced from the moral law, because the rule of morality is what serves the general good.[91] Morality and the law of the land are therefore intimately related in Berkeley's moral philosophy.

For the most part, the important conclusions Berkeley draws about

[89] PO, 53
[90] BBTM, pp. 77-87
[91] D. p. 203

the relations between moral philosophy and theology are not found in *Passive Obedience*. From this point until the beginning of the next section I shall be referring largely to those other works where he does discuss these matters. A principle almost theocratic in nature arises in Berkeley's writings when he speaks about religion, the general well-being, and the corresponding responsibility of public officials. Religious opinions have an immense influence upon the actions of men, and therefore they cannot be excluded from the class of events which affects the public weal. Sound religious principles ought therefore to be propogated by public officials.[92] Objections were raised against this, especially by the Deists, because they did not like the ascendancy of the clergy which followed upon their assumption of civil responsibility under the system of state religions. But Berkeley replies that objections against the position of the clergy are no argument against the thesis that sound principles of good behavior ought to be taught to the young and to others not capable of knowing whether the principles are well-founded. Secondly, in his view, truth and utility cannot be divorced in moral matters, nor in others.

I have already observed that a point's being useful, and inculcated betimes, can be no argument of its falsehood, even although it should be a prejudice; far otherwise, utility and truth are not to be divided; the general good of mankind being the rule or measure of moral truth.[93]

In both the first chapter and in this one I have argued that Berkeley's theory of truth is related to the Pragmatic or Instrumentalist view, and remarks like this seem to support that assertion. The theocratic tendencies of his politics and moral philosophy should not seem strange to anyone who recalls his view of science, which has also been mentioned before:

... it is the searching after, and endeavouring to understand those signs instituted by the Author of Nature, that ought to be the employment of the natural philosopher, and not the pretending to explain things by corporeal causes; which doctrine seems to have too much estranged the minds of men from that active principle, that supreme and wise spirit, in whom we live, move, and have our being.[94]

Berkeley has philosophical arguments which he offers in support of the doctrine of the soul's immortality, but here too his remarks have an obvious theological tinge, especially when he is speaking of the utilit-

---

[92] D. p. 201
[93] D. p. 211
[94] P., 66

arian value of religion. But Berkeley never ceased to emphasize the primacy of reason in moral matters:

... it is highly needful that all the motions, and passions of the soul should be under the regulation and influence of Reason, whose office it is to see that they are placed on proper objects, that they spring from worthy motives and are contained within a just degree.[95]

Yet at the same time, he saw evidence for eternal life in our dispositions, instincts and natural desires. He thought that the desire for happiness was "wrought into the original frame of our nature", and indeed that it was to be found in all of animate nature. In man, because of our superior rational ability, this desire extends to the happiness of all men as well as our private well-being.[96] In so far as man acts for this promotion of the well-being of all, just so far does he deserve "well or ill both of the world and of himself." But moral dessert does not end with this life: reason, revelation, the gospels, wise men in all ages, the law, prophets, and our own natural instincts tell us that man will be rewarded according to his works.[97] Yet it is clear that this world is such that, on the whole, we cannot be perfectly happy, and that it was designed to encourage the hope of perfect temporal happiness. This is the message of Christianity: it gives us hope and thus a measure of happiness, because even if we are miserable, we can believe that our good will be rewarded in the hereafter.[98] Thus, if we have an interest in eternal life, we should mind the teachings of religion, if only for selfish motives.[99] Self-love, guided by reason, is sufficient of itself to lead us to a knowledge of the true methods for obtaining happiness.[100]

But all of this presupposes that we are immortal. Is this wishful thinking? Berkeley did not think so. The belief is supported by the inferences of reason (see the next chapter) and by the fact that God has implanted a strong desire for it in us.[101] In addition, eternal life is proclaimed as a fact in the gospels.[102] He admits that instinctive beliefs are not alone sufficient evidence of truth, but argues that they do provide "probable" inferential grounds, when taken in conjunction with other evidence, such as the analogy between our instincts and the principles of coher-

[95] SE II, p. 16
[96] SE IX, p. 214
[97] SE II, p. 22
[98] Alc. V, 5
[99] SE II, p. 24
[100] SE VI, p. 90
[101] SE VIII, p. 109
[102] SE IX, p. 116

ence in the physical universe. Just as the mutual order of the parts of creation demonstrates God's wisdom and goodness, so our social instincts without which man would not survive demonstrate the same thing.[103] Furthermore, we can confirm that action in accordance with these instincts, though not justified by the instincts, is usually both in our duty and our interest, because we know that the end urged upon us by them is social well-being, which is the moral end indicated by God's moral laws.[104]

Not only do our instincts testify to the benefits accruing to morally right action, but God has also indicated the dissatisfactions of evil to us, in a similar way:

... the practice of any vice or the commission of any crime is attended with an immediate punishment in this life. The infinitely wise providence of God hath joyned moral and (natural) evil together. Some inward uneasiness of mind, some outward pain of body, some loss in reputation or fortune, or the like, is visibly annexed to sin to deter men from the practice of it.[105]

The bracketed word "natural" is blurred in the original, but seems to be the logical interpretation.

Nowhere is Berkeley more specific on the subject of innate dispositions than in his sermon "On the Will of God". There he says that in addition to the study of natural law, there is another "natural" way to discover the moral will of God. "Natural conscience", an "inward feeling implanted in the soul of every man", suggests to us independently of reason that morally right actions are attended with "joy and satisfaction", whereas evil actions bring us unhappiness and remorse. This "inward feeling" or "natural conscience" is one of the original dispositions and tendencies of human souls, and Berkeley expresses his belief that these "shew themselves, at proper periods, and in certain circumstances", and he says that because they are universal and "not to be accounted for by custom or education" in any age or nation, they are "properly said to be natural or innate."[106] Other dispositions which we have are the impulse to love our children, the tendency to believe in a superior being, the abhorrence of certain crimes and vices, and the urge to love and "relish" what is good and virtuous.[107] There, are then three ways by which we can know the will of God: revelation, reason, and natural conscience, and they all tell us the same thing,

[103] GE XII, p. 225
[104] GE XII, pp. 226-227
[105] SE III, p. 36
[106] SE X, p. 129
[107] SE X, p. 130

which is that personal and social happiness can be obtained by obeying the moral laws taught us in the language of nature, and that it is God's will that we do this.

... nothing can render our lives more conformable to the will of God than a steady endeavour to promote the wellbeing of his creatures, whose happiness is so constantly uniformly and impartially promoted by the laws of nature, that they sufficiently declare and speak out the will of him that framed them.[108]

Again however, when we consider what is suggested by our instincts and dispositions, we must remember that they *suggest*, and that by themselves they do not constitute sufficient evidence of the moral validity of the courses of action which are suggested. For this sufficiency, reason is always required.

Our knowledge of what God wills us to do is not always sufficient to cause us to do it, and because he believed this, Berkeley also believed in the efficacy of reward and punishment in the hereafter, especially since he could see no way to rectify injustice in our temporal lives without such eternal sanctions. Without this, Berkeley can see no reason why we should not act selfishly:

For what reason is there why such a one should postpone his own private interest or pleasure to the doing of his duty? If a Christian foregoes some present advantage for the sake of his conscience, he acts accountably, because it is with the view of gaining some greater future good.[109]

The "such a one" of whom he asks this question is of course the freethinker, and his reply invokes the ultimate justification of Christianity, which is utility.

4. SOME RULE-UTILITARIAN ELEMENTS

In this section I shall examine some principles of Berkeley's moral philosophy which are strikingly modern. These are some of the tenets of the theory known as Rule-Utilitarianism, a theory which only became popular in the present century with the writings of such philosophers as John Rawls. I do not mean to suggest that Berkeley was a Rule-Utilitarian, nor even that he held most of the tenets of that theory, but I do think that he held the central ones, and that, so far as I know, he was the first to do so.

[108] SE X, p. 133
[109] SE V, p. 200

The most important source for information about this is again *Passive Obedience*, though most of the arguments may also be found in other works as well. As we seen, Berkeley claims that we cannot leave the moral conduct which results from obedience to the moral law to decisions of impulse or instinct, because chaos would be the result, given the variations in individual impulses and the possibility of their abuse. The only reasonable way to achieve the moral end, the greatest happiness, is to obey general rules, discoverable in the natural language, and confirmed by the tendencies of our instincts and reconfirmed in the gospels and revelation. Passive obedience, or loyalty to the duly constituted authority, is one of those laws.[110] It is in the defense of this assertion that he makes the distinction between positive and negative laws which I have already given. But the *most* interesting part of this argument concerns the ways that Berkeley thinks we can serve the moral end. We can accomplish the end in one of two ways:

... first, without the injunction of any certain universal rules of morality, only by obliging every one upon each particular occasion to consult the public good, and always to do that which to him shall seem, in the present time and circumstances, most to conduce to it. Or, secondly, by enjoining the observation of some determinate, established laws, which, if universally practiced, have, from the nature of things, an essential fitness to procure the well-being of mankind; though in their particular application they are sometimes, through untoward accidents and the perverse irregularity of human wills, the occasions of great sufferings and misfortunes, it may be, to very many good men.[111]

He realizes that the second method, the obedience to rules rather than making individual decisions in particular circumstances, may now and then be attended with undesirable consequences. But on the other hand, the wisest of men, whether from lack of ability to predict all of the consequences, or lack of knowledge of the circumstances surrounding the situation, often cannot make an adequate moral decision. It is also easier to judge each act by its relation to a rule than it is to judge it according to the consequences which may follow upon it in some particular situation. In fact, it is impossible to calculate all of the consequences of any given action, and even if it were, the calculating "would yet take up too much time to be of use in the affairs of life."[112] Furthermore, even if we could judge the moral value of acts,

---

[110] PO, 3-20
[111] PO, 8
[112] PO, 9

based on their consequences, within a reasonable period of time, it would still not be acceptable to leave it to the judgment of the individual, because moral opinions vary in wide degree, depending as they do upon each man's circumstances and special interests.[113] In the end, this would mean that we would have no certain moral standards in accordance with which we could judge acts.

For all of these reasons, the procedure by which the individual would apply the utility principle himself upon particular occasions in order to make a moral decision would itself violate that principle, since it would result in a chaos of conflicting moral judgments, vacillation and hesitation in making these judgments, and confusion in the evaluation of acts and moral agents.[114] But God himself, we know from our study of nature, from scripture, and from natural conscience, enjoins upon us the duty to do whatever we can, provided it is not evil, to promote the general happiness. It follows therefore:

... that the great end to which God requires the concurrence of human actions must of necessity be carried on by the second method proposed, namely, the observation of certain, universal, determinate rules or moral precepts, which, in their own nature, have a necessary tendency to promote the well-being of the sum of mankind, taking in all nations and ages, from the beginning to the end of the world.[115]

It is of course still true that in the case of positive precepts, circumstances play a limited role on some occasions, as when we might have to suspend action in accordance with the rule because of conflict with another rule. But in the case of negative rules, no such difficulties arise.[116] Examples of negative precepts again are "Thou shalt not foreswear thyself", "Thou shalt not commit adultery" and "Thou shalt not steal".[117]

In Berkeley's eyes, there are two cardinal objections to this thesis, insofar as it entails that loyalty to a government is a moral obligation. The first objection is that if God enjoins the public good as a moral end, we must be obliged in cases where strict adherence to the precept is obviously contrary to this end, to disobey it. In reply Berkeley says that 1) nothing is a moral law merely because it serves the public good, but because it is willed by God. I have already given reasons for believing

---

[113] PO, 11
[114] PO, 28
[115] PO, 10
[116] PO, 26; cf. also BBTM, *passim*, and BTU, p. 90
[117] PO, 15

that two criteria are not involved here, or to put it another way, that the question of the derivation of obligation is unnecessarily raised here, because the question we are really concerned with is whether there is any such thing as a moral law which does not serve the public good. Berkeley should simply say that there is not. His second reply in effect does raise this point. He thinks that the objection fails to distinguish between particular instances of bad consequences following from accidental circumstances, and the *general* fitness and tendency of the rule to serve the public welfare. These other circumstances, as I have mentioned, are not due to the rule: tyrants are not part of the law of nature enjoining loyalty.[118] Berkeley sums it up this way:

> ... that whole difficulty may be resolved by the following distinction. In framing the general laws of nature, it is granted we must be entirely guided by the public good of mankind, but not in the ordinary moral actions of our lives. Such a rule, if universally observed, hath, from the nature of things, a necessary fitness to promote the general well-being of mankind: therefore it is a law of nature. This is good reasoning. But if we should say, such an action doth in this instance produce much good and no harm to mankind; therefore it is lawful: this were wrong. The rule is framed with respect to the good of mankind; but *our practice must always be shaped immediately by the rule*.[119]

The utility principle is the rule of rules, that whereby we formulate the other subsidiary rules which we discover in nature. Once we have these other rules, we do not justify particular decisions by appeal to the general good, but by appeal to the rules. Hence, "our practice must always be shaped immediately by the rule", and only mediately by the principle of utility.

The second major objection to Berkeley's position is the contention that loyalty as a moral law violates a still more basic natural and moral law, that of self-preservation.[120] Berkeley agrees that self-preservation is a *natural* law, but thinks that we must take care to distinguish between those natural laws which are also moral laws, and those which are not. Those natural laws which are also moral laws are those which we can use as "a rule or precept for the direction of the voluntary actions of reasonable agents", and only such rules imply moral duties. But there are natural laws which are merely "any general rule which we observe to obtain in the works of nature, independent of the wills of men", that is, mere sequences or series of

[118] PO, 41
[119] PO, 31, (my italics)
[120] PO, 33

events which we see in the natural world which do not concern the government of human conduct. It is presumably in this last sense that self-preservation is a natural law. Berkeley says:

I grant it is a general law of nature that in every animal there be implanted a desire of self-preservation, which, though it is the earliest, the deepest, and most lasting of all, whether natural or acquired appetites, yet cannot with any propriety be termed a moral duty.[121]

In his view, self-preservation could not possibly be the fundamental moral principle, for if it were,

. . . it would hence follow, a man may lawfully commit any sin whatsoever to preserve his life, than which nothing can be more absurd.[122]

He does not consider the possibility that self-preservation may be a natural moral law, but not the most fundamental one. Nor does he say anything more about the strange distinction between those natural laws which may be used to guide voluntary acts, and those which may not be so used. This argument surely needs explication and defense, for on the face of it, there seems to be no reason why *any* natural law could *not* be used as a guide for our actions. There is no reason to push someone off a cliff, or to prevent them from jumping, if the law of gravity does not hold.

But Berkeley thinks that there is yet another reason to reject the claim that self-preservation permits us to break the loyalty rule. Even if self-preservation was a moral law and not just a natural one, the fundamental *negative* moral principle which we know is "Evil is never to be committed, to the end good may come of it". From this it follows that in order to save our lives, we are still not entitled to engage in active rebellion because this would be to act in accordance with the *positive* law "To save your life, rebel", or some such law, and Berkeley argues that negative precepts always take precedence over positive ones.[123] His way of stating this is to say that negative precepts are not subject to "limitation", whereas positive ones are. He thinks that moral duties may be limited in two ways: "first, as a distinction applied to the terms of a proposition, whereby that which was expressed before too generally is limited to a particular acceptation." He himself admits that this is not so much a matter of "limiting" moral duties as it is a question of *defining* them, that is, deciding what the range of a moral

---

[121] PO, 33
[122] PO, 33
[123] PO, 35

rule is, by deciding what moral acts count as instances falling under it. Even negative moral rules are limitable in this sense. But there is a second sense of limitation: "it may be understood as a suspending the observation of a duty for avoiding some extra-ordinary inconvenience, and thereby confining it to certain occasions". It is in this sense that he thinks positive duties may be limited but not negative ones. Evidently his reasoning is that in spite of rules enjoining us to partake in a certain sort of action, circumstances may always intervene and prevent our performing the act, or cause us to postpone doing it, or to modify what we do in some other way. But when a negative rule enjoins us *not* to do something, there is nothing circumstantial which can prevent us from doing nothing. This is a position which is simply factually false if one construes an "action" as something, an event, which is the possible object of perception. But all such objects of perception are *not* actions for Berkeley – they are *effects of actions*. I shall discuss this important point later on. For the moment, it is only important to notice that if the latter is true, then Berkeley's position is not on the face of it simply empirically false, as it otherwise might seem. Certainly it is not without its difficulties. Nonetheless, at this point suffice it to say that two principles become evident from his discussion of limitations of moral rules, and the distinction between positive and negative rules. The first is that if negative moral rules always take precedence over positive ones, then no moral action enjoined by the latter sort of rule can ever take precedence over the abstinence from action enjoined by the former kind. Secondly, negative precepts cannot be suspended because of circumstances or particular bad consequences, first of all because empirical consequences cannot causally effect any mental act (though this must also be true of acts enjoined by positive laws, as Berkeley apparently fails to see) and secondly because negative rules prohibit the performance of evil acts, acts known by natural moral laws to tend to the worsening of the human condition rather than its betterment. Thus they could not be performed in any circumstances. Of course, if we could show that a natural law had a tendency to promote our detriment rather than our well-being, we would then have shown that it was not a *moral* law.

Passive Obedience, where most of the material on positive and negative laws and the limitation of moral laws is to be found, appeared for the first time in 1712, and there were three other editions. It was a synthesis of three sermons which Berkeley gave in Trinity College chapel in Dublin, and it was published because Berkeley was accused of being sympathetic to the Jacobites on the basis of the original sermons. I must say that how anybody could gather this from the sermons is beyond me, and in fact he claimed that it was precisely to refute the Jacobites that he gave them in the first place. Nevertheless, because of its clearly political tone and motive, it should not be taken as indicative of Berkeley's true position without further corroboration. Support for the three major points of rule-utilitarianism which arise in *Passive Obedience*, both direct and indirect, *is* forthcoming in the other works. The three major points are again:

1. "Our practice must always be shaped by the rule", not the individual judgment of particular cases.

2. The rule itself is to be judged on the basis of its tendency to promote the greatest good of the greatest number in the long run, for all times and places.

3. Particular judgments of particular issues cannot be the mechanism of moral decision, because a) it is impossible to judge consequences accurately, and b) even if it was, it would be impractical because of limited time and ability.

Modern rule-utilitarianism holds that an act is right if it falls under a rule when practice in accordance with that rule brings about the greatest happiness, because rules themselves bring about nothing. An issue now arises: it is the question of whether an act is right because it is of a certain type which maximizes good, or because it falls under a rule, and having the rule in force maximizes good. I think that Berkeley would say that the type of action which maximizes good is identical with the class of actions which is in accordance with natural moral laws, and that without these laws, we would never know what sort of action it *is* that maximizes good. I am not sure that this constitutes an answer to the rule-utilitarian problem, or whether Berkeley would simply say that it really is not a problem at all. I am inclined to think that his position implies the latter. In all events, it is clear that the three points place Berkeley in the Rule-Utilitarian tradition, though it is odd to speak of someone being in a "tradition" when the tradition did not begin until centuries after his death. Surely the fact that he ennunciated principles used in the modern theory is indubitable, and this is all I wish to claim.

5. A PRELIMINARY SUMMING-UP

The word "system" is misleading. There is no denying that Berkeley has no developed ethical system, if by that we mean that he did not write a book in which we can study his logically organized thoughts and arguments specifically about ethics as opposed to the rest of philosophy. But it is quite another thing to argue that the principles of an ethical system are not to be found in his work, and I think that I have already shown that several such principles are to be discovered there. These principles cannot be separated, in many cases, from their relevance in ontological and epistemological contexts: but that is only to say that the same axiom can be used in more than one theory, and it shows that in Berkeley's case, the traditional divisions of the subjects of philosophy are not cut and dried. The morally relevant principles which have been examined thus far can be conveniently schematized as follows, though I do not suggest that Berkeley did so organize them in the works we do have:

1. Nature is a divine language which is a direct effect of God's willing.

2. There are three ways in which we can discover what God's will is:
   a) Revelation
   b) Natural reason (the study of nature)
   c) Natural conscience

3. By natural reason, we discover that there are two sorts of natural law in the natural language:

Natural Laws	a mere sequence of uniformities	whose purpose is the maintenance of the physical universe, and to witness the wisdom and intelligence of God
	uniformities used for the direction of voluntary agents, which are moral as well as natural laws.	positive moral law / negative moral law — purpose of both is our temporal and eternal well-being.

4. Among the natural laws which are also moral laws are the laws of pain and pleasure. Through the use of natural reason, we discover that there are distinct kinds of pleasure, and that our true interests lie in the achievement of some of these pleasures, but not in others:

Kind of Pleasure:	*Valuable as:*	*Leading to:*
Rational, i.e. natural:	Either as a	a) temporal and
1. of the understanding	means, or an	eternal private
2. of imagination	end *per se*.	and public good
3. of sense		
(highest qualitative		
value is 1, then 2 and 3)		

Irrational, i.e. unnatural and fantastical.	Neither as means nor as ends.	Self-defeating, both temporally, and, if constantly pursued, eternally.
1. of understanding 2. of imagination 3. of sense		

Acting in accordance with natural laws leading to the rational pleasures in their proper relations is acting morally.

5. For the reasons given in this chapter, we should make moral decisions according to the moral law rather than according to consequences in particular cases. Our original investigation of the language of nature teaches us that the ultimate moral end to which all moral laws tend when obeyed is the greatest good etc., and this is the rule of rules, i.e. the criterion according to which subsidiary rules or natural laws are judged to be moral laws, provided they can be used to direct our voluntary actions.

This summary is just that – I cannot in a short space present an adequate representation of all the relations between these principles, and indeed I have ommitted at least two principles which I have mentioned but not investigated in detail, but which are assumed by the first of the five claims above. These principles are that God exists, and that he has morally relevant attributes. There is still a third omitted axiom: that men are free. These are the topics of the next two chapters.

[124] PO, 52

CHAPTER III

ETHICAL ACTS AND FREE WILL

The lost second part of the *Principles of Human Knowledge* was also to provide Berkeley's complete theory of mind, so we do not know a great deal about it. However, he did say enough in the works we do have for us to gather the general outlines of his position. In these works, with the exception of a few remarks in the *Philosophical Commentaries*, Berkeley talks about mind only in connection with its relation to body. Mind is the opposite of body. Bodies are extended, inactive or passive, and dependent upon mind and its activities for their existence. Mind is independent of the changes in nature, though not of God, it is active, it is not extended, and because it is not extended and not subject to natural law, it is immortal. When we know our minds, we apprehend them directly, and as they are in themselves. We can form no image of mind, because mind is not picturable. We know only our own minds directly, and all others indirectly, by analogy. Since all ideas are passive, and possible objects of sense, we have no ideas of minds. In the second edition of the *Principles*, the term "notion", which was first used in section 140 of the original manuscript, is used to characterize our conceptual awareness of minds.[1] The term is also used in the third edition of *Alciphron*, seventh dialogue, section five. Furthermore, Berkeley's theory went through several stages, as the *Philosophical Commentaries* show, and his final position is most likely that given in entry 788. Throughout everything he says on the subject however, some themes are constant. Among these are that minds or spirits are active whereas ideas are not, that God's will is the immediate and only cause of natural things, and that understanding and willing are mental activities. As we shall see, the latter is important for the parallel and constant claim that order in our lives is the effect of judgment, and

[1] P. 89, 140. 142

not of passion or appetite.[2] Another constant claim with obvious moral implications is that:

Men impute their actions to themselves because they will'd them and that not out of ignorance but whereas they knew the consequences, of them whether good or bad.[3]

Further, he thinks that

Actions leading to heaven are in my power if I will them, therefore I will will them.[4]

These related positions are manifested again in his forthright assertion to the American Samuel Johnson that guilt is a function of willing alone.[5] Power or agency implies volition and the effects of volition,[6] and virtue and vice consist in the will.[7] Our freedom consists in spontaneous acts of will, undetermined by anything, including "prior uneasiness", as Locke would have it.[8] Because we have no ideas of our minds or their operations, we must speak in metaphorical terms when talking about them.[9] It is because mind is not an "object of thought", or "something" that it cannot be determined or effected by natural objects, which are inactive and therefore not causal agents. A major cause of the theory that we are determined in our actions, and that we have ideas of minds and can therefore demonstrate propositions about them, is verbal confusion. As Berkeley says;

We are imposed on by the words, will, determine, agent, free, can etc.[10]

The grand Cause of perplexity and darkness in treating of the Will, is that we Imagine it to be an object of thought (to speak with the vulgar), we think we may perceive, contemplate and view it like any of our Ideas whereas in truth 'tis no idea. Nor is there any Idea of it. tis toto coelo different from the Understanding i.e. from all our Ideas. If you say the will or rather a Volition is something I answer there is an Homonymy in the word thing wn apply'd to Ideas and volitions and understanding and will. all ideas are passive, volitions active.[11]

[2] D., p. 203
[3] PC, 157
[4] PC, 160
[5] Correspondence with Johnson, p. 281
[6] PC, 669
[7] PC, 149, 669
[8] PC, 156-161
[9] PC, 176, 176A; P., 144
[10] PC, 627
[11] PC, 643

Or again:

> If you ask wt thing it is that wills. I answer if you mean Idea by the Word thing or any thing like any Idea, then I say tis no thing at all that wills. This how extravagant soever it may seem yet it is a certain truth. we are cheated by these general terms, thing, is etc.[12]

If all our ideas are passive, if we therefore have no ideas of the will and of the understanding, and if the functions of our minds, willing, judging etc., are activities, then it follows that:

> We have no Ideas of vertues and vices, no Ideas of Moral Actions wherefore it may be Question'd whether we are capable of arriving at Demonstration about them, the morality consisting in the Volition chiefly.[13]
> The opinion that men had Ideas of Moral actions has render'd the Demonstrating Ethiques very difficult to them.[16]

Berkeley thinks that a "cure for pride" follows from his theory, namely, that "we are only to be praised for those things wich are our own, or of our own Doing, Natural Abilitys are not consequences of Our Volitions."[15] But in addition to the rejection of the Lockean theory of demonstration, upon which I have commented, this theory entails the radical claim that moral actions are quite strictly acts of will. This is a "radical" claim in the sense that it is seemingly incompatible with the utilitarian strain in his writings.

I. ACTS AND CONSEQUENCES

In traditional utilitarian theories, the motive of the agent provides the ground upon which we can make judgments of moral value about the agent, and the consequences following upon an action provide the criteria according to which we judge the moral value of the action, and the basis of moral obligation. The act of will itself, and the source or cause of the act, is normally considered solely within the context of the problem of free will. This then seems to be a fundamental difference between Berkeley's theory and those of the traditional utilitarians. Consequences for Berkeley are the immediate result of an act of will, ours or God's, and they are morally relevant in ways which seem irrelevant to ordinary utilitarianism. Certainly, for Berkeley, they do not provide the *ground* of obligation. But they *may*, appearances to the contrary,

[12] PC, 658
[13] PC, 669
[14] PC, 683
[15] PC, 964

provide criteria for judging moral acts, and that is what we shall investigate here.

I have already mentioned Berkeley's suspicions of language which characterizes the mind and its activities in object-oriented terms such as "thing", and how he thought that words such as "that", "which" etc. mislead when they are applied to the will. We have also just examined what he means by the word "action" in moral contexts, and it is clear from this that his denial that there are ethical actions must be taken as a denial that there are possible objects of perception which are ethical actions. Given the object-oriented nature of our languages, we find it necessary to speak in metaphorical terms when speaking of our minds and their activities.

But there *are* ethical acts, mental acts, and they are either right or wrong, and their consequences *are* either good or bad for Berkeley. Further, as we shall see, we have a choice in what consequences do follow upon our mental acts, because we are free, and we are entitled to guilt or blame, merit or justification, according to whether or not we acted willfully.[16] I must therefore be able to decide, before I blame or praise myself or others morally, a) whether or not they acted willfully, and b) whether or not what they did, and what they intended, was right or wrong, good or evil. The question is, *how* do I do this? Berkeley is quite specific about this:

We see no variety or difference betwixt the Volitions, only between their effects. Tis One will one Act distinguish'd by the effects. This will, this Act is the Spirit, operative, Principle, Soul etc.[17]

It is understood that part of his intention here is to draw a distinction between acts of the will as opposed to the acts of judgment or understanding. As he says:

Will, Understanding, desire, Hatred etc. so far forth as they are acts or active differ not, all their difference consists in their effects, circumstances, etc.[18]

But at the same time, it has already been noted that he thought the grounds for imputing actions to others consisted in our awareness that we act for consequences reasonably expected to follow from our actions,[19] and that an orderly moral life results from the making of judgments.[20]

[16] Alc. VII, 18, 19
[17] PC, 788
[18] PC, 854
[19] PC, 157
[20] D. p. 203

The issue is, how do we interpret these remarks *vis à vis* the role of consequences in Berkeley's philosophy? I suggest that the only sensible interpretation is the following: a) consequences must resemble one another in some ways which enable us to distinguish those acts which are intentional from those which are not; b) given that they are intentional, it must be possible to tell whether or not the consequences following from them are in accordance with natural moral law, or not; c) a moral motive for Berkeley is the intention to act in accordance with moral law, i.e. to follow God's will, and in accordance with PC 157, this seems to entail acting with the intention of achieving consequences meeting the requirements of the moral law; d) it has been shown that the fundamental moral law is to act so as to achieve the greatest happiness of the greatest number for all times and places; e) consequences of action in accordance with rules meeting this requirement will be good, and those not meeting it will be bad; f) the mental act causing such consequences will accordingly be denominated right or wrong, because we, as observers, only distinguish between acts of will on the basis of their consequences, and therefore, consequences provide the criteria for deciding whether an ethical act was right or wrong; h) a good man is one who does right acts, and conversely, a bad man is one who does evil acts; thus, consequences provide the criteria for making this sort of judgment too.

All of this is consistent with everything Berkeley says, and in addition, so far as I can see, it is the *only* interpretation which enables us to fit his various remarks into a systematic relationship. If it is well-founded, then the difference between Berkeley and the utilitarians on this point is not so much over the role of consequences, as it is over the definition of an ethical act, and this seems to be a question which the utilitarians did not discuss, taking it for granted that everyone knew what an ethical act was. But for Berkeley, the entire question of mental acts cannot be divorced from his ontology and epistemology, for without his fundamental bifurcation of the world into mind and body, his proof for the existence of God has no foundation, and therefore ultimately, neither knowledge nor morals would make any sense for him, because they would have no foundation.

When we come to discuss the *grounds* of obligation rather than the criteria for judging the rightness of an act on the normative level, there is indeed a fundamental difference between Berkeley and most utilitarians. Consequences may provide the criteria for deciding whether or not a practice and the rule governing it are in accordance with the utility principle, and they may allow us to decide whether a given act is in accordance with a given rule, but it is *not* for Berkeley, as it is for the utilitarians, the consequence of an action which is the source of the obligation to do it. Ultimately, the justification for the cardinal normative rule, and thus for all the rules falling under it, is a fact about God. C. D. Broad makes this clear, though I do not agree with his formulation of the point:

> What makes any moral precept binding on us is simply that God has ordered us to act in accordance with it, and that we, as his creatures, have a manifest duty to obey the commands of our creator. Thus Berkeley's doctrine is fundamentally different from ordinary Utilitarianism. For that makes utility the one and only *ground* of obligation.[21]

This issue will be discussed at greater length in the next chapter.

I have developed the arguments presented thus far primarily upon the basis of evidence provided in the *Philosophical Commentaries*. But the same arguments may be supported by reference to the *Principles of Human Knowledge*, and to his other works. In the *Principles*, he takes great care to define spirit or mind, and to differentiate it from objects. Spirit is that which "thinks, wills, and perceives", and this is the total meaning of the term. Therefore, if we have no idea of these operations, then we have no idea of a spirit. Whereas the existence of objects consists in their being perceived, that of spirits consists in their perceiving, their activity. Although we do not have an idea of spirit, we understand the meaning of the term, as is proven by our affirming and denying truths about it. In addition, we know other minds by analogy with our own, of which we have "notions".[22] With a touch of humor he says that he will not stand in the way if the words "idea" and "notion" are used interchangeably, "if the world will have it so", as no doubt the world will.[23] In the same place, he hints that relations, in his view, are not discovered as ideas are, but are rather a function of the activity of the mind, of which we therefore have "notions", not ideas. He did not develop this theory, but certainly it would be consistent with the sort of nominalism I have ascribed to him. And a little later he states quite succinctly the claim that we can know other minds only by analogy based upon their effects upon us:

> From what hath been said it is plain that we cannot know the existence of other spirits, otherwise than by their operations, or the ideas by them excited

[21] BBTM, p. 78
[22] P., 139, 140, 145
[23] P., 142

in us. I perceive several motions, changes, and combinations of idea, that inform me there are certain particular agents like myself, which accompany them, and concur in their production. Hence the knowledge I have of other spirits is not immediate, as is the knowledge of my ideas; but depending on the intervention of ideas, by me referred to agents or spirits distinct from myself, as effects or concomitant signs.[24]

All of these points of course lead to a conclusion which is essential to Berkeley's theory, namely that the soul is immortal. What he means by "immortal" is important; he means "naturally" immortal, that is, that the mind, because it is not an idea or a set of ideas and therefore not an object, is not a part of the natural world, and therefore not subject to the divine rules of grammar in the natural language, natural law. Destruction, decay, dissolution, in a word, death, results from the laws of nature. What follows is this:

We have shewn that the soul is indivisible, incorporeal, unextended, and it is consequently incorruptible. Nothing can be plainer, than that the motions, changes, decays, and dissolutions which we hourly see befall natural bodies (and which is what we mean by the course of Nature) cannot possibly affect an active, simple, uncompounded substance; such a being therefore is indissoluble by the force of Nature, that is to say, the soul of man is naturally immortal.[25]

2. FREE WILL

In the introduction, I mentioned that Berkeley had written in the *Philosophical Commentaries* that the "two great principles" of morality were the being of a God, and the freedom of the will. The first principle has been discussed briefly, though only to the extent that it is presupposed by the subject-matter of the first two chapters, and it will be examined at length in chapter four. I have also mentioned that Berkeley believed in the freedom of the will, but his arguments for this position have not been discussed in any detail.

His actual arguments in favor of free will must be gathered more from his arguments against determinism as it is set forth by others than from his own positive statements. The primary source for both kinds of information is in four sections of the seventh dialogue of *Alciphron*, sections 16 to 20. There he is arguing against four claims made by the advocates of determinism, especially Anthony Collins. (see chapters 8 and 9) The four claims are that 1) the will is mechanically determined,

---

[24] P. 145
[25] P. 141

2) the will is determined by the judgments of the understanding, 3) that God's foreknowledge entails determinism, and that 4) free will and its theory entail an infinite regress. The first claim is set out by Alciphron. He compares man to a puppet. From every object, he says, certain particles are emitted, which compose "rays" or "filaments", and these "drive, draw, and actuate every part of the soul and body of man, just as threads or wires do the joints of that little wooden machine vulgarly called a puppet", the difference between man and a puppet being only that wires are visible whereas the "rays" or "filaments" are "too fine and subtle to be discerned by any but sagacious free-thinkers", the latter remark being no doubt a not very well concealed Berkeleyan *ad hominem* against his opponents. The position being stated here is obviously a crude version of materialism and the determinism attendant upon it. In fact, as we shall see when I discuss the Deists, none of them held such obviously mistaken theories.

Berkeley's first reply is that if the "free-thinkers", i.e. determinists, are right, then morality is nonsense, because this theory "transfers the principle of human action from the soul to things outward and foreign." But the theory has several other things wrong with it, from Berkeley's viewpoint. First, it supposes the mind to be moved, literally, and as a result, it supposes that acts of will are actually motions, where "motions" here is to be understood as we understand the term when applied to material efficient causes in the natural world. I have already pointed out Berkeley's views of natural motion, namely, that in fact, there is no such thing. But the word has another sense, that outlined in *De Motu*: that motion in a natural context is a function of the measurement of the positions of three objects (one being the spatial position of the observer's body) at different moments in time. That there are motions in *this* sense in the natural world is consistent with Berkeley's views, indeed, it *is* his position. But of course, this position, if applied to minds, would assume that minds can have such properties as spatial position, which in Berkeley's opinion is absurd. Thus, if the soul is incorporeal, then motion in the natural sense cannot affect it, and it follows that "motion is one thing and volition another." Or to put it another way, determinism as so stated depends upon the supposition that the mind is an object, which Berkeley has already (in the *Principles*, *Three Dialogues*, *New Theory of Vision* and *Philosophical Commentaries*) denied. In order to support this version of determinism then, Berkeley thinks the question at stake must be begged:

On the contrary, it seems plain that motion and thought are two things as really and as manifestly distinct as a triangle and sound. It seems, therefore, that in order to prove the necessity of human actions, you suppose what wants proof as much as the very point to be proved.[26]

At this stage, Alciphron abandons the materialistic thesis, and turns on another attack. Even if the soul *is* incorporeal, he says, he can still prove determinism. He now bases his appeal on our personal experience. If we observe ourselves when we decide to do one thing rather than another, we will notice that first of all the understanding considers the alternatives involved without making a decision, and then the judgment makes a choice based upon this consideration. This judgment also includes a decision about the means to be employed in the achievement of the chosen course. Once the judgment has made the decision, the will is determined by it, because the function of the will is merely to execute what, in this case, the judgment has chosen. It follows that there is no such thing as freedom of the will, because it is always determined by the last judgment of the understanding. If the will *was* free, then "there should be an indifference to either side of the question, a power to act or not to act, without prescription or control", and since there is not in any case where the judgment has already been made about the choice, the will cannot be free. It does not matter, so far as the question of the freedom of the will is concerned, whether the judgment is free or not: it might be in its turn determined by "the greatest present uneasiness, or the greatest apparent good, or whatever else it be"; so long as the judgment determines the will, the will is not free.[27]

Taking this view, and extending it to all human faculties, there is no such thing as human freedom, because each such faculty is "determined in all its acts by something foreign to it." For example, when the understanding is presented with an idea, it *is* that idea and no other, and so it cannot alter that idea, "but must necessarily see it such as it presents itself." So too with our appetites; they are "by a natural necessity . . . carried towards their respective objects." Reason too is determined by the rules of thought; we cannot infer indifferently "anything from anything" because the laws of causality and the rules of logical inference delimit the bounds of possible inferences. This is as true of the will as of our other faculties, only what determines the will, as he has said, is the judgment, in particular the *last* judgment before the act of will.

[26] Alc. VII, 16
[27] Alc. VII, 17

This position as described by Alciphron is a composite of the views of Locke, Collins and Shaftesbury, and indeed, Alciphron quotes the latter:

Appetite, which is elder brother to reason, being the lad of stronger growth, is sure, on every contest, to take the advantage of drawing all to his own side. And will, so highly boasted, is but at best a football or top between those youngsters, who prove very unfortunately matched; til the youngest, instead of now and then a kick or a lash bestowed to little purpose, forsakes the ball or top itself, and begins to lay about his elder brother.[28]

At the end of this presentation, Alciphron brings in the third argument to be refuted, because it depends essentially upon the same foundation, namely, that causes are necessary, and that what is certain is determined. If God knows everything, then it cannot be the case that he knows an event will happen in the future, and at the same time, that the event not occur. Thus, given that God has known all things from all time, everything must necessarily occur as God knows it will occur. If that is true, then man's choice is either irrelevant, or determined, that is, it can be no other than it is. This theory is also one put forth by Collins in his *Inquiry Concerning Human Liberty*, which I shall have cause to examine at greater length later on.

Berkeley's first reply to the last argument is simplicity itself. God is not only all-knowing, he is all-powerful. Thus, if he can know all things, he can also do all things, and it follows that he can create a free agent without contradiction, and still know what that free agent will do. Such an agent would think that he acted, would condemn himself for some acts and approve himself for others, and on the basis of his acts he would believe himself deserving of either reward or punishment. In fact, all the properties of agents now called free would be properties of this agent, and Alciphron admits this. If this is true, then there must be some property of a supposed free agent which could *not* be found in actual men who do the things and have the thoughts Berkeley has described. If such a property cannot be given, why then do we suppose there is such a thing? And if such a property cannot be given, then . . .

we must conclude that man hath all the marks of a free agent.[29]

In short, what we mean by "free man" is what is included in the properties listed in his description and if the description of Alciphron's necessary agent and Euphranor's (Berkeley's) free agent do not differ, then the dispute about free will is merely verbal.

[28] Advice to an Author, pt. 1, sec. 2
[29] Alc. VII, 18

But one might reply that this answer does nothing to solve the central issue, which is that if our acts are caused by anything, and if causes are certain and necessary (certain because God knows them, necessary because they cannot be other than they are) then further discussion is unimportant, and determinism is true. In reply, Berkeley makes a distinction which only became noted and admired in this century when it was stated by Moritz Schlick.[30] He claims that there is a crucial difference between "certain" and "necessary".

To me, certain and necessary are very different, there being nothing in the former notion that implies constraint, nor consequently which may not consist with a man's being accountable for his actions. If it is foreseen that such an action shall be done, may it not also be foreseen that it shall be an effect of human choice and liberty?[31]

The point is a subtle one, which involves the distinction between properties of states of mind, and properties of natural events. The sentence "God knows every event which will occur" is a sentence saying something about God's state of mind, and we might predicate certainty of this state of mind without thereby predicating anything of what it is that God is certain *about*. On the other hand, "necessity" is a property predicated by determinists of "causal" series in the natural world. But Berkeley has already shown that there are no causes of the sort the determinists imagine in the real world, so predicating necessity of events in the real world is either question-begging, senseless, or simply false. The central point is that the truth or falsity of the two claims, the one about God's mental state and the other about causal sequences in the natural world, are not dependent upon one another.

In addition, since the above is true, it is possible for God to foresee, and be certain about, events which will be the effect of free human choice, without himself determining what it is that the choice will be. From the certainty of God's mental state, it simply does not follow that God *forces* humans to choose what he knows that they will choose.

The point can also be considered this way: causes are mental acts for Berkeley. Knowing is also a mental act for him, involving judgment. But for determinism to be entailed by God's foreknowledge, his acts of knowing would also have to be acts of causing. This entails occasionalism. But Berkeley denies occasionalism. Therefore, he *believed* that the two sorts of act were different. To put it another way, it might follow from God's knowledge of a future event that the event

[30] Schlick, M., *Problems of Ethics*, Prentice-Hall, New York (1939)
[31] Alc. VII, 18

will occur, but it does not follow that God is the cause of the event, and determinism would only be true if this did follow.

Finally, if the above is true, then God can foresee events, and also foresee that they shall be the results of human choice. But this changes the issue from the question of God's foreknowledge back to the question of whether our choice is determined by factors other than God, and the various versions of this problem have already been discussed.

Then Berkeley discusses the other deterministic claim, that even if the mind is incorporeal, determinism is still true, because the will is determined by the last act of judgment. On this issue, Berkeley's reply in Alciphron is not specific or clear. He notes that Alciphron makes much use of terms such as "power", "faculty", "act", "determination", "indifference", etc., and hints that he uses them in such a way as to indicate that they stand for abstract general ideas, abstracted from the particular workings of the mind. If this is so, then Alciphron is guilty of all the mistakes Berkeley has discovered in that theory, plus another important one, given that in this case we are talking about minds. The latter additional mistake would be that since we have no ideas of minds or mental acts, we obviously could have no abstract general ideas of them, even if there were such general ideas in the first place.

His second rebuttal hinges on his conviction that the understanding and the will are not to be considered as two different things; rather, they are but two aspects of the mind's activities. Acts of will and understanding (judgment) are to be distinguished only by their effects.[32] The effects of volition, being ideas, cannot determine other volitions. But since we can only distinguish among the various mental acts by their effects, it is senseless to speak of one mental act determining others.

Finally, apart from arguments depending upon reason, there is the intuitive evidence we have of our own minds, and of their activity. If a man were to argue, however adroitly, that things do not move (here we must understand natural motion in the sense I have given) you would be quite justified in ignoring him, for good philosophical explanations must accord with common sense. (Berkeley himself, due to the misunderstandings of Dr. Johnson, was subjected to just this sort of criticism.) But by this rule, determinism must be false, for as Berkeley says,

If we consider the notions that obtain in the world of guilt and merit, praise and blame, accountable and unaccountable, we shall find the common question in order to applaud or censure, acquit or condemn a man, is, whether

[32] PC, 788, 884

he did such an action, and whether he was himself when he did it. Which comes to the same thing. It would seem, therefore, that, in the ordinary commerce of mankind, any person is esteemed accountable simply as he is an agent. And, though you should tell me that man is inactive, and that sensible objects act upon him, yet my own experience assures me of the contrary. I know I act, and what I act I am accountable for . . . that (man) doth act is self-evident. The ground, therefore, and ends of religion are secured, whether your philosophic notion of liberty agrees with man's actions or no; and whether his actions are certain or contingent; the question being not, whether he did it with a free will, or what determined his will; not, whether it was certain or foreknown that he would do it, but only, whether he did it wilfully, as what must entitle him to the guilt or merit of it.[33]

It will be noticed that in the latter part of this remark, where Berkeley refers to "contingent" or "certain" actions, he does *not* say "necessary" actions, for he thinks he has already shown this issue to be uninvolved in the question of free-will. Further, it must be understood that his appeal to common sense on the subject of the inactivity of man and the action of sensible objects upon us, is to be understood as a conjunction, for it is clearly not common sense to deny that objects have some effect upon us, though given Berkeley's other arguments, it may be true. And this raises the fundamental criticism of this reply, which is that an appeal to "common sense" is often an appeal to a "je ne sais quoi" based upon still more fundamental ignorance. When Berkeley's assertion that the existence of objects consists in their being perceived is explained and unfolded, he thinks it is in accordance with the opinions of the common man; but even that is doubtful, and without explanation, it certainly is not commonsensical. At least this much can be granted him though: if we are *not* free, that is, if determinism is true, then our personal experience with decision-making also systematically misleads us, for surely Berkeley is correct when he says that our everyday lives lead us to believe that in some decisions at any rate, we are free. So if the appeal to experience is not a sound support for the free-will theory, it is at least no support at all for determinism.

This brings us to the last deterministic argument raised, which is that the free-will position involves an infinite regress. The thesis is simply put: the normal meaning of the phrase "a man is free" is that "he can do what he will." The question *about* free-will, that is, the question which expresses doubt about the truth of the statement that a man can do what he wills, is "whether he can will as he wills?" But of course,

[33] Alc. VII, 19

this is an infinite regress not entailed by *Berkeley's* view, but about the theory which would *question* the free-will claim, namely, determinism, and, though Berkeley does not specifically mention him here, the determinism of Anthony Collins in particular. Having pointed out the absurdity of the question, Berkeley simply dismisses it as "idle".[34]

In all of these arguments, Berkeley's own views are constant. Free will, spontaneously free will, is a necessary condition for moral behavior; determinism of whatever variety is false, based either on the mistaken theory of abstract general ideas, or on the equally mistaken view that objects are active causal agents effecting minds, or resulting from verbal confusion. We know our own wills directly, those of other humans and God by analogy based upon the assumption that like effects have like causes, and that therefore other minds resemble our own. We act in the light of expected consequences, which we know to be either good or bad, because they serve the general well-being (and thus are in accordance with God's law), or they do not. Since mental acts are the only acts, agents are to be judged on the basis of whether their acts were intentional, and if they were, whether the acts were right or wrong. There are no ideas of these acts, only "notions". Volitions are distinguishable from other mental acts not in themselves, but through their effects. Were this not so, we could not distinguish moral acts from others.

3. OTHER EVIDENCE, GUILT, AND COMMENTS

I think the argument that Berkeley's theory is not utilitarian in the sense which has been outlined important enough to rally still more evidence against it. I have already tried to show that the difference between Berkeley and more traditional utilitarians lies not primarily in the fact that consequences are not the criteria for judging acts, but rather in the definition of what an act is. It is well to recall again that there is not just one, but three sorts of evidence which support this claim. The first sort lies in Berkeley's explanation of the divine natural language, his discussion of those natural laws which are moral laws, and the end which is served by those laws. Also in this first category of evidence is his examination of why we act, and his analysis of the necessary conditions for our being able to make moral judgments about other agents, i.e. resemblance between minds, like effects implying like causes, etc.

[34] Alc. VII, 19

The second type of evidence is introspective evidence based upon our awareness of innate appetites and aversions. In the tenth *Sermon, Siris, Alciphron I,* the eighth *Sermon,* and in the twelfth *Guardian Essay* references are to be found to innate "social appetites", "sympathy", innate parental love, innate impulses to beneficent actions, and the natural self-hate resulting from the performance of evil acts.[35] In the eighth *Sermon,* whose topic is eternal life, Berkeley points to these properties as grounds for "probable arguments" for the belief in eternal life. It is a probable argument for this reason:

We may add as a further proof of this point that natural appetite of immortality, which is so generally and so deeply rooted in mankind, and which we cannot suppose implanted in us by the author of our beings, merely to be frustrated. This would not be of a piece with the other dealings of God towards man.[34]

The third kind of evidence is revelation, and the truths revealed therein, thinks Berkeley, are consistent with the conclusions drawn from the other two kinds of evidence.

In sum, Berkeley has this to say of vice:

As there is nothing more engaging than virtue so is there nothing more deformed than vice and irreligion, these are spots and stains upon the mind, they are a crookedness in the will and the affections and they are the most pernicious things in the world. Nothing is so destructive of Society, so contrary to the reasonable nature of man, so utterly inconsistent with all the advantages and satisfactions, all the good offices and enjoyments which are truly desirable in life.[37]

There is one other objection to Berkeley's position which may be considered here, and which will come up again in the next chapter. It is that since God is the immediate cause of all natural effects, and since even the effects of other human wills, so far as they are observable by us, depend at least upon the concurrence of God, then God is "the author of murder, sacrilege, adultery, and the like heinous sins."[38] This argument is raised in the *Three Dialogues,* where Hylas has been arguing in favor of the material substance hypothesis. Berkeley's reply is worth examining in full, if only to demonstrate that the arguments I have submitted are found throughout his writings.

---

[35] References, in order: SE X, p. 129; S., 308-309; Alc. I, 14; GE, pp. 226-227; SE X, p. 133; SE VIII, p. 108
[36] SE VIII, p. 108
[37] SE II. p. 17
[38] DHP, pp. 263-237

He begins by pointing out that the nature of the instrument used to commit a moral offense has nothing to do with the guilt or innocence of the agent. It follows that the materialists, who in effect make God act through the instrument of material substance, make him as guilty as does Berkeley by making God act immediately upon nature, without an instrument. But the important thing to know is that the question of moral actions does not concern the world of perception in the first place. ". . . sin or moral turpitude doth not consist in the outward physical action or motion, but in the internal deviation of the will from the laws of reason and religion." Berkeley asks us to consider the examples of slaying an enemy in battle, or putting a criminal legally to death, which he did not count as moral offenses, "though the outward act be the very same with that in the case of murder." The consequences of an action are not that which we call the moral act, for the latter is a mental act. It follows that even if God were the immediate author of all physical acts, he would not thereby be guilty of the mental acts which we might have coincidentally with the occurrence of those physical acts. In short, even if occasionalism were true, it would not imply that God was the author of evil. But Berkeley then says that he has nowhere said that God is the only cause of natural motions, and that in fact, we are also causes of such motions, although our powers are limited, and "ultimately indeed derived from God." Nonetheless, these powers, such as they are, are under the direction of our wills, and this is sufficient to make us morally responsible.[39]

The comparison between murder and legal capital punishment might seem to raise a counterexample to my interpretation of Berkeley, since I have argued that he distinguishes between acts of will on the basis of their effects, and on that basis alone, and here the effects seem to be the same. But this apparent difficulty is easily explained. The solution depends upon noticing other factors about the consequent not specified here. Both the act of murder and that of legal capital punishment are intentional, but intentions are always intentions to *do* something, and what is intended here is not simply to kill someone. Rather, in the case of the legal punishment, it is presumably to kill 1) in accordance with the civil (and in this case moral) law, and 2) is the act if morally right, to act according to a rule which, when followed, serves the public good, thereby also acting in accordance with God's will. The distinction between 1) and 2) collapses for Berkeley if we take it (as he did) that one has a moral obligation to

[39] *Loc. cit.*

obey civil laws. The question of what it is about the resultant acts which would enable us to tell whether or not one or both of them had these motives is not the same as the question of what Berkeley believed about moral acts: it may be that he cannot in fact answer the former query. But that he believes that a) we distinguish between acts of will on the basis of their consequences, and b) that moral praise or blame accrues in virtue of intention, seems to be unquestioned.

There are of course serious difficulties with Berkeley's position here. One has already been mentioned: what properties do the consequences of mental acts have which enable us to know their motives? There are other, equally serious problems. For example, if we are the cause of some ideas and God is the cause of others, we must be able to distinguish between those we cause and those he does. Berkeley tries to do this by using the standard criteria, such as vividness, dependence upon our personal perception, permanence, etc. But this does not always provide a satisfactory explanation. For example, suppose we are speaking about that set of visual, auditory, etc. effects known by me as my wife. I do not cause that set of ideas to occur, but a great part of the set of ideas, perhaps most, are presumably caused not by God, but by my wife: her smiles, gestures, speech, the manifestions of her moods, etc. They meet all of the requirements Berkeley provides for being effects of *God's* will, and I think he would have to say that at least in so far as God's concurrence is essential for the existence of effects, in so far as he is the "ultimate" cause, my wife's mental acts are not sufficient for the existence of those ideas which are part of the set I call by her name. If they are not, then how is it that anyone can be free? Surely if we are, then we are only because of God's sufferance, and that would probably be Berkeley's answer. But the problem of occasionalism again raises its head here, aside from the strange notion of freedom which results. Furthermore, it seems to violate Berkeley's "no second causes" theory. In the *Philosophical Commentaries*, entry 433, he denies that there are second causes of events, referring here to efficient causes in the natural world, claiming that there is only one cause, God. Now if God *and* human minds cause the same effects, another version of the problem seems to arise, namely, the sufficient reason for two, rather than one cause. And this too seems to lead to occasionalism. Since I have criticized Berkeley here, I might add one defensive claim; his arguments against determinism seem to me to be well-founded *if* his analysis of the perceptual world is, and therefore a totally new approach would have to be taken to argue against them, because this analysis is totally new. And as a matter of fact, very few of the criticisms of Berkeley's fundamental ontological claims are successful, the most notable failure being Moore's "Refutation of Idealism". I should have to defend this claim of course, which cannot be done here, but that is my opinion.

4. PRELIMINARY CONCLUSIONS

This brings me to the end of my consideration of Berkeley's normative ethics, and to the beginning of meta-ethical issues in his system. The distinction between normative and meta-ethical questions is itself not clear, but at the least, it can be said that there are questions which are asked on what is called the meta-ethical level which are not asked within the framework of ethical decision-making and justification on the practical level. Such questions are, for example: what do "right" and "good" mean? What is the source or ground of moral obligation? What are the logical structures of propositions in morals? If Berkeley has an acute analysis of the emotive uses of ethical language, what is its role in his overall theory? Is Berkeley a cognitivist, and if so, why? These are some of the questions I shall examine in the next few chapters, especially the next two, but it might be wise to pause here for a moment to summarize.

What sort of evidence would establish that Berkeley had a systematic ethical philosophy? Well, there would be the obvious type, namely, the discovery of studies made by Berkeley and concerning just this subject. No such evidence is forthcoming, if what we are searching for is a carefully *organized* set of arguments from principles analytically established beforehand. However, I should think that it would also count as evidence, if it could be shown that the principles for the arguments are all there in the existent works, that the conclusions can be drawn from those principles, that many of the conclusions were themselves stated by Berkeley, some of them in fact being derived in arguments of obvious import for moral philosophy, and that the relations between the various conclusions are such that they form a coherent set of thoughts on the range of problems thought to constitute the subject of moral philosophy. This second sort of evidence is discoverable in Berkeley's writings. In support of his principle, Berkeley marshals three sorts of evidence: the moral end is witnessed by what we learn from the language of nature, by our innate natural instincts and/or dispositions, and by what is revealed in the gospels. But the natural language is not simple. Understanding it involves an appreciation of the different kinds of pleasurable and painful sensations, their differing qualitative values, and an awareness of the long-term rather than the short-run tendencies of things. We must also distinguish between two kinds of rules or laws of nature – the mere sequence of regularities, and those sequences which can be used for the direction of voluntary actions. This is the significance of the diagram at the end of the second chapter. Furthermore, once we do understand these things, we will understand that decisions must be the result of conscious inference if we expect an ordered moral life, and that particular circumstances preclude such inferences in practice unless we decide according to rules such that practice in conformity with them has a general tendency to serve the moral end, rather than by particular cases. This is assuredly true in cases where "negative" moral rules are in question, but upon occasion, "positive" moral rules allow the consideration of individual cases in their application.

Another principle is presupposed by the ones just given: man is a creature of spontaneous free will. Were this not so, there would be no moral responsibility, and the denial of free-will cannot only be refuted by reason, but also by our personal experience.

The next principle is that man is immortal, or more specifically, that his mind or soul is "naturally" immortal, since it is not subject to natural dissolution.

The final principle is the logical extension of all the rest: our true interests both as individuals and as a society are eternal, and utility therefore dictates that we act accordingly. Since this is the message of religion, religion is useful, indeed, thinks Berkeley, indispensable for morality. And at this point we begin the study of his meta-ethics.

I suggest that these principles are not random assertions by the Bishop of Cloyne. The extensive references support the claim that every one of them is the result of a careful process of reasoning, and that they are consistent throughout the Berkeleyan *corpus*. If this is so, then it only remains to show that the conclusions themselves are so related as to constitute a system, and the criteria for the second sort of evidence I suggested are satisfied. But for that we must wait until the rest of the principles of Berkeley's moral philosophy have been discovered and established.

CHAPTER IV

THE ROLE OF GOD AND THE DEFINITION
OF GOOD

A "definist" in ethics is a person who believes that "ought" can be defined in terms of "is". For example, one might hold that "we ought to do X" means that "Society requires us to do X". There are obviously many sorts of these theories, all variations of the same theme. Naturalism of all varieties, and intuitionism, are two classes of definist theories. "Theological definism" is a theory which holds that the facts in terms of which the basic moral concepts are defined are facts about God or some divine being. I believe that Berkeley held premises which imply what *we* would now classify as a version of theological definism. In this chapter, I shall try to support this thesis, and I shall also criticize Berkeley's views on the subject. I shall also briefly examine the meanings of the basic moral terms for him, and try to relate them.

In order to accomplish these purposes, we must return to a subject which has already been outlined. This is the two part proof for the existence of God and his attributes which was discussed in the first chapter in connection with Berkeley's theory of the natural language. It is now time to examine those arguments in more detail, for on them depends Berkeley's definism, given certain additional premises.

Several fundamental assumptions, some assumed as axioms and never questioned by Berkeley, are at the foundation of the arguments. These assumptions are:

1. Like effects have like causes.
2. Resemblance in proportion is a sufficient ground for arguments from analogy.
3. From a difference in degree, magnitude etc. in an effect, we can infer like differences in causes.
4. Nothing is that is not caused.

Berkeley believes that these axioms, together with the conclusions resulting from his analysis of mind, and what is given in sensation, allow us to generate two arguments about God. The first of these arguments is "necessary", and the second is probable. The first argument purportedly proves that God is the immediate cause of the world of ideas, and the other concludes that God not only exists as the immediate and essential cause, but also that he is benevolent, provident, wise and good. As we shall see, the arguments are not dependent upon one another logically except in so far as they both depend ultimately upon Berkeley's unique analysis of the elements of knowledge.

I. THE NECESSARY ARGUMENT

This first argument can be stated briefly, and in fact it was so stated near the beginning of the first chapter. It is best presented in the *Three Dialogues Between Hylas and Philonous*. This statement ties the proof directly to the *esse est percipi* principle, which is of course a conclusion from Berkeley's analysis of the objects of perception. In that analysis, Berkeley argues that an examination of the data of sense will show that ideas of sense are inactive, can only resemble other ideas, that the relations between ideas are founded on constant conjunction and resemblance, and that there is no such thing as an efficient cause relation in nature. At the same time, an examination of our minds shows that they are active, unextended, causal agents. We do cause some ideas, but we obviously do not cause others, nor does any human mind. It follows that either there are ideas with no causes, or their cause is a mind which is non-human. Because of his acceptance of his version of the principle of sufficient reason, (axiom 4 above) Berkeley concludes that all ideas have a cause, and that therefore the cause of at least those ideas which human minds do not cause is a non-human mind. His name for the activity of mind constituting the relation between minds and bodies is "perception", and he therefore thinks that ideas of sense are dependent upon their perception by some mind, or to put it his way, their existence consists in their being perceived – *esse est percipi*. A perusal of our experience verifies that there are no other causal agents which we know aside from minds, and that of all minds, we only know our own directly. But in order to know *that* there is a non-human cause, it is not necessary to know that non-human cause, or other minds for that matter, directly. In short, we can infer from the seen to the unseen, the directly known to the indirectly known, where "indirectly known" in this case means "known by inference". Therefore, the problem of other minds, and ultimately the entire subject of arguments from analogy, do not enter into the inference from data of sense to their causes. It is an inference based upon just three things; the principle of sufficient reason, the nature of the real world as perceived by us, and the nature of what does the perceiving. The empirical (broadly speaking) investigation of minds and bodies shows that the latter are dependent upon the former, but that most objects are not perceived by humans and that their continuity does not depend upon continual human perception. Hence, they depend upon another mind. This is a necessary inference because it follows from the known nature of minds and bodies, from the meanings of the words "body" and "mind", and its denial is thus a contradiction, for it would be the assertion that bodies do not depend upon minds, which for Berkeley simply demonstrates that you do not understand what a body is. The conclusion is stated succinctly in the *Principles*:

... all the choir of heaven and furniture of the earth, in a word all those bodies which compose the mighty frame of the world, have not any subsistence without a mind, that their being is to be *perceived or known*; that consequently so long as they are not actually perceived by me, or do not exist in my mind or that of any other created spirit, they must either have no existence at all, or else subsist in the mind of some eternal spirit.[1]

In the *Three Dialogues*, the proof is stated at somewhat greater length, and without as much care as it is given in the *Principles*:

Besides, is there a difference between saying, there is a God, therefore he perceives all things: and saying, sensible things do really exist: and if they really exist, they are necessarily perceived by an infinite mind: therefore there is an infinite mind, or God. This furnishes you with a direct and immediate demonstration, from a most evident principle, of the being of a God... that an infinite mind should be necessarily inferred from the bare existence of the sensible world, is an advantage peculiar to them only who have made this easy reflexion: that the sensible world is that which we perceive by our several senses; and that nothing is perceived by the senses beside ideas; and that no idea or archetype of an idea can exist otherwise than in a mind. You may now, without any laborious search into the sciences, without any subtlety of reason, or tedious length of discourse, oppose and baffle the most strenuous advocate for atheism.[2]

This is not as careful a statement as the earlier one because it imports the word "infinite" into the conclusion, which cannot be justified without further argument. At most, a "cosmic cause", as it were, is the conclusion warranted here. The argument is also used in sections 48

1 P., 6; cf. also DHP, p. 230
2 DHP, p. 212

and 91 of the *Principles*, but the most important philosophical premise in it, the necessity for a cosmic cause to explain the *continuity* of the natural world independently of human perception, is not there developed.

The proof has other advantages from Berkeley's view. One of the great disadvantages of the material substance theory was in his opinion that it made God a remote cause, if he exists at all, divorced from the continuity of the natural world and hence from us. Indeed, Berkeley thought that the refutation of idolatry, epicureanism and the theory of Thomas Hobbes was impeded by substantivalism.[3] The "direct and brief demonstration of an active powerful being" as the immediate cause of natural effects overcomes all this.[4] For Berkeley, we in effect witness the immediate results of God's present activity, and in the words of one author, nature is "to that extent a theophany" for Berkeley.[5] There are no second causes in his natural world, just one, single cause.[6] The essence of this cause is will, for power implies volition and its effects.[7] The effects are the ideas of the natural world, my sensations:

Every sensation of mine wch happens in Consequence of the general, known laws of nature and is from without i.e. independent of my Will demonstrates the Being of a God. i.e. of an unextended incorporeal Spirit wch is omniscient, omnipotent, etc.[8]

This is why God is the author of the laws of nature and hence personally involved in my moral life.[9] This claim of Berkeley's never changes throughout his writings, and on it depends his argument, and his evidence, for the benevolence and wisdom of God, and his consequent interest in the course of human affairs.

Assumed in the necessary argument then is the soundness of the refutation of the doctrine of material substance which Locke and his followers held. This theory set it forth that perceptions such as color, odors, tactile sensations etc., the so-called "secondary" qualities, were an effect in us of "powers to produce various sensations in us by their (bodies') primary qualities." These primary qualities were solidity, extension, figure, motion or rest, and number. They produce ideas in us,

[3] PO, 17
[4] PO, 41
[5] NSBP, pp. 106-107
[6] PC, 433
[7] PC, 669
[8] PC, 838
[9] PC, 884

that is, bodies do, through impulse, literally. From external bodies, "some motion must be thence continued by our nerves or animal spirits, by some parts of our bodies, to the brain or seat of sensation, there to produce in our minds the particular ideas we have of them." Both kinds of ideas, primary and secondary, are so conveyed into the mind, but our ideas of primary qualities do resemble their "patterns" actually in the objective bodies, whereas our ideas of secondary qualities do not, because in the bodies to which we attribute them, they are "only a power to produce these sensations in us: and what is sweet, blue, or warm in idea, is but the certain bulk, figure, and motion of the insensible parts in the bodies themselves . . ."[10] But qualities cannot subsist by themselves according to this theory. There must be some "substratum", some material substance, in which they inhere, or which "supports" them.[11]

In Berkeley's view, this was a pernicious theory. It entailed scepticism, because substance was unknowable, so we could never tell whether our ideas of qualities *truly* resembled their causes. It put us in the position of not really knowing whether or not there even was a God. As such, in his eyes, it encouraged atheism and immorality. His attack on it has several points, of which the most salient are the following:

1. Ideas can only resemble other ideas, so if ideas of secondary qualities do not resemble their causes, then neither do those of primary qualities. Moreover, the distinction between the two sorts of qualities is unfounded in the first place, as you can see for yourself if you try to think of an uncolored but extended area, which you ought to be able to do if you could have an idea of the primary quality extension alone.

2. Causes are not ideas: they are active, for example. Thus, no ideas can resemble them.

3. "Material substance" is a general word which stands for a general idea; but there are no general ideas, so the name is meaningless.

4. Since we know only what is given to our senses, our minds, relations and what we can infer on the basis of all three, we could not know material substance even if it did exist, for grounds for the inference to it are not present in any of these sources of knowledge. Thus, it is a useless explanatory entity, even if it does exist.

5. But it cannot exist, since its very concept is contradictory. This is because material substance is defined as an unthinking substance by

[10] Locke, J. *Essay*, Bk. 11, chapter VIII, 7-15
[11] *Ibid.*, chapter XXIII, 1-4

Locke, which is in principle unperceivable. But there are only perceiving minds and inert objects in reality, the existence of the former consisting in its active perceiving and of the latter in being perceived. Material substance is therefore something not a mind, which is not perceived, which is a contradictory concept.

At the same time, Berkeley understood that if the material substance theory is unsound, there must be some other explanation for the origin of our ideas, and his God in effect takes the place of material substance, without, he thinks, being contradictory. In addition, it has the advantage of being immediately inferable from the definitions of the components of reality, whereas Berkeley thought that no such grounds could be presented for Locke's theory. Once again then, the principle that intelligent minds alone can be active causes is a necessary conclusion resulting from the thesis that there are no natural causes when this is conjoined with the refutation of the material substance theory. Inferences founded on these principles are not properly speaking empirically based arguments from analogy, which would stand upon the sign-to-thing-signified relation. There is no such relationship between ideas and their mental causes, for minds are not ideas. It is for these reasons that Berkeley speaks of the "necessity" of God, and it is within this framework that his remarks about the "necessity" of moral laws are to be understood, as I pointed out in chapters two and three. The necessity of moral laws is the necessity of their being caused by the supreme mind, not the necessity of analyticity.

At one point in the *Principles of Human Knowledge* he puts many of these points together in such a way that it may be taken as a transition point from the necessary to the probable argument. There he notes that since there are no efficient causes in nature, the only true cause is a mind or minds. Minds operate for reasons, so we should attempt to explain the course of nature in terms of final causes. There are also no necessary connections in nature, and if there are regularities in the natural world, then they are there because of the free acts of a mind, God. A study of these connections enables us to realize that we could not subsist and prosper without them, and the mind which is the cause of them is therefore concerned with our welfare, and is good and kind. Therefore, it is necessary for us to study nature in an effort to learn how to act for our own and society's profit, even though our knowledge of natural law can only be probable.[12]

[12] P., 107

2. THE PROBABLE ARGUMENT

Although the inference from passive ideas to a supreme cause is necessary, the inference from the regularity of effects in the natural world to the *wisdom* and *goodness* of God is *probable*, because it is based not upon the relation between ideas and effects, but only upon the contingent and observed continuity of nature, which can only be known probably.[13] So the two kinds of arguments must be separated. To know *that* there is a supreme mind which causes the natural world involves but an a priori inference based upon an understanding of the terms "idea", "cause", etc. But the knowledge that this supreme mind has the attributes we normally predicate of God must be based upon our observations of the sign relations in the natural language.

Berkeley realized that the impersonal cause we can infer as a necessary entity is not satisfactory as a concept of God, at least as seen through Christian eyes. For this, God must be an immediate and *intelligent* cause, personally concerned with our well-being, and capable of providing an explanation of the proportion and beauty which he thought to be exhibited in the world. This he thought the material substance theory could not do.[14] In addition, the material substance theory, because it cannot account for the purposive design in nature, is unable to see that purpose manifested in moral rules of behavior enabling us to direct our lives properly, and ultimately to achieve the last utilitarian end, the eternal happiness of rational minds.[15] If God cannot be shown to have a morally relevant nature, then we cannot make sense out of Berkeley's comment:

God Ought to be worship'd. This Easily demonstrated when once we ascertain the signification of the word God, worship, ought.[16]

Berkeley's terms for the proof are rigorous. It cannot be a "dry and jejune" proof of the metaphysical variety, but rather, it must be *a posteriori*, and readily understandable.[17] He believed, in fact, that we know God exists as clearly and with as much evidence, indeed, more evidence, as we have in the case of other human minds.[18] Yet in spite of all this, and the clearly teleological implications of the language

---

[13] LDB, pp. 8-9
[14] PC, 836, 838, 839
[15] Alc. V, 5
[16] PC, 705
[17] Alc. IV, 2
[18] P., 147, 419

metaphor, not to mention the cosmological overtones of a God who is an immediate and first creator of all natural causal chains, the Jesuits accused Berkeley of undermining the proofs for God's existence, as did other bishops of his own church, notably Peter Browne.[19]

The key premise is the language of nature thesis. It must appear that nature suggests and infers God through all our senses ". . . as certainly, and with the *same* evidence, at least, as any other signs perceived by sense do suggest to me the existence of your soul, spirit, or thinking principle."[20]

It may seem from this that Berkeley is here concerned once again to prove *that* God exists, but he is actually much more concerned to show what *type* of being God is. The evidence for this is that the development of the argument depends first of all upon Berkeley's argument for the existence of other minds, which is an argument from analogy. It is not until this argument is accepted that he posits his conditions for the proof of the existence of God, and it is not only necessary to understand his analysis of minds and bodies, but also to study his thoughts about the nature of analogical argument itself. This is because he believed that the notion had been misused in such a manner that equivocation resulted in the predication of properties of God. But unless we preserve the exact meaning of the terms involved in arguments about the attributes of God, then

. . . every syllogism brought to prove those attributes, or (which is the same thing) to prove the being of a God, will be found to consist of four terms, and consequently can conclude nothing.[21]

On this point, Berkeley was thinking of Peter Browne, and the controversy between the two is detailed at some length in Chapter eight. His concern then is to keep God as a knowable entity whose attributes can be known by analogy with human ones.

Originally, the term "analogy" signified a "similitude of proportion." Thus: "2:6::3:9" predicates an analogy or similitude of proportion between the relations involved in the two sets of numbers. At the start, analogy was purely a quantitative notion, that is, the proportions involved were measurable on definite scales, but the term has come to be used to cover any "similitude of relations or habitudes", whether quantitative or qualitative, or indeed, whether there is any real

[19] ERI, chapter I, p. 17; cf. also chapter VIII herein
[20] Alc. IV, 5
[21] Alc. IV, 22

similarity between the things compared or not. The Thomists claimed an analogy between intellect and sight; a prince is "analogically styled a pilot", etc.

The further distinction between proper and metaphorical analogy had also been introduced by that time, an example of the latter being the attribution of human parts to God, as in "the hand of God", or the attributing of imperfect human passions to him. But we should be careful to distinguish between imperfect passions and human parts predicated in metaphorical analogy, and the quite different case, thought Berkeley, of predicating wisdom and knowledge of God.

... in knowledge simply, or as such, there is no defect. Knowledge, therefore, in the proper formal meaning of the word, may be attributed to God proportionably, that is, preserving a proportion to the infinite nature of God. We may say, therefore, that as God is infinitely above man, so is the knowledge of God infinitely above the knowledge of man, and this is what Cajetan calls analogia proprie facta.[22]

In other words, this sort of analogy is not metaphorical, but proper, that is, literal, and Berkeley thinks that these two analogies are comparable:

$$\text{``2:6::3:9''}$$
and

"God: man:: the infinite knowledge of God: knowledge of man". But clearly the similitude here depends basically on a value-judgment; it is God's infinite *perfection* that is the issue. As Berkeley (in this case, Crito) says: "We may, therefore, consistently with what hath been premised, affirm that all sorts of perfection which we can conceive in a finite spirit are in God, but without any of that alloy which is found in the creatures."[23] There is therefore some doubt as to whether Berkeley himself is restricting his use of analogy to the *quantitative* similitude of proportions.

In the case of the problem of other minds, the "similitude of proportion" is roughly equal, the statement of it being:

ideas : my mind : : other ideas : other minds

This statement is the conclusion of an argument which assumes that ideas which are the effects of human minds have certain characteristics which differentiate them from other ideas not so dependent, and this assumption, and the analogical argument from other minds, ultimately

[22] Alc. IV, 21
[23] Alc. IV, 21

depends upon the relation of resemblance. Thus, the ideas I produce are: a) different from some of those produced in nature independently of me, and b) they are *similar* to *some* sets of other ideas I perceive. It is on the basis of this similarity that I predicate the analogy given above, for given the axiom that like effects have like causes, and that I know the relation between my mind and the ideas I produce, then if I perceive a similarity between those ideas and others, I am justified in inferring that their causes are minds like mine, alike at least in certain fundamental relevant respects, such as being active, unextended, perceiving beings. I can also infer, given that from a difference in degree, magnitude etc. in effect a like difference can be inferred in cause, that other minds may be more intelligent or less than mine, more or less moral, etc.

With these premises, we can infer by analogy that as our bodily movements (at least some of them) are caused by our minds, so the bodily movements of others are caused by their minds. But not just any bodily movements will do. In particular, (though not exclusively) we infer the existence of other minds from a set of ideas which we call a "language", for to us, language is a set of sounds or written characters, and thus a set of ideas. It is agreed then, that from the use of language we may infer a mind as the cause of these signs. But nature is a language too, literally.

As with our artificial languages, nature must be composed of "arbitrary, outward, sensible signs, having no resemblance or necessary connexion with the things they stand for and suggest"; these signs must make known an "endless variety of things", in virtue of which we are "instructed or informed in their different natures ... taught and admonished what to shun, and what to pursue ... directed how to regulate our motions, and how to act with respect to things different from us, as well in time as place." If nature meets these requirements, then nature is a language, and if it is a language then there is as much reason to think that it is caused by a mind as there is to think that there are other minds because of our observation of speech etc. in others. It makes no difference that the natural language seems to be primarily visual rather than auditory – it is auditory too, and in any case, the nature of the characters does not determine *that* something is a language, though it may determine its type. Consistency therefore demands that we admit God exists if nature is a language.[24] There is no more reason to deny it than there is to deny that the king or queen of Britain

[24] Alc. IV, 12

exists when you see them with your own eyes, or when you are told they exist by someone who saw them. We do not perceive that "principle of thought and action" by which people are enabled to do things like speaking a language. Nonetheless, we gather that kings and queens have minds, because "the being of things imperceptible to sense may be collected from effects and signs, or sensible tokens",[25] and to the observer, all behavior is a set of signs. The testimony of your senses upon which you infer the existence of another mind or minds is therefore exactly on a par with the testimony of those same senses and the evidence they provide of God's existence, provided that nature is a language.

But God is just not any other mind, and the evidence for this is clear too. Just as we can validly infer the unseen from the seen, and causes from effects, so we can also infer from greater effects to greater causes.

And the wisdom that appears in those motions which are the effect of human reason is incomparably less than that which discovers itself in the structures and use of organized natural bodies, animal or vegetable. A man with his hand can make no machine so admirable as the hand itself; nor can any of those motions by which we trace out human reason approach the skill and contrivance of those wonderful motions of the heart, and brain, and other vital parts, which do not depend on the will of man. Alciphron. All this is true. Euphranor. Doth is not follow, then, that from natural motions, independent of man's will, may be inferred both power and wisdom incomparably greater than that of the human soul?[26]

Further, this "greater power" shows his wisdom in the "unity of counsel and design" in the universe, and in the purpose evident in the whole. But if we admit all this, then:

"Will it not then follow that this vastly great or infinite power and wisdom must be supposed in one and the same Agent, Spirit, or Mind; and that we have at least as clear, full, and immediate certainty of the being of this infinitely wise and powerful Spirit, as any one human soul whatsoever besides our own?"[27]

In sum, we may infer that the cause of nature is a mind. Nature is a more magnificent creation, illustrating more variety, intelligence and scope than artificial languages, so the mind which is its cause is proportionately greater than our minds. Further, just as the relation between our minds and our languages is one of direct and not remote

[25] Alc. IV, 4
[26] Alc. IV, 5
[27] Alc. IV, 5

causality, so it is the same with the natural language. Finally, we decide that a man is good and wise, or evil and stupid, from his deeds, his language not being the least of these. On this basis, we can attribute these properties to the cause of the natural language, whom we call "God". If it is objected that terms used to characterize man may not be predicated of God, because God is *infinitely* above man, the correct reply is that this entails a misunderstanding of the word "analogically", which in its true sense means "proportionably", and that therefore, provided we mean that God possesses such qualities as goodness in proportion to an infinite nature, the terms are indeed predicable of him.

The fundamental analogy from which others such as analogical predications of God's goodness are generated is therefore this one:

Man : his languages : : God : natural language

Anticipating possible objections, Berkeley notes that there is a way we can distinguish between real things, and figments of our imaginations. Ideas of sense, and the real things made from them, are "more vivid and clear" than ideas of the imagination, and they "have not a a like dependence on our will". Moreover, natural ideas are regular and constant, a part of the Language of the Author of Nature.[28] These regularities which we find in nature, the Laws of Nature, are proof of God's wisdom and benevolence, though strictly speaking, this is involved in the second part of the proof, and not the *a priori* first part. The criteria for distinguishing real from imaginary things are also given in the *Principles*, sections 28 to 33.

The difference between the first and second parts of his arguments can be characterized in two ways, one of which I have already mentioned, namely, that the first part is necessary whereas the second is *a posteriori* and probable. The second way is related to the first: stated simply, the second part of the proof requires that nature be a language, the first does not. If there were but one idea, it would still imply a mind as its cause. But from one idea, we could not gather anything about God's intelligence, the magnitude of his power, his moral relevance to us, his "personality" in short. For that, nature must be a language. The natural philosopher should busy himself with understanding the laws of nature.[29] And the theologian ought to take a leaf from the scientist's book, for there is more reason to believe that God exists and has certain attributes from the regular occurrences in nature than on the basis of the occasional miracle, since inconstancy is not a mark of freedom or

[28] DHP, p. 235
[29] P., 66, 72

intelligence, but regularity is.[30] Were it not for the fact that nature had laws, it could not be the "rational discourse" Berkeley thought it was.[31] But of course, we cannot know that God will act the same tomorrow as he did today, and so any inferences based upon our reading of the natural language must be probable. We might not have found ourselves in this difficulty if we could have an idea of the mind of God, but we cannot, any more than we have any idea of other minds. I know my own mind intuitively, and what I know is that my mind is indivisible because it is unextended, that it thinks, wills, perceives. My knowledge of other minds, God's included, is based upon the knowledge that like effects have like causes, and since I know that the cause of all ideas is a mind, I assume that it has some of the properties of my mind. In short, I have a "notion" of God "obtained by reflecting on my own soul, heightening its powers, and removing its imperfections."[32] Knowing *that* God exists is simple: it is a result of a necessary inference. But knowing *what* God is can only be based upon the sort of evidence we use to know what other minds are. Since we come to know God in exactly the same way that we come to know other minds, then if the evidence, though probable, is acceptable in the latter case, why not in the former? From this evidence, we know that God is a spirit, and therefore, like us, active. From the regularity of his actions, we know that he is what we would call a person. From the fact that we can only serve our interests by obeying God's natural and moral laws, it is evident that those laws were made for us, and this shows God's benevolence. From the magnitude and detail of the creation, we know something of God's power and intelligence.[34]

But if we attentively consider the constant regularity, order, and concatenation of natural things, the surprising magnificence, beauty, and perfection of the larger, and the exquisite contrivance of the smaller parts of the creation, together with the exact harmony and correspondence of the whole, but above all, the never enough admired laws of pain and pleasure, and the instincts or natural inclinations, appetites, and passions of animals; I say if we consider all these things, and at the same time attend to the meaning and import of the attributes, one, eternal, infinitely wise, good, and perfect, we shall clearly perceive that they belong to the aforesaid spirit, who works all in all, and by whom all things consist.[35]

[30] P., 57
[31] S., 252, 253
[32] DHP, p. 231
[33] *loc. cit.*
[34] Sillem, E. A., *George Berkeley and the Proofs for the Existence of God*, Longman's, Green and Co., London (1957) (PEG)
[35] P, 146

Without God, we could not even converse with one another, for although I am free to cause the motions of my body, it is thanks to the intervention of God that you are able to perceive the ideas I produce.[36] That God should be this near to us, yet that some men should doubt his existence, is to Berkeley evidence of the "stupidity and inattention of men, who, though they are surrounded with such clear manifestations of the Deity, are yet so little affected by them, that they seem as it were blinded with excess of light." We apparently can't see the forest for the trees.[37]

3. ANOTHER KIND OF EVIDENCE, AND THE MEANING OF "GOOD"

In the first two sections, I have tried to develop Berkeley's views on the basis of the principles developed in his epistemology and ontology, as these are found primarily in the *Essay Towards a New Theory of Vision* and its defense, and in the *Principles of Human Knowledge*. But occasionally, I have mentioned that Berkeley has recourse to *other* sorts of evidence to support his claims. Two of these other kinds of evidence are revelation, and natural conscience. The lessons of all the kinds of evidence are in his opinion that God is entitled to dominion over us, and that we ought to try and make our wills one with God for our own well-being as well as that of others.[38]

There is yet a *fourth* source of information, which leads to these same conclusions, and I am going to consider it here, both because it is almost never mentioned, and because it leads me into the next to last topic of this chapter, which is how God provides the ground of obligation in moral matters for Berkeley.

As Professor Jessop notes in a footnote at the start of the XIIth of Berkeley's sermons, it is a closely reasoned, highly thoughtful sermon, resting on the perception of design in the universe, and on an analogy which Berkeley draws between the forces of attraction and repulsion which maintain the coherence of the universe, and the forces governing our relations within societies. The sermon is called "The Bond of Society", and it is not an isolated example of this sort of thought in his philosophy. A very similar view is set out in *Alciphron I* in a memorable passage in which Berkeley after arguing that the general happiness is

[36] P., 147
[37] P., 149
[38] SE X, pp. 129-136

the most excellent end man can propose, and that natural moral laws have "a necessary connection with the general good of mankind", says this:

Throughout the whole system of the visible and natural word, do you not perceive a mutual connexion and correspondence of parts? And is it not from hence that you frame an idea of the perfection, and order, and beauty of nature? . . .

Ought we not, therefore, to infer the same union, order, and regularity in the moral world that we perceive to be in the natural? . . .

Should it not therefore seem to follow, that reasonable creatures were . . . made one for another; and consequently, that man ought not to consider himself as an independent individual . . . but rather as the part of a whole, to the common good of which he ought to conspire, and order his ways and actions suitably, if he would live according to nature? . . .

Will it not follow that a wise man should consider and pursue his private good, with regard to and in conjunction with that of other men?[39]

What *is* this "union, order, and regularity" in the two worlds? He says that in both the

moral and intellectual, as well as the natural and corporeal, we shall perceive throughout a certain correspondence of the parts, a similitude of operation and unity of design . . . and that the system of thinking beings is actuated by laws derived from the same divine power which ordained those by which the corporeal system is upheld.[40]

The source of the laws which govern the natural world we know to be God, and these sequences are the immediate result of his direct willing. Thus, I conclude that the same is true of the moral world, because as was shown in chapter two, moral laws are but one sort of natural law, that sort which can be used for the voluntary direction of our actions. Nor is it strange, at this state, to find Berkeley speaking of a "unity of design" in both worlds, for once it is given that a benevolent and wise God has created and maintained the world for our interests, as he thought, it would follow that there must be no conflict between our obligation to the moral law, and the impersonal forces of nature over which we have no control. Both must tend to the general well-being.

. . . philosophers are now agreed that there is a mutual attraction between the most distant parts at least of this solar system . . . if we carry our thoughts from the corporeal to the moral world, we may observe in the Spirits or Minds of men a like principle of attraction, whereby they are drawn together in communities, clubs, families, friendships, and all the

[39] Alc. I, 15, 16
[40] SE XII, p. 225

various species of society. As in bodies, where the quantity is the same, the attraction is strongest between those which are placed nearest to each other, so it it likewise in the minds of men, caeteris paribus, between those which are most nearly related.[41]

In order to explain celestial phenomena, we must have recourse to God, "who never ceases to dispose and actuate his creatures in a manner suitable to their respective beings." But the social bonds of man can also never be explained in any other way. The "reciprocal attraction in the minds of men . . . is not the result of education, law, or fashion; but is a principle originally engrafted in the very first formation of the soul by the Author of our nature." Just as the laws of gravity are essential for the explanation of nature so we cannot understand moral phenomena without the principle of social appetite. Social appetite is "that (which) inclines each individual to an intercourse with his species", and urges us to the sort of behavior which best serves the "common well-being". Its manifestations include the sympathy or empathy with which we suffer when our fellow man does, and parental love "which is neither founded on the merit of the object, nor yet on self-interest". Like dispositions urge us to care for the well-being of those yet unborn, to care for those of other nations whose welfare has no direct bearing on our own. Not everyone is born with these tendencies, and those who are not are a sort of "monster" incapable of really understanding this "diffusive sense of humanity". Without these dispositions, the general happiness would not be served as well as it is, and it follows that we ought to develop them as much as we can. It is a duty to do this because these inclinations are an indication of God's will that we act for the common good, and it is in our interest to develop them because "the good of the whole is inseparable from that of the parts; in promoting therefore the common good, every one doth at the same time promote his own private interest."[42]

As objects exist because they are perceived, so *we* are what we are because of God's creation; and just as the laws of nature are the manifestations of God's maintenance of that world, so our instincts are the evidence of his intentions for our well-being, and one of the indispensible means for its achievement. An essential principle of Berkeley's moral philosophy underlies this reasoning: as nature is an immediate effect of God's will, dependent upon him for its existence, so is the

[41] SE XII, p. 225
[42] SE XII, pp. 226-227

good, the moral end of man, and the means by which man can achieve this end.

In the second chapter, I quoted the following definition of the good for man:

... the good or happiness of man consist(s) in having both soul and body sound and in good condition, enjoying those things which their respective natures require and free from those things which are odious or hurtful to to them ... [43]

At the time, I noted that this was an unsatisfactory answer for several reasons. Now we can improve upon this earlier position.

To be a morally good person for Berkeley is to obey moral laws because a) they are in our interest, and b) because they are commanded by God. This is what moral goodness *is*, and so moral badness consists in not obeying these laws. This is so even if there is a basic unresolved tension, as there is, between the motive of being moral because it is in our interest to do so, and being moral because God so commands us. According as we are moral or immoral, we are deserving of merit and demerit respectively, and the currency in which the balance of merit or demerit is settled is *non-moral* good or evil, which according to Berkeley is happiness or unhappiness. In this life, that happiness is defined as above, i.e. bodily and mental health, and these non-moral goods are thus valuable for themselves and not as means to anything else. But Berkeley of course believed in an immortal life for the human soul, and he recognized that good men are not always rewarded with happiness in their temporal lives. Thus, non-moral happiness is also the eternal reward, and unhappiness the punishment, in eternal life. Berkeley nowhere discusses the problem of justice involved here, i.e. whether an act committed in the temporal life can ever be of such horrendous evil that it merits eternal condemnation, i.e. unhappiness. But clearly what he intends, in Broad's words, is that

God's ultimate end for mankind is an *eternal* state of affairs in which non-moral good and evil (i.e., happiness and unhappiness) are distributed among men in accordance with their moral dessert. This moral dessert arises solely from obedience or disobedience to rules of conduct which are enjoined by God as a means to men's *temporal* happiness without regard to dessert. [44]

In the temporal sphere the concept or criterion of dessert does not apply because we are all morally equal in the beginning of this life.

Both moral and non-moral goodness then are involved in Berkeley's

[43] Alc. II, 9
[44] BBTM, p. 85

analysis of complete goodness, the former arising solely from obedience to God's moral laws, and the latter being given as a reward for attaining moral goodness. No description of eternal non-moral goodness can be given for obvious reasons. But the source of both non-moral kinds of goodness is ultimately God. He is the *sole* source of eternal non-moral goodness, and because of his necessary concurrence in our actions in this life, and the dependence of the laws of nature upon his will, he is at least a cooperating cause of temporal non-moral goodness. Moral goodness alone, however, seems to depend solely upon human agents, since it arises only in conjunction with our behavior in accordance with moral rules. The central meta-ethical question is therefore how to define non-moral goodness in terms of a fact or facts about God, or at least, if Berkeley is a theological definist, or holds a related theory, then this is the central question.

The only answer I can give to the question is not satisfactory, but that is because Berkeley does not give an answer to it that is satisfactory. Good is that which, as Professor Orange puts it, "is present to the mind of God." God's will *is* morality, and to say that one can act for the good, and not act in accordance with God's will, is surely a contradiction for Berkeley. "Right" as it applies to mental acts is defined in terms of good, for right acts are those mental acts which are in accordance with moral law, and a moral law is a law such that practice in accordance with it tends to serve the general happiness. But it is *because* the general happiness is "present to God's mind" that it *is* the moral end, so ultimately, goodness is identical with whatever God wills. This is I believe, the import of a remark I quoted earlier in this chapter:

God Ought to be worship'd. This Easily demonstrated when once we ascertain the signification of the word God, worship, ought.[45]

It is no accident that Berkeley's favorite scriptural quotation is Paul's famous characterization of God as the being "in whom we live, and move, and have our being." It is a fact for the Bishop of Cloyne. Without God, there is no natural world, no human world, no minds, no moral end, no means to achieve that end, no reason in the universe, no purpose in life, no answer to injustice, no foundation for morality, no reason to treat one another with respect rather than trying to satisfy our most selfish desires.

Why then ought we to do what God wills? Why should we live

[45] PC, 705

morally? Because we cannot serve our own and the public interest in any *other* way.

Since God is perfectly free, he need will no particular thing, and it follows that even if we cannot conceive how, he could have willed something other than the general happiness to be the moral end. Thus, the sentence "Happiness is good" must be sythetically true, and for the same reason, "x (an ethical act) is right" is also synthetically true. The "is" in terms of which "ought" is defined for Berkeley is therefore the will of God, and if this is true, then Berkeley held a position similar to theological definism.

I must emphasize again that I do not intend to imply that Berkeley would have called himself a theological definist, nor that he would have been aware of the issues involved in the sort of propositional analysis I have briefly indulged in. But one can claim with justice that a man holds the conclusions derivable from his premises if he holds the premises, and I think I have correctly derived these conclusions.

4. CRITICISMS

It is one thing to discover the moral philosophy of a man, and quite another to defend it. It would be silly to expect a full blown defense from Berkeley for something he never formulated precisely but from what has been said, it seems clear that his theological definism at least is indefensible. More of this will come up in the conclusion, and in chapter eight, but it seems appropriate to mention some of the difficulties in this chapter.

The first criticism will be pursued at some length when I discuss Berkeley's argument with Peter Browne over the use of analogy in theological arguments. Here it need only be said that Berkeley admits we have but a very deficient, incomplete knowledge of God. At one point he goes so far as to say: "God is a being of transcendent and unlimited perfections: His nature therefore is incomprehensible to finite spirits." If we are to take the word "incomprehensible" literally, Berkeley is in trouble. But even if we treat it sympathetically, it does seem that there is little ground for the second part of Berkeley's argument for the existence of God, the part which is based upon probabilities. This is not to question the inductive base, but rather the possibility of forming any concept at all of God. At bottom, I think

---

[16] DHP, p. 254

Browne was right when he said that when all was said and done, God's attributes for Berkeley remain but perfect human ones.

Secondly, no matter what emphasis Berkeley places on reason and common sense, in the end he denies that these methods are to be extended to revelation and the propositions of scripture. In these matters, he thinks "... an Humble Implicit faith becomes us just (where we cannot comprehend and Understand the proposition) such as a popish peasant gives to propositions he hears at Mass in Latin." If this be called irrational, Berkeley replies that he thinks it more irrational "to dispute at cavil and ridicule holy mysteries i.e. propositions about things out of our reach that are altogether above our knowledge."[47] However much this might strike chords of sympathy in the apologists' breast, it is certainly not acceptable philosophy. This would be unimportant were it not so obvious that Berkeley's philosophy of morals and his theology cannot be separated, or at least, not easily. The one hope might be that none of the mysteries are morally relevant, and that those non-mysterious propositions ennunciated in scripture are also confirmed in the language of nature, and by our knowledge of ourselves. In fact it seems to me, though this is little more than speculation, that Berkeley had more in common with the Deists on the subject of scripture than with his contemporary orthodox bishops. But more on that subject later on.

There are some clearly fallacious inferences in his ethics. Thus, from the fact that injustice is not always punished here, nor good rewarded, it does not follow that it must be somewhere else, and though this is the message of revelation, it is hardly good "reason" unless all of his arguments about God are valid.[48] Furthermore, his arguments for the intelligence of God which are based upon the design in the natural language often seem to be close to circular: design in the universe implies an intelligent being and an intelligent being is one who puts design in the universe. But this circularity might well be repaired. The anthropomorphism of the designer probably could not be avoided, and at bottom this problem brings us back to the use of arguments from analogy in theological contexts.

God is the cause of the natural world, and maintains it through his perception and will. But what this "perception" is, is a conundrum indeed. Berkeley says, for example, that although God knows what pain is, and sometimes causes us to suffer pain, he does not himself suffer it. Compared to God, we are "limited and dependent spirits". We have sense impressions, sensations, which are the "effects of an external agent", God, and occasionally these impressions are produced in us quite contrary to our own wills. This cannot be true of God, for he cannot be affected by any other being. God perceives nothing by sense, for he has no senses. God's will is the cause of all things, and it is "absolute and independent", as well as irresistable. Our perceptions are tied to our bodies, and these bodies themselves are but collections of ideas whose existence depends upon a perceiving mind. When we speak of the connection between ideas of sensation and our bodies, we are in effect speaking of nothing else than "a correspondence in the order of Nature between two sets of ideas, or things immediately per-ceivable." Since God is a pure spirit, this is not true of him. "God knows or hath ideas; but His ideas are not convey'd to Him by sense, as ours are."[49] Similar points are made in entry 675 of the *Philosophical Commentaries* and in *Siris*, among other places. In *Siris* he says:

All those who conceived the universe to be an animal must, in consequence of that notion, suppose all things to be one. But to conceive God to be the sentient soul of an animal is altogether unworthy and absurd. There is no sense nor sensory, nor anything like a sense or sensory, in God. Sense implies an impression from some other being, and denotes a dependence in the soul which hath it. Sense is a passion; and passions imply imperfection. God knoweth all things as pure mind or intellect; but nothing by sense, nor in nor through a sensory. Therefore to suppose a sensory of any kind – whether space or any other – in God, would be very wrong, and lead us into false con-ceptions of His nature.[50]

At times he states, quite straightforwardly, that there are "arche-types", or forms of corporeal things in God's mind.[51] At least one of his close correspondents, the American Samuel Johnson, understood him to be making this claim. Johnson saw Berkeley as holding that there is a "two fold existence of things or ideas, one in the divine mind, and the other in created minds; the one archetypal, the other ectypal." If this is so, Johnson says, then the "real and permanent existence of things is archetypal", and it would seem to follow that our ideas are somehow copies of them which correspond to the Ideas of God to the extent willed by God as manifested in the laws of nature. Nature under this interpretation becomes "ideal in the mind of God", which is compatible with the claim that there is no material substratum, while

49 DHP, p. 241
50 S., 289
51 DHP, p. 254

at the same time avoiding the solipsism which would be entailed by claiming that things were dependent upon finite created minds for their existence. Things would be "external to any created mind" in their "originals", so that, for example, the Ideas or divine archetypes of light and heat, whiteness and softness etc. would exist in God's mind, and our sense ideas of the same qualities, which when found together we call a "candle", would in some way or other resemble them.[52]

There are places where Berkeley seems to confirm this view, or one much like it. In the *Three Dialogues* he admits that he believes that God "knew all things from eternity", and that consequently all things "always had a being in the Divine Intellect". With respect to God's mind, it therefore follows that "nothing is new, or begins to be." But he also wants to distinguish, as he did in the case of perception and awareness of ideas of sense, between existence in God's mind and in ours. He says that when we speak of objects existing because they are perceived by human minds, we may "call this a relation, or a hypothetical existence if you please", and he clearly intends that it is relative when compared with the status of objects with regard to God, in which relationship they presumably have an absolute existence.[53] Mabbott has argued that this view is related to the problem of the *meaning* of the natural language, for we normally expect a "distinction of status . . . to separate a language from what it means".[54] But Berkeley is not unequivocal about the issue: at points he tells us that sense-data signify (mean) other sense-data; at others he says that the language of nature reveals the "attributes" of God to us; but according to Mabbott, nowhere in any of his works, does he say that our ideas "stand for" God's Ideas, and in the *Theory of Vision Vindicated and Explained* he seems, again in Mabbott's view, to deny this claim. It is instructive to consider the passage that Mabbott uses to support his argument:

The objects of sense . . . are called ideas . . . From our ideas of sense, the inference of reason is good to power, cause, agent. But we may not infer that our ideas are like unto this Power, Cause, or Active Being. On the contrary, it seems evident that an idea can be only like another idea, and that in our ideas . . . there is nothing of power, causality, or agency included . . . Whenever, therefore, the appellation of sensible object is used in a determined, intelligible sense, it is not applied to signify this absolutely existing outward cause or power, but the ideas themselves produced thereby. Ideas which are

[52] Philosophical Correspondence with Johnson, p. 274
[53] DHP, pp. 251-252
[54] PGB, pp. 26-27

observed to be connected together are vulgarly considered under the relation of cause and effect, whereas, in strict and philosophic truth, they are only related as sign to the thing signified.[55]

I do not think that the quote supports Mabbott's claims, simply because it is one thing to deny that our sense ideas can resemble their cause, God, and another to say that they cannot resemble God's Ideas, whatever they might be. The quote does assert the former, but not the latter, and to support the view that both propositions are asserted, one would have to hold that God is identical with his Ideas, which would be rejected by Berkeley. It is also necessary to distinguish between God's Ideas and his *attributes*. As I have noted previously, there *is* some sense in which the concept or notion we have of God is identical to our notion of his attributes, among which are perfect goodness, providence, knowledge and wisdom. But these are not "Ideas", divine or otherwise. Furthermore, in Berkeley's reply to Johnson's letter, he seems to be objecting more to the realist's claim about the existence of what are known as "universals" than to the thesis that there are divine archetypes:

I have no objection against calling ideas in the mind of God archetypes of ours.
But I object against those archetypes by philosophers supposed to be real things, and to have an absolute rational existence distinct from their being perceived by any mind whatsoever; it being the opinion of all materialists that an ideal existence in the divine Mind is one thing, and the real existence of material things another.[56]

But this remark does not answer the question raised by Johnson about the resemblance between our ideas and God's.

It might be thought that the reply to Johnson, when conjoined with Berkeley's thoughts about the Mosaic account of creation, supplies a solution. My earlier discussion of objects existing eternally in the mind of God was taken from Berkeley's analysis of this theory of creation. In that place he goes on to hold that creation might be interpreted as follows:

. . . things, with regard to us, may properly be said to begin their existence, or be created, when God decreed they should become perceptible to intelligent creatures, in that order and manner which he then established, and we now call the laws of Nature. You may call this a relative, or hypothetical existence if you please. But so long as it supplies us with the most natural, obvious, and literal sense of the Mosaic history of the Creation; so long as it

[55] PGB, p. 27
[56] Correspondence with Johnson, p. 292

answers all the religious ends of that great article; in a word, so long as you can assign no other sense or meaning in its stead; why should we reject this?[57]

Apart from the rather blatant pragmatism involved, this theory seems to imply that a) matter is co-eternal with God, and b) what we perceive, when we come to perceive it, is somehow identical with God's Ideas. If this is a correct interpretation, then about all that can be said for it is that it solves none of the problems I have raised, especially those concerned with the dual meanings of "Idea" and "idea", "perception", "sensation" and "existence" when applied in human and divine contexts. At bottom, the key issue, as it is in so many philosophical problems, is the problem of resemblance and difference, and their explanation. Berkeley must eventually explain what the relation between my ideas and God's is. But Berkeley is dead, and the lost second part of the *Principles*, where these sorts of issues were to be discussed, has never been recovered. We can only say that the solution would not have been the traditional recourse to independent universals, and it is obviously not the substantivalist's answer. So far as I have been able to discover, there are no premises in Berkeley's writings aside from those which I have given, which give a hint to his possible approach. But if he does not solve the problem, then his meta-ethics is unsound, because without a solution he cannot explicate the relation between the language of nature and its author, which is the cornerstone of his system. For the same reason, his entire epistemology and ontology are likewise inadequate.

There is another intriguing situation which arises in conjunction with the existence of Ideas in the mind of God, when this theory is used to explain creation and in particular the Mosaic account of it. We have seen that in answer to a query about this. Berkeley claimed that he could account for the book of Genesis by holding that creation consisted in God's willing that the natural world become perceptible to finite minds, presumably in the *order* given in Genesis. This would seem to entail that our minds existed *before* creation, or at least came into being contemporaneously with it. If creation consists ". . . in God's willing that those things should be perceptible to other (finite) spirits, which before were known only to Himself"[58] then there seems to be no other alternative to this conclusion. Was a new world, albeit one which exists "relatively" to us, created for each new succeeding

[57] DHP, p. 253
[58] Letter to Percival, p. 36

generation? Whether true or false, and I shall not debate the question here, this is surely an odd position for a *Christian* theologian to espouse!

His "solutions" to the problem of natural evil are usually the traditional ones, put forever to rest by David Hume. The "excesses, defects, and contrary qualities conspire to the beauty and harmony of the world".[59] Pain is "indispensably necessary to our well-being" and when we consider it as evil "our prospects are too narrow":

. . . if we enlarge our view, so as to comprehend the various ends, connexions, and dependencies of things, on what occasions and in what proportions we are affected with pain and pleasure, the nature of human freedom, and the design with which we are put into the world; we shall be forced to acknowledge that those particular things, which considered in themselves appear to be evil, have the nature of good, when considered as linked with the whole system of beings.[60]

God is not responsible for evil, because guilt consists in the will, and since we are free, he cannot be responsible for our acts.[61] What he means is that God could indeed have dispensed with pain, but only at the cost of depriving us of our freedom, which would defeat the purpose of our earthly lives. But of course, this does not account for *unnecessary* suffering, nor does it stand up to the traditional "either all-powerful or all-good but not both" argument.

On the question of whether or not Berkeley is guilty of the so-called "Factualistic Fallacy", the derivation of "ought" from "is", I remain undecided. Certainly, if there was any inference as obvious as "God commands us to do X, therefore we ought to do it", I should have to accuse him of this mistake. But though he comes close, he is not quite this blatant, and in any event, there is some doubt as to whether the "fallacy" is really a mistake after all. I think Berkeley would simply say that "ought" is senseless outside the context of "good" (we are speaking of the moral uses of terms of course) because they are analytically tied, and that happiness is causally, though not logically, tied, to God's will. Or to be more precise, the *particular* good at any time is dependent upon what is present to God's mind. There is not enough further material to decide whether or not his authoritarian theory of the derivation of moral obligation is deductive in nature.

Thus, there are problems, some of them probably, nay, certainly fatal, with Berkeley's moral philosophy. But hindsight is simple, and it

---

[59] S. 262
[60] P., 153
[61] DHP, p. 237; Correspondence with Johnson, p. 281

should not surprise us to discover that a bishop of the Church of England who died in 1753 held views in moral philosophy which, though stunningly original and fruitful in some respects, were at the same time rather traditional and ordinarily mistaken in others. And it is well to keep in mind that Berkeley was truly an experimentalist: fruitfulness as a criterion of value was of the highest value to him, as his remarks about the Mosaic account of creation show, whereas truth by correspondence was not. This attitude of mind enabled him to see things without the hindrance of previously accepted dogmas in many cases, one of which is his acute and at the time novel examination of the way terms which do not apparently denote or name ideas function in ethics. The next chapter will investigate this last topic.

CHAPTER V

BERKELEY AND THE EMOTIVE USES OF ETHICAL LANGUAGE

In the first chapter I discussed some of the problems concerned with the meaning of "truth" in the Berkeleyan system. I argued that he rejects the "idea-correspondence" theory of truth, giving two principal reasons for this: first, in sentences such as "Melampus is an animal" no correspondence of ideas is relevant to their truth or falsity because only one idea is involved. Secondly, in the case of sentences about minds, mental acts, or relations, no ideas at all are involved – only "notions". I also mentioned a third claim, but only briefly. This was that the primary importance of such ethically relevant terms as "goodness", "justice", "grace" etc., lies in their use to influence action and emotion rather than in some correspondence with ideas, notions or things. I argued that these issues are closely related to the refutation of the doctrine of abstract ideas for Berkeley, and it was suggested that his theory of truth was probably very similar to modern pragmatic and instrumentalist views. In the present chapter these matters become central, because astonishingly enough some philosophers seem to have thought that Berkeley was an emotivist! If I am correct he must of course be a cognitivist, though perhaps a pragmatist or an instrumentalist so far as his theories of truth and meaning are concerned.

In their milestone work *The Meaning of Meaning*, Professors Ogden and Richards make this claim:

"When language is once grown familiar," says Berkeley, "the hearing of the sounds or the sight of the characters is often immediately attended with those passions which at first were wont to be produced by the intervention of ideas that are now quite omitted." From the symbolic use of words we thus pass to the emotive; and with regard to words so used, as in poetry, Ribot has well remarked that "they no longer act as sounds; they are musical notations at the service of an emotional psychology."[1]

[1] Richards, I. A. and Ogden, C. K., *The Meaning of Meaning*, Harcourt, Brace and World Co., New York (1923), p. 42 (TMM)

Berkeley's acute understanding of the emotive and other practical uses of language in ethics has been noticed elsewhere, though not widely. H. D. Aiken in an article in the *Kenyon Review* notes that the twentieth century analytical philosophers questioned whether or not such ethical terms as "good", "ought" and "right" should be understood to be denoting qualities of things or acts, but he then says that they were not the first to discuss the issue, because:

Berkeley contended that the characteristic use of the primary terms of ethics and theology (such terms, for example, as 'good', 'right', 'divine', and 'grace') is not to distinguish and identify objects of perception, but to express attitudes, to formulate rules, announce aims, and to guide and to control the practices essential to the conduct of life.[2]

Still others, such as Harry M. Bracken[3] and Avrum P. Stroll have also commented upon the subject, though strangely enough, neither A. J. Ayer nor C. L. Stevenson mention Berkeley, though they are among the founders of modern emotivism or non-cognitivism. The question is then, is Berkeley a non-cognitivist, and if he is not, then how do I account for his strange remarks about the emotive uses of ethical language?

I. ABSTRACT GENERAL IDEAS AND THE "FAMILIAR" USES OF WORDS

Of all the remarks about Berkeley's discussion of the ethically relevant uses of language, the most accurate are Avrum Stroll's. He argues that Berkeley distinguishes between "pure" and "impure" emotive meaning. When a term causes an emotive reaction without the occurrence of any ideas "between the term and the emotive reaction", that is pure emotive meaning. When the term is "accompanied by an idea that helps to produce the emotive effect", the emotive meaning is impure.[4]

Stroll notices that it cannot be held that Berkeley was an emotivist, and he mentions that Berkeley's purpose in discussing the uses of language in ethics was part and parcel of his attack on the doctrine of abstract general ideas. Berkeley saw that expressions "may have significance without designating either particular ideas or abstract ideas", and Stroll argues that Berkeley has a theory of "indifferent

---

[2] Spring, 1962, "The Fate of Philosophy in the Twentieth Century", p. 235
[3] ERI, p. 76
[4] Stroll, A. P., *The Emotive Theory of Ethics*, Berkeley and Los Angeles, The University of California Press (1954), p. 24 (ETE)

signification" according to which "terms may be significant because they may function like variables in algebra, in that they may signify indifferently particular values of the variables without necessarily being individual names."[5] Since a purely emotive term signifies nothing, the "indifferent signification" theory must be distinguished from cases in which there is no signification.

The most important points in Stroll's analysis are in my opinion that Berkeley is not an emotivist and that although some terms have emotive meaning, whether pure or impure, because they cause an emotive reaction, they may also signify some particular idea at the same time, though not necessarily the same idea at all times. But I think that Berkeley's views are much more complex than Stroll makes them seem. It seems to me that although no *ideas* need be denoted by some of the terms used in ethics, and though no notion, no particular notion, need be designated or connoted by such terms at any given time, these terms must be at least *potentially* "significant" if Berkeley is to remain a cognitivist. I place quotes around the word "significant" because of course no sign relationship, strictly speaking, can exist for Berkeley anywhere but in the world of ideas, or between words and other words and ideas. Stroll and others fail to realize the *dispositional* nature of Berkeley's theory and they do not see the important role of metaphor in the ethical uses of language. It remains for me to prove these contentions, but if I succeed, then the Ogden-Richards theory will clearly be mistaken.

Before I proceed to a discussion of these issues, one other theory should be mentioned. Ian T. Ramsey argues that the logic of such terms as "grace" for Berkeley differs from the logic of mathematical terms such as "number" because "grace . . . being a construct from activity, involving activity, is *notionally* given. The word 'grace' like 'God', is significant though its distinctive reference extends beyond ideas."[6] There is truth in this comment, but it is very misleading. The truth is that words designating, referring to, or connoting etc. notions are significant, though we must take care to keep in mind that this is a different *type* of signification than that involved in the relations of words to *ideas*. But the claim is misleading for many reasons. For one thing, there are mathematical terms which refer to or connote relations, and they too are therefore in some sense "notionally given". If this is so, then their "logic" might be quite similar to terms such as

[5] ETE, p. 25
[6] NSBP, pp. 28-29

"grace", and so far as the practical guidance of our actions is concerned, I think that this is true. Secondly, our notions are of our minds, other minds, God and relations. Berkeley's theory of notions is difficult and obscure, and I cannot discuss it at any length here. But this much can be said: grace might well be some sort of relation for Berkeley, but clearly God is not, nor are heaven, hell, rewards and punishments, etc. In short, there is no reason to speak of all notions as though they were alike, and consequently one must discuss the terms of ethics, or those which refer to nonempirical contexts, in the framework of the *type* of notions to which they refer. Obviously, the "logic" of these terms might well vary according to the type of notion involved, the logic of one usage being more similar to that of mathematical terms and of another, to the uses of terms as signs in the world of concrete ideas. Furthermore, it is well to remember that not *all* of the terms used in ethics refer to or connote notions: for example, all those terms which refer to the visible effects of our actions in the world of ideas are used non-notionally. But I do agree with Ramsey that for Berkeley no ethical terms (indeed, no terms at all) connote abstract general ideas, and that *some* of the terms used in ethics and theology connote notions. This is of course true of non-ethical discourse as well: a word such as "I" does not refer to a mere set of ideas in Berkeley's view.

As I have noted, these problems must be considered within the context of Berkeley's attack on abstract general ideas. The foundation of this attack was a simple truth which Berkeley saw clearly: there are many words to which there are no corresponding ideas at the time when we use them. The believers in the idea-correspondence theory held the opposite view. They thought that when we use general words such as "man", "triangle" etc., such words must refer to ideas. Given that these words are general, these theorists thought that they must have a general referent, and hence, there must be general ideas. These general ideas are formed as a result of an intellectual process called abstraction, which is the method whereby the mind forms a concept of what is common to the members of a given class, and this is what is denoted by the general word – hence the name *abstract* general idea. A proposition composed of general terms is a general proposition. But if, as Berkeley thought, there are no abstract general things, ideas or not, and if there are many words which not only do not denote ideas when they are used, but never denote them, and finally if there are words which denote, connote, or signify only analogically and metaphorically, then the theory of abstract general ideas is not only mistaken, but inadequate as an explanation of the multitudinous uses of languages.

Berkeley of course does not deny that there are general words. Nor does he deny that there is general knowledge, and that this is expressed in general propositions. But a general word is not general because of what it stands for; it is general because of the special sort of *function* it plays. As opposed to particular words, which may signify only one thing at one time, or, in the case of proper names, but one thing at any time, general words may signify many things at any time. The many things must be related however; they must *resemble* one another. We do not have some sort of "general concept" or idea which results from abstraction and which is named by the word: rather, there are things in the natural world, and in languages, which resemble one another, and we use some particular word which need not resemble what it signifies in any way to stand for or represent each of these things. General propositions are formed from such signs. General knowledge is either about general words, or about general signs which are not words, since as we have seen signs do not have to be artificial for Berkeley. In considering general signs, we consider them

. . . in their relative capacity, and as substituted for others, (rather) than in their own nature or for their own sake.[7]

It is not the sign *per se* that is the object of general knowledge, but the many things for which it stands, and the relation between the sign and these referents. All ideas, whether particular or general, are themselves particulars. There is no such thing as a triangle, real or ideational, which is neither isoceles nor scalene nor some other shape, but rather "all of these and none at once." There are no men, nor ideas of men, which are neither black nor white, tall nor short, thin nor fat, but all of these and none of these at once. If there are no such things, then there are no words which signify them. The explanation of general signification concerns the nature of signification itself. Particular words are those used to signify particularly, that is, words whose use is to point to one single thing at all times or at some times. General words then signify generally, that is, they can be used to denote this man, or that one, or any particular man, the only requirement being that all the things signified must resemble one another in certain decided respects. The nature of the sign-vehicle is usually unimportant: "Black line one inch long" may be used as a sign, but so may _____, and

7 Alc. Appendix I, pp. 334-335

they may signify the same thing or class of things. In earlier chapters, especially the first one, I discussed at length the way words come to be signs, or at least, I discussed *one* way they do, and that way was constant association with the signified. This association is of course necessary in the case of general words as well. But in general signs, the added element of resemblance among a number of particulars becomes important, and Berkeley does not say much about this problem. I have discussed its importance, primarily in the last chapter. Here I should like simply to mention one point which might be the source of some fruitful speculation about Berkeley's views: resemblance may be a relation for Berkeley, and relations, he gives us some reason to believe, are posited by a mind. In the case of the language of the Author of Nature, the mind is probably God's. But if a relation is the foundation for general signification in the case of classes with resembling members, then the general terms in the artificial languages of men *do* depend upon something beyond the nature of the signification: their use depends upon the objective resemblance of objects, independently of *their* minds, though not of God's. Were this not so, there would be no explanation of the origin of general terms. But this fact does not, I think, bear upon his theory of the nature of general signification, and upon the central contention that all signs are themselves particulars which signify other particulars.

The second aspect of the attack on abstract general ideas which is crucial for an appreciation of Berkeley's views of the ethical uses of language concerns the *times* at which ideas occur to us upon the use of signs. Berkeley is very clearly denying that ideas must occur to us *every* time we use a sign, whether the sign be particular or general. Whether reading or speaking, the idea of a particular man does not occur to me every time I use the word "man". But why should anyone think that some idea *would* have to occur every time we use a sign? The first reason is that we are falsely convinced that the only purpose of language is the communication of ideas.[8] But if this is not the only purpose of language, then what are the others, and how are they served? This is the context of the seventh dialogue of *Alciphron*. The particular issues at stake in the dialogue are the truth and utility of the Christian religion, and hence, indirectly, the meaning of "truth". Alciphron represents the free-thinkers, Anthony Collins in particular, and indirectly he stands for what Berkeley thought Locke's theory to be. Alciphron argues that Christianity cannot be true because some of

[8] *Loc. cit.*

its propositions, in fact, most of them, are literally meaningless. For example, propositions containing terms such as "grace" are meaningless because this word denotes no idea, and "words that suggest no ideas are insignificant".[9] If this were not so, we could not communicate, because the purpose of using words is to raise in the hearer those ideas which are in the mind of the speaker. If we fail to accomplish this then our words "serve no purpose", because again, communication consists in having "the same train of ideas (in the hearer's mind) as in the mind of the speaker or writer."[10] But if there are no ideas which correspond to the words used, or if the ideas do not occur to the hearer, then this is impossible.

This must be the case even if faith is relevant to religious belief. Faith requires assent to propositions, but if the propositions themselves are senseless, how can one assent to them? And would they not be senseless if they denote no ideas?[11] Here then, the question of a theory of *meaning*, not just a theory of truth, is raised. It is difficult to separate the issues of truth and meaning in Berkeley's philosophy.

The first part of Berkeley's reply, that general words do not stand for general ideas, has already been discussed. The next moves concern his analysis of how some terms influence action, passion and emotion directly, without the intervention of ideas at that time. This amounts to a theory about uses of language *other* than that of simple communication of ideas, though as we shall see, the latter function remains the fundamental role of signs. Before we begin to discuss this in detail, the reader should understand two facts: the first is that Berkeley is not clear, and he is occasionally contradictory, in what he has to say about the pragmatic roles of language in ethics and theology. The second fact is that he nowhere defines the range of *cognitive* responses to signs. Thus, a certain amount of guesswork in the interpretation of his position is going to be inevitable. I shall try to indicate whenever I am guessing!

In Berkeley's view, some roles of language are similar to the role of faith. The central role of faith is not to examine truths or to clarify them, but rather to govern our conduct. Faith is therefore primarily important as a "practical" rather than as a cognitive state of mind. This does not constitute grounds for a criticism of faith however, because in essence, the role of science is similar to that of faith. The purpose of science is to promote our well-being. To accomplish this, science does

9 Alc. VII, 1
10 Alc. VII, 1
11 Alc. VII, 4

not deal with ideas directly. It deals with, it consists in, the manipulation of signs, and in particular, general signs, rather than concerning
itself with the ideas to which the signs ultimately refer. In addition,
there are some signs with which science deals which refer to no ideas
at all, such signs as "force" for example. For this reason, if we were to
understand science as a system of propositions denoting ideas, we
would have as many mysteries to solve as we do when we take faith in
this way, and the moral of the story is to understand both faith and
reason as practical as well as cognitive. This makes it more difficult to
understand both faith and reason, but the fact that it is hard to understand the meaning of "grace" is in itself no more reason to reject
religion than is the difficulty of understanding the role of the sign
"force" a good reason for refusing to use it in science.[12]

Words, of course, are but one kind of sign. Through the examination of other types of signs, it is possible to illuminate the various roles of
words. One other type of sign is a counter, that is, something like a
poker chip which is used as a substitute for money in card games.
Berkeley's idea in using this type of sign as a point of discussion is
because of its similarity to words: the counter is a substitute for money,
as words are substitutes (some of them) for ideas. If we consider the
purpose of using counters, and the roles which they play in a game, we
will see that not only are they substitutes for money, but during the
game, *no idea* of the money which they represent normally occurs to us.
In fact, it is not stretching a point to say that one of the reasons for
using counters is that having to compute amounts at each step of the
game makes it too difficult to play, whereas the counters provide a
means for doing this only when it counts – at the end of the evening.

Now instead of thinking about counters, think of monetary signs.
When we are computing a sum of money, using the signs known as
numbers, does an idea of the actual currency represented by the
number occur to us with each step in the computation which involves a
different number? Certainly not, any more than in the case of the
counters. Now if numbers, counters, and words are but three different
kinds of sign, why must ideas occur to us every time we use words, but
not in the other two cases? Berkeley's answer is of course that ideas
do *not* always occur when we use words. It simply is not necessary, after
we are familiar with the signs. The reason it is not necessary is that the
purpose of using such signs in many situations is not to communicate
ideas, but to "direct our actions with respect to things." There are

[12] Alc. VII, 11

several ways that this influencing of our conduct may be accomplished through the use of signs. Among them are the "forming of rules for us to act by, or by raising certain passions, dispositions, and emotions in our minds." When these effects of the use of signs happen, though no ideas accompany such use, the signs are "significant", and "useful". Now this sounds very much like the beginnings of an emotive theory. But in the same passage where these remarks are found, Berkeley lays down a condition for the significance of such signs which belies any obvious non-cognitive interpretation. He says "words may not be in-significant, although they should not, every time they are used, excite the ideas they signify in our minds; it being sufficient that we *have it in our power* to substitute things or ideas for their signs when there is occasion."[13] We should note that he is here speaking of signs which do and did stand for ideas, rather than those which stand for other signs such as words, or those referring to notions. But although this is true, I think it justified to assume that he would hold the same position with regard to these other signs, because he begins the passage by referring, as we have seen, to counters and numbers. It seems therefore that a necessary condition of our being able to use signs to form rules of conduct, or to raise passions, dispositions and emotions affecting con-duct, is that we be *able* "when there is occasion" to provide the things or ideas for which the signs stand. This necessary condition in turn presupposes a high degree of familiarity with the use of the signs in question, for it is a true psychological statement that when we are first learning such signs, the ideas they stand for do occur each time we use them. There is then a sort of *two*-fold interpretative process going on here. C. M. Turbayne, speaking of this subject, says

Being directed how to act or to get ready to act by means of signs is inter-pretation of them just as well as being minded of other things by their means. It is knowledge. It is knowing how to act or to prepare for action.[14]

It is interesting that as support for this claim, Turbayne refers to section 253 of *Siris*, where Berkeley is claiming that a true knowledge and understanding of the natural language entails an ability to "raticinate", that is, to be able to foretell or predict what will occur upon the basis of the present and past occurrence of groups of signs – natural laws. In that passage. Berkeley concludes: "Nor is this manner of reasoning confined only to morals or politics, but extends also to

13 Alc. VII, 5 (my italics)
14 MM, p. 73

natural science." Now I think that when we consider the remarks about being able to "cash" signs in things and ideas, together with Berkeley's claims about what it is to understand natural signs and how familiar signs can affect action, passion, dispositions and emotions without the occurrence of ideas, a general theory of "significance" (meaning?) begins to appear in outline. The cardinal principle of this theory is that the *same* sign may have, depending on its context, different *kinds* of significance, and that in some cases at least, the types of significance depend in specifiable ways upon one another. Take the case of the counters. Counters as signs are significant in at least two ways: they are significant because they are signs of various amounts of currency, and they are significant because they direct us to act in certain ways. The two kinds of significance are different, but they are also related. They are related because the fact that the signs (counters) stand for specified amounts of currency is the *reason*, the explanation, of why they direct our actions in certain ways. If in the case of the counters we were unable to provide, when the occasion arose, the amounts of currency which the chips represent, our action would be absolutely senseless. In short, only when we retain this "cashing" ability is our action directed towards some object, and being directed towards some object is one of the traditional criteria for cognitive conduct. I shall return to this theme in later sections.

2. MORE ABOUT BERKELEY'S THEORY OF TRUTH

There are some signs which *cannot* denote ideas, among which are all those which refer to (in the broadest sense) relations and notions, syncategorematic terms, etc. It would seem that such signs cannot be ostensively defined. Of these signs, Turbayne has this to say:

> We could say that their meanings are placed in the will and affections rather than in the understanding... the way we respond is part of our understanding of them.[15]

We place them in a context, and we react to them. They have a "pragmatic" rather than or in addition to a communicative function.[16] But the issue is more complex than this, because among other things, many of the signs of mathematics fall into this category, and of all intellectual pursuits, doing mathematics has always been held to be the epitomy of cognitive activity. Berkeley says this:

[15] MM, pp. 89-90
[16] MM, pp. 92-93

... the algebraic mark, which denotes the root of a negative square, hath its use in logistic operations, although it be impossible to form an idea of any such quantity. And what is true of algebraic signs is also true of words or language, modern algebra being in fact a more short, apposite, and artificial sort of language, and it being possible to express by words at length, though less conveniently, all the steps of an algebraical process.[17]

Since this is so, perhaps we can learn more about the perplexing relationship between the two kinds of significance I have mentioned by studying Berkeley's views of mathematics a little further. One of the results of such a theory will be to demonstrate that for Berkeley, it is difficult, if not impossible, to separate questions about truth from those about meaning.[18]

Berkeley's primary purpose in attacking traditional mathematics and science was again to refute the doctrine of abstract general ideas. His conviction about both mathematics and natural science is evident from his description of them as "the two great provinces of speculative science conversant about ideas received from sense."[19] His attack on the doctrine of materialism and mechanism, based upon his denial of efficient causality in the physical world, has already been discussed, as has its relation to the argument against abstract general ideas. The primary target to which he directed his energies in the case of the "infidel mathematicians" was the theory of infinites, and the reason for his animus on this subject was again the theory of abstract general ideas. Numbers, in Berkeley's eyes, were not the magical things, the abstract entities, some thought them to be.[20] There are no "general or abstracted triangles or circles", and they are therefore not "the subject of all the eternal, immutable, universal truths."[21] But because of his denial of a possible realm of mathematical "forms", and his arguments against material substance (which some thought to be the source of our ideas of number) he felt it necessary to explain how general proofs are possible without abstract general ideas. Part of his effort in this connection is directed toward showing that mathematical terms or signs are not necessarily connected with, or do not necessarily signify, anything which is not another mathematical sign, yet at the same time, they are meaningful. The tenor of his attack on traditional mathe-

---

[17] Alc. VII, 14
[18] I owe considerable thanks for the development of what follows to Mr. R. J. Baum, a graduate student at the Ohio State University.
[19] P., 101
[20] P., 119
[21] TV, first edition, 125

matics can be gathered from this remark, where he is speaking about the thesis that geometry deals with abstract general ideas called "lines", "triangles", etc.:

I do not find that I can perceive, imagine, or anywise frame in my mind such an abstract idea as here spoken of. A line or surface which is neither black, nor white, nor blue, nor yellow, etc., nor long, nor short, nor rough, nor smooth, nor square, nor round, etc., is perfectly incomprehensible.[22]

He feels the same way about the mathematical idea of "unity", which some, notably Locke, had claimed to accompany all other ideas, and to be perceived, in Berkeley's words, "by all the ways of sensation and reflection". In his eyes, he simply has no such idea, and by definition, it is just another abstract general idea.[23] Nonetheless, we do after all have mathematical concepts, and Berkeley certainly does not want to deny this. The problem is to explain what mathematics is about, and how it has meaning. For him, mathematics, both geometry and arithmetic, are comprised of arbitrary signs which are manipulated by arbitrary rules, and it is through their *signification* that they derive their meaning. Just as, in the *New Theory of Vision*, visible lines have no significance or meaning apart from their function as signs of tangible objects, so visible figures play the same roles in geometry that words do:

... the one may as well be the object of that science as the other; neither of them being otherwise concerned therein than as they represent or suggest to the mind the particular tangible figures connected with them.[24]

The origin of numbers is the same as that of names:

... the notation of the Arabians or Indians came into use, wherein, by the repetition of a few characters or figures, and varying the signification of each figure according to the place it obtains, all numbers may be most aptly expressed; which seems to have been done in imitation of language, so that an exact analogy is observed betwixt the notation by figures and names. . .[25]

And from this it follows that the ground of the relation between mathematical signs is the same as that in other artificial languages – constant association – though of course, overt stipulative definition plays a relatively larger role in mathematics. Moreover, the *generality* of mathematics is explicable in the same context as is the general signification of normal words. Mathematical knowledge, like all true knowledge and demonstration, concerns "universal notions". But these

[22] P., 123
[23] P., 13
[24] TV, 152
[25] P., 121

notions are not formed by abstraction: universality does not consist "in the absolute, positive nature or conception of anything, but in the relation it bears to the particulars signified or represented by it."[26] Mathematical signs are themselves particulars: they become general in the same ways as other signs: "by being made to represent or stand for all other particular ideas of the same sort."[27]

At this point an important distinction between geometry and algebra arises in Berkeley's philosophy. Geometry for him is the study of the relations between visible signs and tangible signs signified. As such, it is part of the Language of the Author of Nature. We have already seen that humans cannot know with certainty that the sign-relationships in the natural language will remain constant, for this would imply that we know the intentions of God. Hence, the truth of the laws of geometry depends upon God's will, and in this sense they are arbitrary. Arithmetic is arbitrary too, much more so than geometry, for it is the creature of the mind of man. Geometry, if you will, is a part of the natural language while arithmetic is an artificial language. Indeed, the relativity of arithmetic extends even to individual minds and their use of these signs: ". . . the same extension is one, or three, or thirty-six, according as the mind views it with reference to a yard, a foot, or an inch. Number is so visibly relative, and dependent on man's understanding, that it is strange to think how anyone should give it absolute existence without the mind." What the number stands for is what the mind counts as a unit; but what that unit is, is arbitrary. As Berkeley notes, we say "one book, one page, one line", and all of them are "equally units", that is, objects named by "one".[28] Numbers then, and the units they stand for, are alike "creatures of the mind".[29] The rules by which arbitrary units are assigned the same name (number) are likewise arbitrary – they are invented for convenience, just as numbers were invented to take the place of word-names for the same reason. Arithmetic consists in the manipulation of these signs according to rules specifying their application to many ideas or units having certain properties in common. Thus, since the terms in any mathematical proof only apply to the properties the units have in common, they will have the required generality, without having to posit the existence of abstract general ideas in order to explain this fact.[30]

---

[26] Intro. to P., 15
[27] Intro. to P., 12
[28] P., 12
[29] TV, 109
[30] Intro. to P., 16; also Alc. VII, 12

As with other artificial languages, once we become familiar with arithmetical calculations, we carry them out without considering what is signified. In the end, the calculations direct us how to act with regard to things, exactly as the counters in the card game do; but during the calculations we do not have the occurrence of the units (ideas) corresponding to the numerical terms, and in fact, given the universality of mathematical proofs, this is in practice not possible. Another way of stating the same fact is to say that the immediate objects of mathematical calculations are but other signs, not units themselves, though in the end, should practical result be desired, the numbers are actually applied.[31] Is there perhaps a clue to a theory of meaning here? Is there some crucial difference between signs and the manipulation thereof when they *do* name units, and when they do not? I think so. Signs *per se*, and hence any demonstration involving their use, are "perfectly arbitrary and in our power – made at pleasure". It is in virtue of this fact that demonstrations succeed, as I argued in chapter two. But such demonstrations are but games, having little importance for human affairs. The "eternal truths" which in the minds of some are expressed in mathematical permutations which do not name units are empty and meaningless:

Let any man show me a demonstration, not verbal, that does not depend either on some false principle or at best on some principle of nature which is the effect of God's will and we know not how soon it may be changed. Qu: What becomes of the aeternae veritates? Ans: They vanish.[32]

And what of verbal demonstrations? Are they meaningful?

When words are used without a *meaning*, you may put them together as you please without danger of running into a contradiction. You may say, for example, that twice two is equal to seven, so long as you declare you do not take the words of that proposition in their usual acceptation but for marks of you know not what.[33]

And there is no guarantee, when one begins to interchange symbols according to mathematical rules, that the symbols in the conclusion will denote units in the world of perception – not even if the symbols in the premises do this. Well then, how can we tell whether or not the conclusions of our proofs *do* apply to reality? Or, to put it in another way, how can we tell when the signs of mathematics are

[31] Alc. VII, 13
[32] PC., 732-735
[33] P., 79 (my italics)

meaningful? Several of Berkeley's remarks taken together provide us with the answer:

In Arithmetic, . . .we regard not the things but the signs, which nevertheless are not regarded for their own sake, but because they direct us how to act with relation to things, and dispose rightly of them . . . those things which pass for *abstract* truths and theorems concerning numbers, are in reality conversant about no other object distinct from *particular numerable things*, except only names and characters, which originally came to be considered on no other account but their being signs, or capable to represent aptly whatever particular things men had need to compute. Whence it follows that to study them for their own sake would be just as wise, and to as good purpose, as if a man neglecting the true use or original intention and subserviency of language, should spend his time in impertinent criticisms upon words, or reasonings and controversies purely verbal.[36]

It is then our *intention* which gives significance to computation. Signs originate in mathematics because they are "apt" for representing "whatever particular things men had *need* to compute". To study mathematics apart from the ways it serves our needs, fulfills our intentions, is to think about that without meaning, about "controversies purely verbal." When we combine ideas together to make units, we do it in that way which "experience shows it to be most convenient".[35] Convenient for what? There seems to be no other answer than, convenient for whatever the needs of men are.

. . . theories . . . in Arithmetic . . . abstracted from the names and figures, as likewise from all use and practice, as well as from the particular things numbered, can be supposed to have nothing at all for their object; hence we may see how entirely the science of numbers is subordinate to practice, and how jejune and trifling it becomes when considered as a matter of mere speculation.[36]

In mathematics, we relate signs to things by rules of practice, and we judge the meaningfulness of our computations in the light of whether or not they enable us to operate about things in such a way that we fulfill our intentions. A sign therefore has meaning only if it has what I might call "intentional utility".

The case is, as one might expect, slightly different for geometry, for in this case God is the author of the sign-to-thing-signified relations. Visible ideas which are the signs of tangible ones, are not, for the most

34 P., 122
35 TV, 109
36 P., 120

part, dependent upon our wills but upon God's. It is the world of perceivable ideas which is the sole source for concepts which are applicable to that world within the context of geometry. This is why the theory of infinitesimals is mistaken in Berkeley's eyes: it has no application, and is an unnecessary hypothesis because it cannot explain anything. In fact, the attempt to use it is a practical contradiction.[37] But for my purposes here, the important fact is that meaningful geometrical propositions are those which have practical application, and which enable us to fulfill our intentions accordingly. In fact, of all the sciences, it is the best (most effective) for our ends, since it is the most complete. This is because God has provided all the signs necessary for it in his natural language. One result is that although concepts derivative from geometry may be used to solve problems in other disciplines, the converse is not true.[38]

    In all of this, the question raised by the title of this section, the nature of truth, rests uneasily in the background. To be blunt, I can find no body of statements in Berkeley's writings which can plausibly be taken to constitute a theory of truth. There are in fact many places where he hints that truth is an abstract general idea. For example;

In the ordinary affairs of life, any phrases may be retained, so long as they excite in us proper sentiments or dispositions to act in such a manner as is necessary for our well-being, how false soever they may be if taken in a strict and speculative sense.[39]

    I would be the first to admit that Berkeley is not consistent in his philosophy. But certainly enough evidence has been presented, at least in the area of mathematics, especially arithmetic, to justify the claim that "speculative truth", that is, analytic truths, are for Berkeley practically unimportant *per se*. We already know that he rejects the Lockean theory of truth, and I have argued that Berkeley's intention in the case of sentences such as "Melampus is an animal" is to interpret them as directions concerning the use of words. If this is so, meaning, not truth, is the cardinal point at stake here. Moreover, where there are no ideas concerned, as in the case of such signs as "I", "myself", "will", "love", "hate", *ad infinitum*, it seems clear that no correspondence theory then known (and I think this is still true) would have satisfied Berkeley. Some version of a coherence theory might have been

---

[37] PC, 354; P, 132
[38] DM, 17-18
[39] P., 52

acceptable to him, but I suspect that he would view such theories as he views "speculative truth", and that he would hold them to be unimportant but for purposes of verbal demonstration. I do not mean to imply that Berkeley thought the entire question of truth and falsity trivial or unimportant. Rather, I want to emphasize his awareness of the *complexity* of the maze of language, his continuing insistence that simple-minded explanations in terms of correspondence to ideas or what have you simply do not do justice to the variety and scope of language, nor to the diverse functions of the creature which uses it. The topic in connection with which this theme is most obvious is his treatment of our "assent" to propositions whose terms do not denote ideas, particularly propositions about religious matters. It is from *this* account that Ogden and Richards draw their conclusion that Berkeley is speaking about emotive meaning rather than cognitive. Berkeley claims that a) if the terms of propositions such as those used in "the Father, the Son, and the Holy Ghost, are God, and . . . there is but one God" do not denote ideas, and b) if it is sufficient for a sign or signs to be "significant" that they "regulate and influence our wills, passions, or conduct", and if c) the terms in propositions such as the one given in a) do influence us as described in b), then "the mind of man may assent to propositions containing such terms, when it is so directed or affected by them, notwithstanding it should not perceive distinct ideas marked by those terms".[40] The specific reactions produced in us by the proposition given are enumerated by Berkeley as love, hope, gratitude and obedience, and these dispositions enable us to achieve the end of ourselves, if Christianity is correct, which is eternal salvation.

Now from such remarks as these, when they are taken out of their particular context, and when they are considered separately from Berkeley's other remarks about the various functions of signs, it is easy to argue that he was an emotivist. But what appears to be is not always what is. In the same dialogue of *Alciphron* where this issue is raised, Berkeley moves on to speak about mathematical signs (which I have already examined) and then to some revealing general remarks about the roles of metaphors, analogies, models, diagrams, "figures" and "types". He concludes the discussion with a summary about signs in general, attempting to tie the uses of signs in science, mathematics, religion, ethics and normal discourse all together. A complete examination must therefore take account of these factors.

Berkeley's view of the uses of metaphor, allegory, etc. rests on the

[40] Alc. VII, 8

contention that they serve to acquaint us with what we do not know through what we do know, and that they make what is less familiar more readily understandable by presenting it in familiar forms. We are, according to him, better acquainted with those objects we first come to know than with those we later come to know; some objects "strike (the mind) more sensibly" than others, and it is natural for us to let these objects represent those which are more difficult to conceive or understand. This is the way in which we "explain and represent things less familiar by others which are more so." There is in fact an heirarchy of symbols, the ranking depending upon the order in which we come to know things, and the clarity and distinctness with which the sign-vehicles in this presentation are known. What we know first is what is given to sense, and of all the data of all the senses, those which are clearest and most distinct, those which have the widest range of possible uses, and which are most "agreeable, and comprehensive", are the data of sight. After sight, though Berkeley does not specifically say so, I imagine that he would list the data of touch. But the point is obvious. After sense, imagination occurs, and then reflection. In the process of coming to know, we try to clarify and make understandable the objects of each succeeding level by using the objects of the level or levels beneath it for purposes of illustration, representation and ex- planation. As Berkeley says, "it is natural to assist the intellect by imagination, imagination by sense, and other senses by sight."[41] The forms of language in which these representations, theories, or ex- planatory devices are expressed are called figures, metaphors, types, emblems, symbols, hieroglyphics, models, diagrams, allegories etc., depending upon the type and relations of the signs used, and the purposes they serve.

We use what is corporeal to illustrate what is spiritual. We use sounds to stand for thoughts, and written, visible letters to represent sounds, though there is no resemblance between them. Small things are employed to make it easier for us to understand big ones, and on the contrary, large models represent to us what is too small to understand or perceive readily. What is present to us serves to illustrate what is ab- sent, and what is stable and permanent is used to capture the fleeting and perishing. The visible helps us to formulate concepts about what is invisible. Berkeley gives us the examples of Plato's winged chariot, with the driver representing the rational faculty of the mind and the two horses being will and appetite. Others are as numerous as your

[41] Alc. VII, 13

capability for discovering and inventing them: Locke's *tabula rasa*; Descartes's pilot in the ship; Plato's State; Aristotle's race-course; Plato's stepped arch; plastic models of atoms; the curved roof of a planetarium; Hobbes' "man is a wolf"; the Newtonian-Cartesian machine view of the world; printing in a book; lines used to represent velocity; maps; visual representations of hellfire and the beatific vision; particular good things for all good things; ect. etc.[42] When we speak of the less readily understandable, we "cash" our words and concepts in the currency of the more understandable, or at least, we sometimes do. Often, the reasons offered for justification or explanation are couched in metaphorical terminology, or in allegory.

Signs and symbols sometimes cause emotions to be aroused, and they produce "certain dispositions or habits of mind". They direct our conduct "in pursuit of that happiness which is the ultimate end and design, the primary spring and motive, that sets rational agents at work." They may suggest or even imply relations or proportions among things which can only be understood by means of signs, and when so expressed these relations and proportions enable us to manipulate things for our well-being. This is true of the uses of ideas in *all* areas of knowledge in Berkeley's view: "that the true end of speech, reason, science, faith, assent, in all its different degrees, is not merely, or principally, or always, the imparting or acquiring of ideas, but rather something of an active operative nature, tending to a conceived good."[43] This conceived good may well be achieved through the manipulation of signs and their ultimate application to the world of ideas even though the signs do not at every step in the process of manipulation denote ideas, as the example of algebra clearly shows.

There is not then, the distinction between clearly emotive and clearly cognitive meaning in Berkeley that one might expect from more modern theorists. Happiness is the spring and motive that "sets *rational* agents at work", and the good for which such agents act must be a *conceived* good. Science and faith, reasoned argument and religion, alike serve their purposes, which are eventually one, by the same means. But to accomplish this, we must know *what* it is that we are acting for. Random mathematics is senseless, as is random action about anything. But purely emotive language is random: the emotions it excites need tend to no conceived good, nor need they enable us to act about things. They have no reasons, though they have an explanation.

---

[42] Alc. VII, 13
[43] Alc. VII, 14

This is not to say that at *all times* when we use signs, or react to them, we must have an idea or notion of the conceived good for which we are acting present to us, or an idea or notion of the ways in which signs must function to achieve this end. We can be affected by the promise of a good thing "though we have not an idea of what it is."[44] Perhaps the best thing to do at this point is to investigate more fully his psychological analysis of what happens in such cases, and then relate this to my interpretation of the role of reason in ethics according to Berkeley.

3. AN IMPORTANT PASSAGE, AND A WORKING EXAMPLE

One of the most remarkably acute analyses of the psychological processes of conditioning which occur once language has become familiar is to be found in the draft of the introduction to Berkeley's *The Principles of Human Knowledge*. It begins by setting the problem, which is simple: what follows upon "mention of reward to a man for his pains and perseverance in any occupation whatsoever"? The answer is, many things do. First of all, one thing that *may* happen is that "there may be excited in his understanding an idea of the particular good thing proposed for a reward." Secondly (though not chronologically of course) "an alacrity and steddiness in fulfilling those conditions on which (the reward) is to be obtain'd" may follow, and with this a desire to please and render good service to the person giving the reward. It is not necessary that these things follow, but sometimes, indeed very often, they do. But now Berkeley notes that the "alacrity and steddiness" and the desire to please may follow *without* the idea of the particular good thing occurring, and that indeed they may follow "tho' . . . there be excited in his mind no other idea than barely those of sounds or characters". There is an explanation for this:

When he was a child he had frequently heard those words used to create in him an obedience to the commands of those that spoke them, and as he grew up he has found by experience that upon the mentioning of those words by an honest man it has been his interest to have doubled his zeal and activity for the service of that person.[45]

It is because of this "customary connexion" that has been established between the very hearing of the sounds in which the reward is men-

[44] Intro. to P., 20
[45] Draft, pp. 137-139

tioned and the activation of the disposition to obey it that the latter may occur without any idea of the particular good thing occurring at the same time. The same sort of situation arises in the case of many other morally relevant terms.

I ask any man whether when he tells another that such an action is honourable and vertuous he has at that instant the abstract ideas of honour and vertue in his view; and whether in reality his *intention* be to raise those abstract ideas together with their agreement to the particular idea of that action in the understanding of him he speaks to. Or rather whether this be not his full *purpose* namely that those words should excite in the mind of the hearer an esteem of that particular action and stirr him up to the *performance* of it?[46]

In the interpretation of this passage, a number of points should be noticed at once. The first is that the part just quoted concerns the intent of the *user* of the signs, the man who mentions the "good thing" or the honorable or virtuous action, whereas the earlier part concerns the reaction on the part of the *hearer* of the sounds. Secondly, it should be mentioned again that the second part is obviously directed against the doctrine of abstract general ideas and the idea-correspondence of truth. Third, it should be emphasized that when speaking about the hearer's reaction, it is necessary to emphasize that the reaction follows upon the association between the pronunciation of certain words by an *honest* man, and the subsequent receipt of the reward. Finally, I would ask you to keep in mind Berkeley's remark that we must "have it in our power to substitute things or ideas for their signs when there is occasion"[47] and to recall my remarks about the cashing of certain sorts of signs in metaphors, allegories, etc. With these preliminaries out of the way, some very important conclusions can be derived about this passage.

The first conclusion is that a necessary condition for the occurrence of the action and the exciting of the dispositions is that the idea *did* occur at some time in the history of the hearer, and that the agent did actually *receive* the particular good thing or things proposed by the user of the signs. Had these two things not happened, there would be no explanation for the establishment of the customary connection between hearing the ideas and acting. Secondly, the hearer is using the signs, to speak loosely, much as the player in the card game uses his counters: he uses the sounds as direct cues for action, signs enabling

---

[46] Draft, pp. 137-139
[47] Alc. VII, 5

him to act about things, but in the end he must cash them. This needs further explanation, because it is true of *both* the user of the signs and the person who reacts to them. The purpose of the user is to cause the hearer to *do* something, that of the hearer to *get* something. Although Berkeley did not say so, there is no more reason to suppose that the specific ideas of the hearer's ultimate action should occur to the user of the signs than there is to suppose that the hearer has an idea of some specific reward, at the time when the signs are used. This is because, or provided that, a disposition has *also* been established in the *user's* mind between using the signs and seeing the subsequent action upon the part of the hearer, just as there is such a set of circumstances in the hearer's case, concerning the hearing of the sounds and being disposed to act. But they *both* have purposes, in the one the action or the end it accomplishes, in the other the reward. These are the reasons which the user and the hearer would respectively offer were they asked for an explanation or justification of their respective behavior. Responsible actions are, after all, whether moral or non-moral, acts of will done in the light of expected consequences. If an agent cannot give reasons in support of his action, then he is not a responsible actor. But he need not give them *every* time he acts, nor need he have the *idea*, or notion, corresponding to his reason or reasons every time he acts. The only requirement Berkeley provides is that he be *able* to provide them "when there is occasion". Berkeley held that moral action is responsible action, and it follows that it must be of that type for which the agent can give reasons.

Consider the following situation: suppose that a user of signs wishes to accomplish an end, which in this case is having his car washed. To this end, he says to a hearer of the signs "If you wash the car, then I shall give you a dollar". These signs contain both a mention of a particular reward, plus a specification of the conditions necessary to obtain it. Assuming that in the case of the hearer, a) he has heard the words (or similar ones) many times before, b) that he has heard them from this man before, c) that upon mention of the words, then upon performing the action, he has in fact received the dollar, Berkeley says that the following may happen: a) an idea of the particular good thing (the dollar) proposed might occur in the mind of the agent; b) "an alacrity and steddiness in fulfilling those conditions on which the re- ward . . . is to be obtain'd" might happen, that is, the disposition to wash the car might be activated; c) "a zealous desire of service and pleasing the person in whose power it is to bestow that good thing" might arise. Now once the hearer is *very* familiar with the hearing of the words, (b) and (c) may happen without (a). An exactly similar situation could be set up for the user of the signs.

Now whether one gives the reasons for acting before or after the action is usually not important, but if anyone became so accustomed to washing cars upon hearing words such as those above that he no longer cared if he got the dollar when he was finished, we should say that that person was not a responsible agent. Such a person would have given us evidence that he is no longer able to justify or explain his action, and in that event, we should say that the action had become reflexive. But surely Berkeley is not speaking of reflexive action (as he would be if he were speaking of "sounds . . . at the service of an emotional psychology" à la Ogden and Richards) for if he were, how could he claim that moral action (which is one sort of action in which these kinds of situations arise) is responsible? Moral action implies order and regularity in our lives, which is "not an effect of appetite or passion", but of judgment.[48] When we "balance low and sensual pleasures with those of a higher kind, comparing present losses with future gains";[49] when we calculate the social benefits of a moderate as opposed to a profligate life;[50] when we speculate about the pleasures appropriate for rational creatures as opposed to brutes;[51] when we attempt to justify choice of a pleasure by reference to the judgments of experts in the field,[52] and affirm that the truly valuable ends of human conduct cannot be estimated by those who "judge of pleasures by sense",[53] are we merely reacting to "sounds . . . at the service of an emotional psychology"? It would seem not, for in all the former processes, inferences are involved at one time or another, but not in the latter. And there can be no judgment, and hence no ordered life, and therefore no moral life, without inferential thought for Berkeley. No one, Berkeley included, would want to claim that we make inferences *every* time we act. Berkeley's purpose in the quotations I have been discussing seems to be to explain how *that* is possible. But he insists that we be able to give our reasons, and that this ability is presupposed by the performance of the act, instead of being explicitly given or thought of every time we act. That the reasons must be understood is obvious from the fact that we soon stop washing cars upon hearing certain sounds if

[48] D., p. 203
[49] Alc. III, 5
[50] Alc. II, 5
[51] Alc. II, 14
[52] Alc. II, 15
[53] Alc. II, 18

the dollar is not forthcoming soon after the action, and in the same way, the user of the sign would soon ask someone else to wash his car, or raise the reward, if nothing happened when he said the words. But if Ogden and Richards were correct when they analyzed Berkeley, then the good bishop would have to hold that we keep right on scrubbing, and the user keeps right on talking, once the customary connections are established.

Words such as "heaven", "hell", "eternal reward" etc. present special problems, but I believe that they too are analyzable in the way I have analyzed "good thing" and "If you wash the car then I shall give you the dollar". The additional mechanism needed is Berkeley's theory about the uses of metaphors, types, figures, allegories, etc. I think that "eternal reward" would be analyzed for Berkeley on the model of "good thing"; it would be understood that although we can have no idea of what the hand of God has prepared for us in heaven, we can and do have an idea of what particular good things are, and we can therefore have at least an analogical or a metaphorical idea or notion of the concept *that* there will be given to good Christians an eternal reward. If this sort of explanation be taken within the context of my remarks about the pragmatic or instrumentalist theory of meaning and truth which Berkeley espouses, I see no objection *in principle* against it, and it certainly seems to me to be consistent with everything that Berkeley says. In such cases of metaphorical explanation and justification, exactly the same sort of psychological association could be established between the hearing of the sounds and the performance of the requisite actions, or the arousing of the required dispositions, as was found in the case of literal or non-metaphorical instances of the uses of signs. I shall not attempt to give examples of what I think such reasoning would be like, because Berkeley's specific remarks about such matters are few and far between, and too general to be of much use in the construction of specific cases. But I think that the principle is clear enough.

The conclusion of this section is that for Berkeley, virtuous action is a habit only in the sense that in a good man it happens regularly. It is not habitual if that term connotes thoughtless reaction to stimuli, and indeed, this is true of all responsible conduct.

CHAPTER VI

BERKELEY AND SHAFTESBURY

Anthony Ashley Cooper, third Earl of Shaftesbury, was the man with whom Berkeley disagreed more than any other in his writings. In many ways, he misunderstood Shaftesbury, taking him as a representative of the free-thinking and deistic movement of the time without question. In addition, he treated this amiable writer with unwarranted abuse in some of his comments, though this was the style then. But as we shall see, Berkeley and Shaftesbury actually agreed with each other more than they disagreed, though no doubt the good bishop would be surprised by that comment. A hint of its truth is given in this remark of Shaftesbury's, which could have been made by Berkeley himself:

All Nature's wonders serve to excite and perfect this idea of their author. 'Tis here he suffers us to see, and even converse with him in a manner suitable to our frailty. How glorious is it to contemplate him in this noblest of his works apparent to us, the system of the bigger world![1]

Shaftesbury lived from 1671 to 1713, and John Locke was the attending physician at his birth. He spoke Latin, Greek and French fluently, and he was a member of the house in King William's second parliament. His health was never good, and when he became the third earl upon the death of his father in 1699, he entered the House of Lords. All

Note: The great majority of the notes in this chapter are references to Shaftesbury's *Characteristics of Men, Manners, Opinions, Times*, edited by John M. Robertson, with an introduction by Stanley Green, Library of Liberal Arts, Indianapolis (1964). All references have in turn been checked against early editions of the work. Since it has several distinct parts, I shall adopt the following system of abbreviations for the footnotes: all references to the Characteristics will begin with the letters "CH" followed by
"AA" for Advice to an Author
"EW" for An Essay on the Freedom of Wit and Humor
"LE" for A Letter Concerning Enthusiasm
"IV" for An Inquiry Concerning Virtue or Merit
"MR" for Miscellaneous Reflections
"M" for The Moralists.
[1] CHM, pt. III, see. 1

his life, he was an ardent whig. He married in 1709, to one Jane Ewer of Hertfordshire. The marriage was arranged by his friends, and Shaftesbury had never seen the bride before the wedding. They had one son, and apparently it was a very happy union. In 1711, Shaftesbury went to Naples because of his bad health, and he died there on February 15, 1713. In many ways, he was a contradictory personality. He hated priests, but attended church regularly; he was frugal himself but generous with his friends; he was opposed to formal metaphysics, yet a convinced Platonist. Early in his life he was greatly influenced by Locke, who had supervised his education from 1680 on, but later turned against Locke's philosophy when he came under the influence of Whichcote, Cudworth and Cumberland, the Cambridge Platonists. Historically, he is most noted for his "moral sense" theory, which influenced his disciple Hutcheson, and through him, Butler, Adam Smith, and Hume. Moreover, he had a powerful influence on the Deists, especially John Toland and Anthony Collins, which is what led Berkeley to think of him as just another Deist. In Germany, his theories became especially important in the field of aesthetics. Aside from Berkeley and much of the church establishment of the time, another notable critic of Shaftesbury, though far friendlier than Berkeley, was Bernard de Mandeville, whom I shall discuss in the next chapter.

I. SHAFTESBURY'S ETHICAL SYSTEM

Shaftesbury's ethical system is frankly platonistic in tone. In brief, he held that the distinctions between right and wrong, virtue and vice, and all our moral ideas, are to be explained in terms of our own natures, and that morality is independent of God. Actions are not right or wrong because God by *fiat* says so, but because they possess some quality in virtue of which they are in fact right or wrong. The ultimate criterion for telling whether or not an action is right, for telling whether it has the property rightness, is whether or not it promotes the general well-being. We know the moral quality of an action because we have a moral sense, which Shaftesbury often compares to aesthetic taste. Through this moral sense we also discriminate between good and bad men. It is because of this moral sense, and because of a love and reverence of a good God, that good men (by which he meant the eighteenth century upper class man of taste) do what is right. Finally, he thought that both our appetites and our reason cause us to act.

These specific conclusions were the result of careful thought, which I shall now investigate in more detail.

The question "What ought man to be?" and the question "What is man?" are not separable for Shaftesbury. Man is what he ought to be, and he ought to be what he is. Man is a system related to larger systems of which he is a part, and the parts of his own system are appetites, passions, affections and reason. The value of any system is a function of the harmony of its parts. Members of the same system are related in virtue of their sharing in a common nature or "form":

But this I should affirm, "that wherever there was such a sympathising of parts as we saw here in our real tree, wherever there was such a plain concurrence in one common end, and to the support, nourishment, and propagation of so fair a form, we could not be mistaken in saying there was a peculiar nature belonging to this form, and common to it with others of the same kind." By virtue of this, our tree is a real tree, lives, flourishes, and is still one and the same even when by vegetation and change of substance not one particle in it remains the same.[2]

Order is a property of nature, and order is the product of an ordering mind, nature in general thus having a "general mind", and we individuals having particular ones. From a study of the whole of nature we discover that the public and private interests are coextensive, that without a harmonious whole, the parts suffer, and that the harmonious whole depends upon the relations between the parts.[3] Knowing this,

... it cannot surely but seem natural "that the particular mind should seek its happiness in conformity with the general one, and endeavour to resemble it in its highest simplicity and excellence."[4]

Nature is an intelligent machine, its regularity testifying to that intelligence, making miracles unnecessary as testimony to its divinity.[5] The problem for ethics then is to find out what the interest of the whole is, because:

Thus the wisdom of what rules, and is first and chief in Nature, has made it to be according to the private interest and good of every one to work towards the general good, which if a creature ceases to promote, he is actually so far wanting to himself, and ceases to promote his own happiness and welfare. He is on this account directly his own enemy, nor can he any otherwise be good or useful to himself than as he continues good to society, and to that whole of which he is himself a part.[6]

[2] *Loc. cit.*
[3] *Loc. cit.*
[4] *Loc. cit.*
[5] CHM, pt. II, sec. V
[6] CHIV, conclusion

That interest, whatever it is, is not personal pleasure. ". . .pleasure is no rule of good, since when we follow pleasure merely, we are disgusted, . . .condemning that at one time which at another we earnestly approve, and never judging equally of happiness whilst we follow passion and mere humour."[7] Either all pleasure is good, or only some, and since the latter seems to be the case, there must be something differentiating good pleasures from bad, and *this* must be what is good, not pleasure.[8] What this something, the good, is we can discover from an examination of ourselves, and our relations to the larger systems of which we are an inextricable part, the animal system, the world, the universe. Only in reference to these relations is anything called good. If we know the good of the system of which we are a part, and act from an "affection" towards satisfying that good, then we act well and rightly. If we act only from "self-regarding" affections, and not for the good of the system or whole, we cannot because of this be called good. We all know that each of us has a "private good and interest" and that there is a "right and wrong state of every creature," both for his own goodness and the goodness of others. For example, if a man drinks excessively, that is doing ill to himself, and at the same time, presumably it does ill to his companions. Thus, that which does ill to him does ill to his species, at least in this case, and one can easily find examples in which one does good to himself and also to his species by the same actions. But upon closer examination, *nothing* which affects us is irrelevant to the well or ill-being of our species, and nothing affecting the species is irrelevant to the world, and the universe. Of course, it may be that in some particular cases, though obviously not the majority, the ill-being of an individual benefits the whole, but if that is true, then

. . . the ill of that private system is no real ill in itself . . . So we cannot say of any being that it is wholly and absolutely ill, unless we can positively show and ascertain that what we call ill is nowhere good besides, in any other system, or with respect to any other order or economy whatsoever.[9]

But again, the good or ill must be done from affection, for to use Shaftesbury's example, we do not say that a man is evil if he has the plague, nor good if he does not do evil because we have tied him down. Things not done from any affection are neither good nor ill, so the question now becomes, what is a good or evil affection? Or what is the

---

[7] CHAA, pt. III, sec. II
[8] CHM, pt. II, sec. I
[9] CHIV, pt. II, sec. I

same thing for Shaftesbury, what affections are "natural" and what "unnatural"?[10] The answer to this question presupposes an investigation into the structure of ourselves, which discloses three elements in our moral natures: self-regarding affections, benevolent affections, and the "moral sense". Reason directs our affections, or it ought to do so. The moral sense is reflective, and both types of affections are independent of one another, thus avoiding the possibility that altruistic action is merely disguised self-interest.[11] It is also important to notice that the affections are not merely passive, but rather impulsive and active. The good man is therefore to be defined in terms of his good or bad affections.

Yet at the same time, ones' affections can contribute toward the good of the whole, while the agent remains "vicious". As he says:

Whatsoever therefore is done which happens to be advantageous to the species through an affection merely towards self-good, does not imply any more goodness in the creature than as the affection is itself good. Let him . . . act ever so well, if at the bottom it be that selfish affection alone which moves him, he is in himself still vicious. Nor can any creature be considered otherwise when the passion towards self-good, though ever so moderate, is his real motive in the doing that to which a natural affection for his kind ought by right to have inclined him.[12]

The operative word in this passage is "merely", for Shaftesbury is not saying that we must not act from self-good on any occasion. He believes on the contrary that self-regarding affections are also essential to the public good or the good of the whole, for the whole cannot be preserved without the preservation of the parts.[13] In the ideal good man, *all* his affections, benevolent and self-regarding, are suited to both the public and private good, and when this is so, "then is the natural temper entirely good". But how is one to know when this is the case? In rational men, that is, creatures "capable of forming general notions of things", we discover that our affections themselves become the object of reflection, and thus "there arises another kind of affection towards those very affections themselves", and this meta-affection, at it were, is the object of the moral sense, it is what is known to be fitting or not, agreeable and disagreeable, regular and irregular, soft or harsh, harmonious or dissonant.[14]

[10] Loc. cit.
[11] CHIV. bk. i, pt. iii,#i
[12] CHIV, bk. II, pt. ii, sec. ii
[13] CHIV, bk. II, pt. i, sec. iii
[14] CHIV, pt. ii, sec. iii

The analogy with aesthetic perception now becomes more obvious. The balance or harmony of our affections is the object of the moral sense, just as the proportion, harmony and relations of the objects of the senses are the object of our aesthetic perception. In both cases, the sense involved "readily discerns" whether or not this harmony is present, and immediately and disinterestedly approves or disapproves the action or object.[15] Virtue therefore consists in "a certain just disposition or proportionable affection of a rational creature towards the moral objects of right and wrong", and as a result, vice is anything which takes away this "natural and just sense of right and wrong", or which inculcates a mistaken idea of it, or which causes opposition to it.[16] The factors which can cause such effects, and which are therefore the properties of a vicious character, are "weak or defficient" public (benevolent) affections, private or self-regarding affections which are too strong, or unnatural affections which are neither self-regarding nor benevolent, and which serve neither the public nor private goods. The good man will be the one whose affections have none of these characteristics.[17]

In all of this, there is a certain confusion between the criteria for good men, and for right actions. Right actions seem to be those performed by a good character, recognizable by the agent through his moral sense. But the analysis is circular, because as we have seen, a good character is one such that its moral sense is "natural". This criticism is somewhat diminished, though not totally overcome, by the fact that the moral sense must be educated, and thus, even though it becomes more or less automatic with practice, there must be some rule or principle in accordance with which the sense must be, or ought to be, educated. The reason the argument remains circular is that the rule or principle itself is for Shaftesbury based upon a property or properties of characters again, namely those properties or dispositions which tend to the ultimate common good of the species and of the whole. The rule of the common good is thus at bottom Shaftesbury's test for both good characters and right actions.[18]

After appropriate education of the moral sense, the "gentleman of fashion" results. These people are "those to whom a natural good genius, or the force of good education, has given a sense of what is naturally graceful and becoming." Some of them are "masters of an

[15] *Loc. cit.*
[16] CHIV, pt. iii, sec. i
[17] CHIV, bk. II, pt. i, sec. iii
[18] CHLE, sec. iv; CHIV, bk. i, pt. ii; CHM, pt. iii, sec. iii; CHIV, bk. I, pt. iii

ear in music, an eye in painting, . . . a judgment in proportions of all kinds, and a general good taste in most of those subjects which make the amusement and delight of the ingenious people of the world."[19] Such a man is "incapable of doing a rude or brutal action", and does not need to deliberate about his moral acts and decisions because "He acts from his nature, in a manner necessarily, and without reflections".[20] And this man is obviously the 18th century gentlemen of culture and social class.

The analogy between moral sense and aesthetic taste is never far below the surface of Shaftesbury's thought, and it is mostly in aesthetic terms that he frames the development of The moral sense theory. His concept of beauty is clearly platonic and formalist. It consists, in an object, in an harmonious relation between the parts involved, and in a moral character, in a virtuous character, the affections, passions and reason standing in harmonious relations, together contributing to the good of the species and the whole. The "proportionate and regular state is the truly prosperous and natural in every subject", he says, and "the same shapes and proportions which make beauty afford advantage by adapting to activity and use." Beauty, truth, and utility are therefore inseparable.[21] Just as natural health consists in "the just proportion, truth, and regular course of things in a constitution", so it is in the mental and moral worlds; there is a "tenor, tone, or order of the passions or affections" and in this harmony does morality consist.[22] The true artist is a "moral artist" who "imitates the Creator" by knowing the "inward form" of the world and himself.[23] The apprehension of form in art objects is intuitive, and so for Shaftesbury is the apprehension of moral beauty and truth, involving the disinterested attitude, the overcoming of the distinction between the subjective and the objective, and immediate enjoyment. It is in this sense, I believe, that we should understand Shaftesbury's claim that the particular mind must seek its happiness in conjunction with the general one. The universe as mind is revealed in its harmony and purpose, and we must enter into that harmony, become part of it, to be happy. The good of this organic whole is thus a concept far wider than mere human happiness for Shaftesbury. Our good, the good of social systems, must be gauged in terms of what is good for the universal system. But this does not entail

[19] CHEW, pt. IV, sec. 11
[20] CHEW, pt. IV, sec. 1
[21] CHMR, sec. 11
[22] CHMR, sec. 11
[23] CHAA, pt. 1, sec. 111

ethical relativism. On the contrary, the laws which enable the achievement of harmony are unalterable and objective. Considering moral and universal organic law as a property of the universe as a whole, individual human ills are seen not to be ills at all, unless, of course, they are violations of these laws, destructive of this harmony.

2. MORE ABOUT MORAL SENSE, AND ENTHUSIASM

The most distinctive feature of Shaftesbury's system, and the one with which Berkeley most often disagrees, is the claim that we have a moral sense. It is original, that is, innate, in us; it can be educated, and destroyed by vicious habit; some of us are unfortunately born without it; it is more emotional than rational, though reason plays a role, in a way Berkeley thought seriously mistaken. The relative roles of reason, appetite and will are characterized in this famous passage:

Appetite, which is elder brother to Reason, being the lad of stronger growth, is sure, on every contest, to take the advantage of drawing all to his own side. And Will, so highly boasted, is, at best, merely a top or football between these youngsters; who proves very unfortunately matched, till the youngest, instead of now and then a kick or lash bestowed to little purpose, forsakes the ball or top itself, and begins to lay about his elder brother. 'Tis then that the scene changes. For the elder, like an arrant coward, upon this treatment, presently grows civil, and affords the younger as fair play afterwards as he can desire.[24]

The objects of the moral sense are independent of it, just as the harmony in, say, architecture, is there independently of the eye. Even disagreement among men over moral matters proves this, for the "fit and decent" is itself presupposed by such argument. Men agree about what good is, but disagree about the application of the standard of it in particular cases, because not all moral senses are equally developed.[25] The symmetry and proportion found in nature is there no matter how barbaric we become in our occasional fads and manners. In the same way, there is a harmony and proportion of affections in a good character.[26] In the case of our concepts of our own affections, the perceived harmony or disharmony may result from the play of our imaginations on our concepts, but nonetheless, the material of the concepts, that upon which the imagination acts, still originates in nature, so the object of the moral sense is still independent.[27]

[24] CHAA, pt. i, sec. ii
[25] CHM, pt. iii, sec. ii
[26] CHAA, pt. iii, sec. iii
[27] CHIV, pt. iii, sec. i

The role of reason *vis à vis* the moral sense is hard to pin down. Aside from the occasional admission that rationality plays some part in moral decisions and the moral sense, Shaftesbury makes no systematic attempt to say what the role of reason is. He does speak on occasion of what would be "offensive" to a "rational" creature, for example, "To have the reflection in his mind of any unjust action or behaviour which he knows to be naturally odious and ill-deserving; or of any foolish action or behaviour which he knows to be prejudicial to his own interest or happiness."[28] But then he speaks of this awareness as "Conscience". Yet his insistence that the moral sense can be educated and changed dictates that reason plays some role, even if it is unclear.

Shaftesbury insists that the object of the moral sense is independent of the fear of God, God's will, and rewards and punishments. "Religious conscience presupposes moral or natural conscience" he says, because if moral values depend upon God's arbitrary will, then they are meaningless because they may change as that will changes. As Professor Fowler states it:

If what is right and wrong, good and evil, depends solely on the Will of God, how can we speak of God Himself as good? Goodness, as one of the Divine attributes, must, on this hypothesis, simply mean that conformity of God to His own Will.[29]

Further, rewards and punishments presuppose something worth rewarding and punishing; if virtue is to be rewarded, then it must be good and right in itself. But if this is true, then rewards cannot be good reasons for being virtuous, because

If the inclination be right, 'tis a perverting of it, to apply it solely to the reward, and make us conceive such wonders of the grace and favour which is to attend virtue, when there is so little shown of the intrinsic worth or value of the thing itself.[30]

Justice and injustice, truth and falsehood, right and wrong, must be independent of both God and rewards in order to say that God has these properties, and to say that they are worthy of praise.[31]

The point about rewards and punishments was much more important at that time than we think it is today. It was then a foundation of religion and morality that rewards were the proper motivation for moral conduct, and punishment the only fit deterent. This was one of

[28] CHIV, bk. II, pt. II, sec. I
[29] Fowler, T., *Shaftesbury and Hutcheson*, London (1882), p. 88 (STF)
[30] CHEW, pt. II, sec. III
[31] CHIV, pt. III, sec. II

the keystones of the orthodox churches of the time, and it was shared by several liberal thinkers such as Locke and John Tillotson. Shaftesbury became the leader of the dissident group. External sanctions are not as important as the built-in sanction we all carry with us-the approval or disapproval of the moral sense. The remorse of conscience and its delight in virtue is combined, in those with a true sense of religion, with the love of God, but one may be moral without being religious. Rewards and punishments may be effective in causing conduct by appeal to private interest, but since that is the way they operate, such conduct cannot be called right and virtuous. Indeed, in so far as such incentives place the emphasis on private and personal rather than on public good and interest, they may be quite harmful, for such motivation "must insensibly diminish the affections towards public good or the interest of society, and introduce a certain narrowness of spirit, which . . . is peculiarily observable in the devout persons and zealots of almost every religious persuasion." Such motivation is also the cause of loss of true piety, which is love of the valuable in itself, for action because of reward ignores the actual value of the act.[32]

This view (the rewards-punishments theory) has a profound effect on politics as well as morals. The magistrates of the country are now expected, thinks Shaftesbury, to be the moral arbiters of the nation, a job for which he thinks them ill fitted:

The saving of souls is now the heroic passion of exalted spirits; and is become in a manner the chief care of the magistrate, and the very end of government itself.
If magistracy should vouchsafe to interpose thus much in other sciences, I am afraid we should have as bad logic, as bad mathematics, and in every kind as bad philosophy, as we often have divinity, in countries where a precise orthodoxy is settled by law. 'Tis a hard matter for a government to settle wit.[33]

Morals cannot be enforced on a people – this comes "only from a social feeling of partnership with human kind". Morality and good government do go together, but they both rest upon the knowledge of public good, and "where absolute power is, there is no public."[34] In his eyes then, the moral sense of individuals is the source of morality and sound government, based upon the independent existence of good, and the free worship of God for his goodness, aside from the incentive

[32] CHIV, sec. 111, pt. 111
[33] CHLE, sec. 11
[34] CHEW, pt. 111, sec. 1

of rewards and punishments. The pursuit of true goodness and virtue is disinterested. We are putting the cart before the horse when we "prove merit by favour, and order by a Deity."[35]

Shaftesbury is often classified as a Deist. It is certainly true that he held some things in common with them. Among these are the views, explicit or assumed, that reason takes precedence over faith, that natural religion is either more important than revealed, or at least, that everything learned in the latter can be known in the former, that optimism for the human condition is more justified than pessimism, that supernaturalism, superstition, special revelations and miracles should be looked upon with doubt, and the criticism of scripture is not only justified but essential. Further, as we have seen, he separated religion from morality. But he was also a theist, which differentiates him from some Deists, and he did not put so much faith in the *consensus gentium* and the equality of the rational faculties of men as did the Deists in general. For Shaftesbury, the expert still takes precedence over the uninformed. Shaftesbury accepted the argument from design for God's existence, and he argued against zealotry and in favor of a sense of wit and humor in matters of religion – something Berkeley did not like in his writings because he thought it frivolous. Shaftesbury also wrote as though God was immanent in creation – often he sounds almost like a pantheist – while the Deists more often spoke of a transcendent God.

Without good humor, we cannot be free in our studies, and reasoning freely about trifles is better than dogmatic restraint in investigations.[36] Scepticism is not as harmful as many see it; rather, it is preferable to the dogmatic frame of mind, for it maintains the curiosity necessary for continued investigation.[37] But this attitude does not impede discovery of the truth. For example, it allows us to ascertain the hand of the designer in the universal system, to see in it the "unity of design and order of a mind" which witnesses God.[38] And one who believes that "everything is governed, ordered, or regulated for the best, by a designing principle or mind, necessarily good and permanent" is a theist.[39] We can achieve such conclusions by our own reason, not needing special revelations.[40] One result is that the pro-

---

[35] CHM, pt. II, sec. III
[36] CHLE, sec. IV
[37] CHMR, sec. II, chap. II
[38] CHM, pt. II, sec. IV
[39] CHIV, pt. I, sec. II
[40] CHM, pt. II, sec. III

bability of the truth of revelation rests upon rational investigation and not alone upon faith.[41]

But such studies are nonsense if we are going to take the truth to be a function of mob opinion – opinions based on the attestations of "a set of Lancashire noodles, remote provincial headpieces, or visionary assemblers".[42] Our opinions in morals should rest on the testimony of experts, as in other fields:

Consider, pray, in mathematics whose is the better reason of the two, and fitter to be relied on? The practiser's, or his who is unpractised? Whose in the way of war, of policy, or civil affairs? Whose in merchandise, law, physic? And in morality and life, I ask still, whose? May he not, perhaps, be allowed the best judge of living who studies life and endeavours to form it by some rule? Or is he indeed to be esteemed most knowing in the matter who slightly examines it, and who accidentally and unknowingly philosophises?[43]

3. BERKELEY VERSUS SHAFTESBURY

Berkeley's attack on Shaftesbury is not the most gentlemanly thing he every wrote. It is often severe, and several times unjustified, because he either misrepresented or misunderstood Shaftesbury. Professors Leslie Stephen, Fowler, Jessop, and Luce all agree that it is the least desirable of Berkeley's writings. Fowler says:

To insinuate that Shaftesbury was a man "without one grain of religion," and to represent him as so little in earnest about virtue as only, "after a nice inquiry and balancing on both sides," to conclude that "we ought to prefer virtue to vice," are sheer calumnies, which the violence of theological partisanship can alone excuse. And even that can hardly excuse *the personal attack on Shaftesbury, under the name of Cratylus,*[44]

So uncharacteristic of Berkeley is this sort of thing that in 1734 a pamphlet appeared entitled "A Vindication of the Reverend D_____B_____y from the scandalous imputation of being author of a late book entitled Alciphron or the Minute Philosopher," based on the grounds that Berkeley could not possibly have been so scurrilous! But in spite of this, the first thing that struck me when I compared the two philosophers was not how much they disagreed, though that disagreement in some particulars is fundamental, but how

[41] *Loc. cit.*
[42] CHEW, pt. IV, sec. 11
[43] CHM, sec. 111, pt. 111
[44] STF, p. 148

much they had in common. The simplest way to state their points of agreement is to give a list of them:

1. They both use a version of the argument from design.

2. Both assert that the utility principle is the ultimate normative test, though for Shaftesbury it is a test of moral acts, and for Berkeley a test of rules.

3. Both use the metaphor of the "Author of Nature".

4. Both believe that personal and public good are in the long run identical, though Berkeley lays more emphasis on the "eternal happiness with God" interpretation of this good, while Shaftesbury inclines more to a platonistic view of goodness as the harmony of the whole universal system.

5. Both assert a qualitative difference among pleasures, and neither believes that pleasure in itself is the *summum bonum*.

6. Both are antipathetic to the *consensus gentium* as a source of authority or truth.

7. Both believe that man is necessarily a part of a social system, and that his moral good is meaningless apart from his role in that system.

8. Both believe that moral judgments of agents must be based upon our knowledge of their motives.

9. Both believe that a balance between our reason, appetites and passions is an essential condition for a virtuous life.

10. Both believe in the universality of moral law, and argue against relativism, though in Berkeley's case these laws are *a posteriori* and not *a priori*, as they are with Shaftesbury.

But although this is certainly a significant number of instances of agreement, Berkeley's disagreements were as numerous, and for my purposes, more revealing of his ethical views.

Among the criticisms Berkeley offers of Shaftesbury, or what Berkeley thought his position to be, are the following:

1. He thought that Shaftesbury virtually ignored the place of reason in ethics, and argued that this is the central fact of moral life.

2. He thought that there was no evidence to support the claim that we have a moral sense.

3. If we did make judgments by some such sense, Berkeley thought that this would entail relativism, to which he was opposed.

4. Berkeley thought that all kinds of values are known by the understanding and not by sense.

5. He believed that the beauty in the world is inexplicable without

Providence, though here he misread Shaftesbury, for the latter would no doubt have agreed, with some provisions.

6. He was sure that leaving moral judgments to individual agents, or rather, leaving the justification for acts in the hands of individual tastes, was ineffective as an active social moral principle, partly because of the vagueness of the idea of "moral beauty."

7. He believed that free-thinking was not a good in itself, nor even good as a means, if it leads to the disparagment of religion, because in so doing it destroyed just that much of the motivation for right conduct.

8. Disinterested virtue he did not understand – if it is not in our interests to be moral then why should we be?

9. He thought that the external sanctions, rewards and punishments, were of great importance, though he also agreed that we do suffer from internal sanctions when we do evil, and that this is important. But the external ones are, in Berkeley's eyes, among the absolutely essential supports for society. Hence, he also disagrees with Shaftesbury's non-too-flattering opinions of the roles of magistrates.

10. Berkeley believed that God's will is the source of the moral law, and that the attempt to separate morality and religion was mistaken.

11. In so far as Shaftesbury often seems to be claiming that our wills are determined by our appetites, Berkeley's arguments against determinism apply to him, and were intended to do so.

Fowler thinks that the most effective thing Berkeley says against Shaftesbury is that "his principles are inadequate to influence the mass of mankind."[45] I think this is an effective comment, but it seems to me that some of Berkeley's other comments are far more important from the philosophical viewpoint. Thus, he argues that:

... to make all the inward horrors of soul pass for infallible marks of sin were the way to establish error and superstition in the world; so, on the other hand, to suppose all actions lawful which are unattended with those starts of nature would prove of the last dangerous consequence to virtue and morality. For these pertaining to us as men, we must not be directed in respect of them by any emotion in our blood and spirits, but by the dictates of sober and impartial reason.[46]

Alciphron (Shaftesbury) claims that moral beauty is "an object, not of the discursive faculty, but of a peculiar sense . . . the moral sense . . . being adapted to the perception of moral beauty, as the eye to colours, or the ear to sounds." But Berkeley replies that although there are in-

[45] STF, p. 150
[46] PO, 21

deed dispositions, appetites and passions in men which are of moral value in certain respects, some of these are predominant in some men, and others in others.

Should it not therefore seem a very uncertain guide in morals, for men to follow his passion or inward feeling? And would not this rule infallibly lead different men different ways, according to the prevalency of this or that appetite or passion?[7]

Berkeley believes that this is a fact of experience.[48] Moral matters are not a subject for decision by emotion, but by reason, and if this is true:

... will it not follow from hence that duty and virtue are in a fairer way of being practised, if men are led by reason and judgment, balancing low and sensual pleasures with those of a higher kind, comparing present losses with future gains, and the uneasiness and disgust of every vice with the delightful practice of the opposite virtue, and the pleasing reflexions and hopes which attend it? Or can there be a stronger motive to virtue than the shewing, that considered in all lights, it is every man's true interest?[49]

It is not simply that moral decision by reason is more practical, as Fowler seems to think, but rather that given the variation in men's appetites and passions, the moral sense theory leads to moral anarchy and relativism. This would be true were there such a sense, but at bottom, Berkeley thinks there is no such thing, for if there were, surely we would be aware of it, or could be upon self-examination. But Berkeley can find no such sense in himself, and for myself, neither can I.[50]

Furthermore, Berkeley thinks that Shaftesbury has been led into the moral sense theory by his failure to realize that both moral and physical beauty are not perceived by sense, but by understanding. His argument in favor of this is interesting for both ethics and aesthetics, for it entails a necessary connection between beauty and utility, and it also involves an interesting use of the argument from design. He believes that the "notion" of moral beauty is "an object of the discursive faculty". It is to be noted that he does not question Shaftesbury's claim that virtue is beautiful; on the contrary, he affirms it, and uses the affirmation to Shaftesbury's disadvantage quite simply: beauty, consisting in proportion, is a function of the relations between sizes and shapes which results in a perfect and complete whole of its kind. That which is a

[47] Alc. III, 5
[48] D., p. 209
[49] Alc. III, 5
[50] Alc. III, 6

perfect thing of its kind is that which "answers the end for which it was made."

But the comparing parts with one another, the considering them as belonging to one whole, and the referring this whole to its use or end, should seem the work of reason. . .[51]

If this is true, then strictly speaking, if virtue is beautiful, it must be perceived by the mind, not the senses, moral or otherwise. The eye alone cannot perceive proportion, for proportions are relational, and not presented as ideas but as notions, in this case, inferred notions. Beauty cannot be separated from utility, because, for example, that which makes a good chair is necessarily related to the end served by a chair, and hence the end is the standard by which the chair's proportions are to be judged. The same is true of clothes and architecture, animals and men. And we will find, thinks Berkeley, that the finest shapes and proportions, considered as related to their ends, are natural shapes, and

nature . . .in her creatures . . .referreth them to some end, use or design.[52]

God, of course, is the author of nature, and the designer of it, the final cause of all things. Thus,

I would fain know what beauty can be found in a moral system, formed, connected, and governed by chance, fate, or any other blind unthinking principle . . . without thought there can be no end or design; and without an end there can be no use; and without use there is no aptitude or fitness of proportion, from whence beauty springs.[53]

Shaftesbury might object that this is all well and good, but that in order to agree, we do not have to assume that this vital principle is an inspecting, punishing, rewarding agent, nor do we need to assume that the soul of man is immortal and shall be rewarded or punished in the eternal hereafter. That is, "what is commonly called faith, worship, and religion" need not be assumed. But what *is* religion? Berkeley asks this question in the *Theory of Vision Vindicated and Explained*:

So long as we admit no principle of good actions but natural affection, no reward but natural consequences; so long as we apprehend no judgment, harbour no fears, and cherish no hopes of future state, but laugh at all these things, with the author of the Characteristics, and those whom he esteems the liberal and polished part of mankind, how can we be said to be religious in any sense?[54]

[51] Alc. iii, 8
[52] Alc. iii, 9
[53] Alc. iii, 10
[54] TVVE, 4

How can anyone believe that a moral system in which the supreme intelligence at the head of it "neither protects the innocent, punishes the wicked, nor rewards the virtuous" is beautiful, asks Berkeley.[55] And how can such provisions be satisfied unless we are immortal and life eternal? In a passage reminiscent of Augustine he says:

To suppose indeed a society of rational agents, acting under the eye of Providence, concurring in one design to promote the common benefit of the whole, and conforming their actions to the established laws and order of the divine parental wisdom: wherein each particular agent shall not consider himself apart, but as the member of a great City, whose author and founder is God: in which the civil laws are no other than the rules of virtue and the duties of religion: and where every one's true interest is combined with his duty: to suppose this would be delightful: on this supposition a man need be no Stoic or knight-errant, to account for his virtue.[56]

In such a system, we can indeed account for the purpose of the whole, and the proportion in the universe can be related to its end, which is "the complete happiness or well-being of the whole"-Shaftesbury's moral end too. But on Shaftesbury's principles, we cannot do this.

Of course, this schema, if correct, also proves the utility and beauty of religion, for its purpose in the over-all design of the universe now becomes one of the means to the total end: it instructs us in the ways to achieve the universal well-being, teaches us moral laws, and informs us about the designs God has for us. In this way does Berkeley think he has shown a) that reason is central and indispensible to morality, b) that without God and eternal life, there is not only no morality but no beauty and utility, all of which are necessarily tied together by the cosmic design, and c) that religion and morality are inseparable. His position also entails the rejection of the "disinterested virtue" theory of Shaftesbury, for two reasons: 1) if it were not to our interests and that of the whole to live virtuously, wrong would go unrequited, in which case it would be an unjust, and therefore according to Shaftesbury himself, an ugly universe. But it is a beautiful universe, therefore, etc.; 2) it is wishful thinking to believe that men will act virtuously unless they believe they will gain from it, and to this end;

Punishments and rewards have always had, and always will have, the greatest weight with men; and the most considerable of both kinds are proposed by religion, the duties whereof fall in with the views of the civil

55 Alc. III, 10
56 Alc. III, 10

magistrate: it undeniably follows, that nothing can add more strength to a good and righteous government than religion. Therefore it mainly concerns governors, to keep an attentive eye on the religion of their subjects. And indeed it is one lesson to magistrate and people, prince and subject, "Keep my commandments and live; and my law as the apple of thine eye."[57]

I am not going to go into detail about Shaftesbury's arguments in favor of the claim that the will is determined by the appetite, nor Berkeley's criticisms of them, because his arguments have already been explained, as have Berkeley's, in Chapter Four. For exact reference, the reader might like to note that Shaftesbury's claims are represented by what Alciphron says in sections 17 and 18 in the seventh dialogues of the book. Nor shall I discuss Berkeley's arguments that God's will constitutes the moral law, for I have already covered that topic in the fifth chapter, and Shaftesbury's arguments in the present one.

What then can be drawn from this chapter about Berkeley's moral philosophy? The first conclusion is general in nature, but I think justified. I have been arguing that Berkeley did indeed have a systematic moral philosophy, though it is not formally articulated in his extant works. This chapter seems to bear out that conclusion. It is hard to believe that the neat dovetailing of Berkeley's remarks in *Alciphron III* about moral and physical beauty, knowing both by reason, relating both to utility, and private utility to that of the whole, the moral and logical necessity for immortality and eternal rewards and punishments, the utility of religion, and the systematic nature of the universe, are accidental. It is still harder to believe that these are isolated examples of moral thought by Berkeley, given that I have come to the same conclusions on independent evidence in his other works, and other parts of *Alciphron*, all of which are consistent with his criticisms of Shaftesbury and his own sketch here of his positive views. The conclusions of the third dialogue are those reached in the *Three Dialogues*, the *Principles*, the *New Theory*, *Siris*, etc., and in those cases where the conclusions are not stated in these other works, premises forming part or all of the foundation for them are to be found.

Secondly, his arguments with Shaftesbury seem to reconfirm four other central claims I have made about Berkeley: 1) moral decisions require rules; 2) the teleogical view of morality, specifically, utilitarianism, is the correct one; 3) Berkeley is a cognitivist; 4) morality and religion cannot be separated, and moral goodness depends for its

[57] D. p. 207

existence on the will of God, as do natural moral rules in the language of nature.

I cannot here evaluate Berkeley's criticisms of Shaftesbury. Obviously some of them are mistaken, others seem to me to be sound. It is clear that he was unjustified in accusing Shaftesbury of holding certain positions, for example, of claiming that morality has *nothing* to do with religion, and of favoring atheism. One reason for this may be that Berkeley did not have Shaftesbury's letters, which are quite clearly theistic, and sympathetic to religious belief.

CHAPTER VII

BERKELEY AND MANDEVILLE

Bernard de Mandeville was born in 1670 in Dort, Holland. He was educated in Leyden, where he received a Doctor of Medicine degree, and for some reason he then settled in London. He was apparently a rather coarse and conceited fellow, not noted for impressing people with his charm and good manners. He supposedly knew Benjamin Franklin. In 1705 he published a poem called *The Grumbling Hive, or, Knaves turned Honest*. It was not very long, but for some reason it caught on immediately, and by 1714 it had been republished, together with preface, notes, explanatory essays, and some dialogues, now under the title *The Fable of the Bees, or Private Vices Public Benefits*. A second edition appeared in 1723, and as of 1755, there had been nine editions. The poem and its essays became the target of heated and very partisan debate, and among those who criticized Mandeville, aside from Berkeley, were John Dennis, William Law, Frances Hutcheson and John Brown.

I. MANDEVILLE'S THEORY

Mandeville had some things in common with the Deists, though most of them would have disowned this. He believed in the primacy of reason, and was tempted by determinism as was Anthony Collins. He thought that religion had little to do with morality. But most of the Deists were optimists, whereas Mandeville was a cynic and a pessimist in the Hobbesian tradition, at least on the subject of human nature. Throughout his work, a constant theme is that man is at bottom thoroughly selfish and that even those actions which seem altruistic are ultimately to be explained in terms of our selfish desires. Because of this, with Hobbes, he thought that society was the result of a compromise with our worst natures, and that in truth even our love of society was the result of our many desires and the difficulty we have in satisfying them. Because of this, society is founded upon vice, and since virtues only arise within society, virtue depends upon vice. Man was not somehow designed for society, as revelation would have it. Rather, man is dispositionally social, as grapes are for wine. As wine is an invention of man, though he needs grapes to make it, so society is also artificial, though it could not arise without our attributes.[1] Societies, furthermore, require the concurrence of human intelligences, as opposed to natural phenomena, and this means that societies "must have a dependence; either on mutual compact, or the force of the strong, exerting itself upon the patience of the weak."[2]

Throughout his theories, a number of consistent and relatively simple mistakes prevail. One of these is the failure to realize that even if the origins of society were as he described them, what we once were might have relatively little to do with what we now are. Mandeville virtually ignores qualitative change, both through social time and among classes of men. Further, there is not much evidence to suggest that he, and Hobbes, are correct about the origins of our society in any case, and as Jessop and others have pointed out, he persistently identifies "actually" with "really". Hobbes and Mandeville were the favorite bugbears at the time Berkeley wrote, along with the Deists. But in spite of this, they did have some allies. Certainly not everyone agreed with Berkeley's criticisms of Mandeville. One author, speaking of the second dialogue of *Alciphron*, has this to say:

For instead of answering what the *Author of the Fable of the Bees* really says, he supposes him to have said Things which he does not say, and answers them; which is carrying his Zeal for *Orthodoxy*, and his *Knight-Errantry* against *Free-Thinkers* and *Free-Writers* so far, that it puts one a little in mind of *Don Quixote*, who fancy'd he saw Giants and Magicians in every Passenger he met upon the Road; and by this means (never seeing any thing in its true Light, or calling any thing by its true Name) was perpetually fighting with *Phantoms* of his own raising, and the unsubstantial *Scarecrows* of his own disturb'd Imagination.[3]

Mandeville's argument is worth considering in more detail. He begins from what he thinks is a factual base, namely, the proposition that there never were any societies without vice, and that it is impossible to

---

[1] *Remarks on a Book entitled The Fable of the Bees*, by John Dennis, London (1724), pp. 104-105 (RFB)

[2] RFB, pp. 206-207

[3] Hervey, Lord John, *Some Remarks on the Minute Philosopher*, London (1732) pp. 42-43 (HR)

conceive such a society. This fact does not imply that vice is good, nor that Mandeville approves of vice, as some have said. Rather, he wishes to show that approval and disapproval are irrelevant to the question of whether or not vice is essential to the foundations of societies, even great ones.[4] The founders of society were at considerable pains to teach that we must subdue our appetites in favor of public rather than private interests. To do this, they had to convince us that in the long run, it was more to our own interests to do so than not, and to accomplish this, they had to provide some sort of reward for doing it. Clearly, this is impossible in the case of each and every action, if a reward is to be something which will cost someone something. But there is one reward which meets the test, and costs nothing, though in Mandeville's view it satisfies and charms everyone, and that is praise or flattery. And conversely, contempt is the most effective universal punishment.[5] Furthermore, if it seemed at times that the sacrificing man was not receiving his due in this world, this could be remedied in the next, where an eternal reward was waiting. Thus does Mandeville hint that eternal rewards are the invention of men. Here on earth however, flattery remains the most effective "argument" men can use to persuade others to act in any given way. Emulation is also effective, and to accomplish this, Mandeville claims that the founders of society divided men into two classes. The first consisted in "low-minded people", who searched after "immediate enjoyment", were incapable of self-denial, and were completely selfish. They were "enslaved by voluptuousness", and used thought only to intensify the pleasures of sense, and this class of people were said to be no better than brutes. The second class thought the improvement of mental skills the highest aim they could choose, and that man's excellence consisted in his unique rational faculty. These people despised all they had in common with the first class, and always sought to overcome their lower sensibilities in order to provide the peace and quiet necessary for contemplation, which necessitated their continual effort to achieve better relations with their fellow men, through the conquest of their own passions and the search after the public welfare.[6]

---

[4] *Some Remarks on the Minute Philosopher by an anonymous Author*, in RFB. This is probably a reprint of Hervey's attack, though in this event the publishing date of RFB could not have been changed by the printer in its later editions, because Alciphron was not published until 1736, p. 34

[5] *The Fable of the Bees, or Private Vices, Public Benefits*, by Bernard de Mandeville, London (1714), p. 245. (FB)

[6] FB, pp. 26-27

Of what has been said thus far, Mandeville says this:

This was (or at least might have been) the manner after which savage man was broke; from whence it is evident, that the first rudiments of morality, broach'd by skillfull politicians, to render men useful to each other as well as tractable, were chiefly contriv'd; that the ambitious might reap the more benefit from, and govern vast numbers of them with the greater ease and security.[7]

Men strive for the higher class, and this is the foundation of politics, which is the set of rules according to which a man can change social classes, and by which the higher can keep the lower in submission.

The lower class presumably benefits from the efforts of the upper to achieve the public good, and action toward that end is the subject of flattery, while selfish conduct is not. Since the upper class is in a better position to do such acts, their flattery accumulates, as it were, causing the lower strata of society to wish them well, but to wish also to emulate them. Furthermore, reflection on themselves convinced the lower class that "none were so obnoxious to them as those that were most like themselves." Thus, a sort of morally schizophrenic social personality arises, in which on the one hand the lower classes praise those who act in the public interest, in order to benefit from it, while endeavoring to practice the indulgence of personal appetite without anyone knowing about it. The lower class agreed, with the higher, to call public-spirited conduct "virtue", and selfish conduct "vice".[8]

But at once the irony of all this is apparent to Mandeville, for he wants to know how the upper class who act for the public welfare are enabled to do so, if they cannot maintain their position through the proceeds gained by feeding the appetites of the lower class. This is how the upper class keeps the lower in submission – they cater to their passions and appetites, the very things they preach against, whether they know it or not. At the very roots then, society is a great hypocritical moral hoax for Mandeville, and his cynicism is evident in this passage from the *Fable*, and the commentary on it:

> And Virtue, who from Politicks
> Had learn'd a thousand cunning Tricks,
> Was by their happy Influence
> Made Friends with Vice ———.

[7] FB, p. 30
[8] FB, p. 30

Page 8. Line 9. It may be said, that Virtue is made Friends with Vice, when industrious good People, who maintain their Families and bring up their Children handsomely, pay Taxes, and are several ways useful Members of the Society, get a livelihood by something that chiefly depends on, or is very much influenc'd by the Vices of others, without being themselves guilty of, or accessary to them any otherwise than by way of Trade, as a Druggist may be to Poysoning, or a Sword Cutler to Bloodshed.[9]

It is in this way that private vices become public benefits, which was of course part of the title of the *Fable* from 1714 onwards. Vice enables virtue to prosper because without such activities as trade in sugar, wine, silk, tobacco, etc. (Mandeville had a rather broad classification of "vices" in mind) society cannot prosper. It will not do to say that these things can be used in moderation, he thought, for in that case, either "no degree of luxury ought to be call'd a vice", or luxury cannot be defined.[10] It is *possible* to have a society where this is not the case, but not a great and powerful one, for without luxury trade, social systems remain primitive. Without great appetite and the encouraging of it, there will never be great wealth, and thus no great power.[11]

It is for all these reasons that Mandeville concluded that "the Moral Virtues are the Political Offspring which Flattery begot upon Pride",[12] and a society in which this is true is described as Mandeville saw it as follows:

> Thus every Part was full of Vice,
> Yet the whole Mass a Paradise;
> Flatter'd in Peace, and fear'd in Wars,
> They were th'Esteem of Foreigners,
> And lavish of their Wealth and Lives,
> The Ballance of all other Hives,
> Such were the Blessings of that State;
> Their Crimes conspir'd to make them **Great**:
> (F.) And Vertue, who from Politicks
> Had learn'd a Thousand cunning Tricks,
> Was, by their happy Influence,
> Made Friends with Vice: And ever since
> (G.) The worst of all the Multitude,
> Did something for the Common Good.[13]

[9] FB, p. 61
[10] HR, p. 42
[11] FB, pp. 162-163
[12] FB, p. 34
[13] FB, p. 8

The moral of the piece is simple:

> Fools only strive
> (T.) To make a Great and honest Hive.
> (V.) T'enjoy the World's Conveniencies,
> Be fam'd in War, yet live in Ease
> Without great Vices, is a vain
> Eutopia seated in the Brain.
> Fraud, Luxury and Pride must live,
> Whilst we the Benefits receive.[14]

So far as the nature of individual good is concerned, Mandeville is specific, but not clear. For Englishmen at any rate, he thought that a pleasure is what pleases a man, and given this, "we ought to dispute no more about men's pleasures than their tastes."[15] He is aware that throughout history men have argued that true pleasure and happiness comes only to the temperate, thoughtful man who has subdued his passions, become humble, and cultivated his intelligence. But though this is what men have *said*, it is not what they have done, and Mandeville thinks that we should judge on the basis of what is done.[16]

Mandeville hints that the immortality of the soul is doubtful, and his reasons are respectable. If matter and mind are quite different, how does the one act upon the other? Surely this is as difficult to explain as is the proposition that thought is the effect of matter and motion, as the materialists believe. The thesis that the mind is incorporeal and immortal thus does not help us one wit in explaining the cause of thought.[17] Perhaps because of this, he seemed inclined to determinism and materialism. "In the choice of things men must be determined by the perception they have of happiness . . .".[18] And although he did not approve of atheism, he did not think that it was necessarily harmful to virtue.

> . . . there are atheists of good morals, and great villians superstitious . . . I have no greater opinion of superstition, than I have of atheism; what I aim'd at, was to prevent and guard against both;[19]

He believed that a man must be judged on the basis of his motives rather than on the effects of his action.[20]

---

14 FB, p. 19
15 FB, p. 114
16 FB, pp. 118-119
17 RFB, p. 190
18 RFB, pp. 195-196
19 RFB, p. 377
20 RFB, p. 42, vol. 2

In all of this, he does not recommend vice, nor claim that men cannot be virtuous, and he resented the criticism that he had held these positions.[21] He believed that he was describing the facts, not propounding some theory, and that in the face of the facts, it was nonsense to claim that the private and public goods were identical, since there were so many glaring exceptions.[22] He thought that Shaftesbury was a noble man, and that his theories were high-minded, but that they were idealistic and romantic, though beautiful. In the end, by favoring Deism, he thought that Shaftesbury had harmed the foundations of revealed religion, even though he might not have meant to do so. In short, he offers some of the same sort of criticisms of Shaftesbury as Berkeley did.[23] But that is about as close as the two ever come to agreement on anything.

2. BERKELEY VERSUS MANDEVILLE

The major arguments Berkeley offers against Mandeville, and from which we can learn his own position, occur in the first two dialogues of *Alciphron*. In the second dialogue, Mandeville is Lysicles. I have already made use of the central argument in the second chapter of this book, but when the criticisms are considered together, they again seem to underline the systematic character of Berkeley's thoughts in moral philosophy, and the unity of this philosophy with his ontology and epistemology. The attack hinges on a few cardinal issues: the meaning of "natural", and the implied significance of this for what a fact is; the role of reason in ethics and its importance as a distinguishing feature of man as opposed to the rest of creation; the qualitative distinction among pleasures, and the realization of the consequences of searching after one kind rather than another; the criticism of free-thinking (by which Berkeley meant Deism) in so far as it seems to recommend the life of the dilettante, and to the extent that it lessens our awareness of moral responsibility through its emphasis on determinism.

Berkeley argues that something can be natural but not uniform throughout the natural world. For example, it is natural for orange trees to produce oranges, but not in England, and the same plant produces different grades of fruit in different climates and agricultural

[21] HR, p. 16
[22] HR, p. 49
[23] RFB, p. 432

conditions. Similarly, there are natural human qualities which vary with different men in different places, for example speech is natural to man, but obviously not all men speak the same language. It follows that a property need not be "original, universal and invariable" to be natural, though some natural properties may have these characteristics. One property which man has which is natural to him is rationality, and as with most other characteristics, it varies with the individual and the environment. Just as the fruits of the best trees in the best environments are preferred, so we ought to prefer the products of the best minds — the "choicest productions of the rational nature of man" are the fruits of the "best and most improved understandings". When we examine such thinkers, we find that they act with planning and design for some end, demonstrating their wisdom in choosing both the end and the fit means to it. But in order to discover the proper end in morals, the natural end, we must "follow nature . . . propose her as a guide and pattern" for our example. The study of nature teaches us that it too is rational, the product of a cosmic mind working for certain ends or purposes, though we may not know what all those purposes are. Mankind being a part of nature, we should be able to tell how to serve our happiness by studying nature, and so we can, and the results of such a study are the utilitarian themes I have already discussed. The achievement of these ends depends upon our success at controlling our appetites, and our ability to distinguish between short run pleasures and long run benefits and act accordingly. Experience teaches that if we fail at this endeavor, we will fail to be happy both as individuals and as a society. Thus, temperate action seems to be natural and rational, and the fact that there are intemperate and irrational men does not alter this fact.[24] Intelligence, cohesion and planning are as essential in the moral world as in the natural, physical realm, and emphasizing the sensual to the detriment of the rational simply ignores this fact. In short, if we are, as Mandeville insists, to found our moral principles on what is instead of what ought to be, then Berkeley thinks that we will come up with his system, not Mandeville's. His disagreement with the latter is then a fundamental disagreement over the nature of the facts underlying moral life.

This disagreement is given practical illustration in the argument between Euphranor and Lysicles in the second dialogue of *Alciphron*. Mandeville says that vice "circulates money and promotes industry", which is an essential conditon for a flourishing society. Berkeley agrees

24 Alc. I, 14-16

that the circulation of money and the stimulation of industry are essential, but disagrees that vice is the essential condition for achieving these means to social well-being. His reasons for the disagreement are not philosophical but factual: that sobriety and temperance contribute to health and longevity, thereby enabling more consumption in the long-run; that society is composed of family units, which are individually not helped by vice, and thus there is no reason to think that society as a whole would be helped; that money spent innocently circulates just as well as that spent upon vice, so that vice seems to be inessential. Further, money, that is, material wealth, is not alone sufficient to make a society prosper. More important are mental and bodily health, for the man with these attributes is the only happy man. Debauchery of course does not contribute to health of body and mind, so it cannot contribute to a flourishing society. Berkeley's argument can be put in this form:

1. Public well-being implies the well-being of the members of the public. (With this, Lysicles agrees)

2. Private well-being implies bodily and mental health.

3. There is no bodily and mental health in a debauched individual.

4. Therefore, there is no bodily and mental health in a debauched society.

5. But a society depending for its well-being upon vice is debauched.

6. Therefore, etc.

Lysicle's (Mandeville's) failure to realize this truth is based upon his failure to understand the different sorts of pleasures and their relative values, in addition to his misunderstanding of what is "natural" and the consequent misinterpretation of how to achieve social happiness. If the satisfaction of sense appetites is happiness, then we can never be happy. If it is said that man should follow his "natural" appetites, then fine, provided we realize that man's natural pleasures include those of reason and imagination in addition to those of sense. As we have seen, Berkeley believed that we learn about at least three different sorts of pleasures from the language of nature coupled with self-examination. If one replies that this is all well and good, but that the common man does not so act, the proper reply is to ask if the common man is the expert rather than the student of the subject. If we are to pay attention to the expert, we find that sense pleasure is "a short deliverance from a long pain", and that sense cannot judge of future pleasures, nor of the pleasures of the understanding. Thus, true pleasure or happiness presupposes that reason must be used to gain it, and what reason teaches is, again, that vice does not promote happiness, and that what we call virtue does. The man of vice is not only mistaken, he is stupid, for he does not even see that his actions harm himself. The moral is that the rational man can only act temperately if he follows his judgments.

Furthermore, if we were to act simply upon the basis of sense-pleasures, and if society rested upon the rock of gratification of appetites, then we are nothing but machines, for action resting on this foundation can be determined as surely as the hands of a clock are determined by its works. Yet determinism, Berkeley thought, is false, for the reasons I have given in the fourth chapter.[25] And since machines or puppets are not moral creatures, determinism implies that men are not either. Because of this Mandeville's views are not only mistaken, but morally pernicious. They lead to the downfall of religion and the furthering of atheism, and for reasons which have been given, Berkeley thought that religion was essential for morality.

Aside from the criticisms of Shaftesbury, there is only one thing I can find upon which Berkeley and Mandeville agree: that we impute guilt on the basis of our knowledge of motives.[26]

All of these criticisms by Berkeley rest on the secure foundation of the divine natural language. This is so because for Berkeley, it is the structure of the Language of the Author of Nature which proves its rationality, and it is because of this rationality that we can learn the proper modes of behavior for the accomplishment of certain purposes, among them the moral purpose. It is because of the radical difference between causes (minds) and effects (ideas) that determinism must be false and eternal life a fact. For Berkeley, an epistemological analysis of the natural language shows that the world is a theophany, thereby integrating religion into the very fabric of our moral existence. *Alciphron* had been written by 1731, and the theory of the natural language had been outlined as early as the *New Theory of Vision*. In all his works, the principles of morality are without foundation unless God speaks to us, teaching us and leading us to temporal and eternal happiness, the while leaving us free to choose. Berkeley's criticisms of Mandeville must be considered in the context of all of *Alciphron*, including the arguments establishing the natural language theory, for without it there is no justification for his factual disagreements with

[25] Alc. II, *passim*
[26] PC, 157

Lysicles. When we keep this in mind, and when we consider that the same conclusions are proven and discussed in the *Principles* and other earlier works in just the same way and on the same premises as those in *Alciphron*, it becomes difficult not to believe that Berkeley's moral philosophy constitutes a systematic study.

CHAPTER VIII

THE DEISTS

In the last two chapters, I have tried to show as much as I could about Berkeley's theory by describing the theories of two of his rivals, and then discussing Berkeley's criticisms of them. Now I am going to consider a group of philosophers and theological critics known collectively as the Deists. Berkeley criticized the Deists on several fronts relevant to morals and theology, and most of these criticisms are based firmly in his ontology and epistemology. One of my claims in this book has been that Berkeley's moral philosophy is systematically related to these other two branches of his philosophy, and by showing how he criticizes the Deists, I hope to adduce further evidence for this thesis. We shall also see that there are several critical issues on which Berkeley is in agreement with the Deists. In this chapter, I shall discuss what deism is, and I shall present some summaries of the views of some of the more prominent Deists. Berkeley's criticisms are presented in the next chapter.

It is often difficult to say just what a Deist is. As Rosemary Colie notices, they could have many different traits and believe many different things. A Deist could go to church or even be a minister, he could be a conservative or a liberal, a radical, an aristocrat or a philosopher. The one thing he could not do was remain silent![1] But they usually shared certain traits as well. They wanted a Protestant succession in England, and freedom of conscience; they were consumed by the pursuit of religious and political liberty; they were free-thinkers, and for the most part believed in the primacy of human reason, and the ability of each man to discover the truth for himself; generally they were in favor of natural rather than revealed religion, and were opposed to mysteries. Most of all they were concerned to show that

---

[1] Colie, R., "Spinoza and the Early English Deists", *Journal of the History of Ideas*, vol. XXII, no. 2 (1961), p. 29 (COL)

Christianity must be reasonable if it is to be of any significance, and that there were rational proofs for the existence of God. Often they taught that although God as a first cause exists, he is distinct from and unconcerned with his creation, which led to their denial of providence and God's immanence. They were influenced by Descartes, Locke, the new physics, and the multiplicity of religious sects, which they found obnoxious. But in truth they were more united by an attitude of mind toward the solutions of the current problems, rather than by basic principles which they all held. They were true men of the enlightenment, and their significant writings begin about 1600 and end about 1750. Thus, they were contemporaries of Berkeley.

The term "deism" originated in France in the 16th century. Although I am not going to discuss all of them, it might be worth something to list the most prominent Deists, and their dates: they were: Lord Herbert of Cherbury, 1583-1648; Charles Blount, 1645-1693; Mathew Tindal, 1657-1733; William Wollaston, 1659-1724; Thomas Woolston, 1669-1733; Junius Janus (John) Toland, 1670-1722; Viscount Bolingbroke, 1678-1751; Anthony Collins, 1676-1729; Thomas Morgan, ?-1743; and Thomas Chubb, 1670-1747. Shaftesbury, for better or for worse, is usually included in the list.

I. THE PRINCIPLES OF DEISM

The very first of the Deists, Cherbury, held views which could hardly be thought to separate him from the mainstream of English thought. Among these were that God exists, that we ought to worship him and that worship consisted in a virtuous and pious life, that one must repent and cease his sins, and that God instituted rewards and punishments here and in the hereafter as incentives to correct behavior, and in the interests of justice. But although this does not seem startling, the seeds for a revolt had been laid, for inherent in Cherbury's teachings, and overt in the later writings of Blount, were the principles that the old testament interpretations of the day were inconsistent with science, that the purpose of the testaments, old and new, was to eliminate polytheism etc., and that they ought to be understood as ethically relevant practical exhortations rather than as factual descriptions. Blount went so far as to claim that a great deal of religion was invented for the purposes of government and the interests of specific classes.[2]

Shaftesbury himself was not terribly interested in their problems, and

[2] *Brittanica*, 11th edition

was probably used by the Deists for his popularity and unorthodox opinions. As we have seen, he did not believe in the literal truth of scripture, and he thought that a man could be moral, but not a theist. Moreover, he was opposed to the rewards-punishments theory which so many theologians found congenial, and the later Deists especially disliked this. Finally, he criticized "enthusiasm" or religious zeal, which the Deists interpreted as support for freedom of thought in religion, and this made him quite popular with them.

The central points of John Toland's thought, for my purposes, were that he denied the theological functions of mysteries, and claimed that the value of religion could not lie in unintelligible or self-contradictory claims. He thought that the essential God was unknowable, but that we could know *that* God exists, and that any truths we know about him must be consistent with reason. This led to Anthony Collins' claims that the main truths of the testaments cannot be known as literal truths, especially if we study the so-called fulfillments of the prophecies, but rather must be interpreted in terms of allegories, metaphors, etc. Furthermore, Collins saw no way for man to fulfill his destiny unless determinism of a sort was true, and he has been called a necessitarian.

Probably the two most important works written, so far as the Deists themselves were concerned, were Tindal's *Christianity as Old as the Creation*, and Toland's *Christianity Not Mysterious*. But again, it is important to realize that Deism does not constitute a particular organized systematic philosophy or theology, but rather an attitude of dissent, an opposition to prejudice and ignorance, and a distrust of the mysterious doings and theories of the then current theology. Often, ther personal lives were prejudicial to the movement itself, and invited the genetic fallacy. For example, Blount loved his dead wife's sister, which was then anathema, and he committed suicide, and Toland had been a Catholic as a youth, and was accused of writing for the purpose of founding a sect.

The best study ever done of the Deists is to be found in Professor A.O. Lovejoy's *Essays in the History of Ideas*. It is worth discussing the principles given there, and then observing how they were carried out in certain of their writings, and criticized by such people as Berkeley. First, the Deists believed in *uniformitarianism*, that is they believed that reason is uniform or qualitatively identical in all men. If there were some men who seemed less capable than others, this was because of physical impediments. Thus, the life of reason must be one which, barring special obstacles, is attainable by all, and it must be a life which is similar for all men. It must be uniform and universal, and this, uniformity and universality, is what the Deists meant by "natural". Because of this, the Deists believed that natural religion, a religion which was universal and attainable by all, must be the true religion. There were two ways in which the knowledge of this religion might be achieved. The first way is described by Professor Lovejoy as "*Rationalistic Individualism*". One might think that this is a contradiction of uniformitarianism, but it is not, for individualism is uniform once it is granted that our rational capabilities are alike, which is a postulate of the first principle. Given this, it may be granted that "truth is to be attained by every individual for himself, by the exercise of his private judgement uninfluenced by tradition or external authority".[3] The Deists sometimes stated this by claiming that each man was empowered to seek the truth by the "natural light of reason". If one was to obey tradition or authority, one would (or might) be ignoring the natural light of reason, that is, ignoring one's own capabilities.

The second way the knowledge of truth might be obtained is related to the first. It is the appeal to the "*consensus gentium*". This is justifiable on the same grounds as the natural light of reason, for if reason is universal and uniform, that which is reasonable is presumably discoverable from an analysis of those beliefs which have in fact been common to all men, or most men, in all ages. This claim was of course not new. It had been a part of the folklore and religion of men since the beginning of time. What *was* new about the Deists' position was their *exclusive* emphasis upon the uniform and the universal, to the exclusion of the learned interpretations of theologians and philosophers. In fact, these two marks, universality and uniformity, at times approaching one another in meaning, became for some of the Deists the *only* valid mark of the teachings of God, the author of nature (a phrase which they used not infrequently, as we shall see) and consequently as the signature of authenticity for a religious truth.[4]

The third characteristic of deism follows again from the first two. Lovejoy calls it "*Cosmopolitanism*", by which he meant the common deistic conviction that if the gifts of reason were uniformly shared, then nationalism and provincialism were obviously mistaken. As a result, they believed that theories about the central place of a given people or planet in the scheme of creation were mistaken.[5] There followed five

[3] Lovejoy, A. O., *Essays in the History of Ideas*, Johns Hopkins Press, Baltimore (1948), p. 82 (AOL)
[4] AOL, p. 83
[5] AOL, pp. 83-84

natural offsprings as axioms emanating from these three foundations: an aversion to original thought and "enthusiasm", that is, private revelation; antipathy to intellectual superiority, or to put it Lovejoy's way, a bias in favor of "intellectual equalitarianism"; suspicion of intellectual systematization; a conviction that early man was closer to the truth than we are in matters of religion, or again to use Professor Lovejoy's terminology, a belief in "rationalistic primitivism"; and finally, "a negative philosophy of history", which will be explained in a moment.[6]

The antipathy to so-called original thought is easy to understand. If reason is uniform and the truths of religion discoverable by all, then revelation becomes unnecessary and suspicious, the latter because uniquely known truths fly in the face of the natural light of reason. The role of the genius is not to tell us previously unknown truths, but to clarify them, and to remove the obscuring prejudices from truths which are essentially simple and knowable by all. Obviously, one cannot accept this view without also agreeing that men are fundamentally equal in their rational capabilities, at least in so far as this means that they are equally capable of knowing the difference between what is true and false, and that is why the Deists believed, to put it colloquially, that one man's opinion is as good as another's in matters of religion and morals. But because they believed this, it is also easy to see why they distrusted intricate and complex systematization, for if the truth is accessible to all men, it must be simple and easy to understand, again at least in the matters of morality and religion. The mysteries of science might be knowable only to those who had mastered the tools, but how could God expect a simple man to be morally good unless the truths of morality were accordingly simple? And if this is true, the next point follows automatically: if the truths of morality and religion are knowable to all men, and must therefore be simple, then early man must have known them too, and in fact, he must have known them better or at least as well as we do, for in those times, he did not have to contend with all the more modern forms of obscuranticism. Thus, the Deists were "rationalistic primitivists." This was Tindal's major message – that if God makes moral truth available to all men, he must have done it from the start, and to do this, he must have provided clear and evident moral rules which we can all, then and now, understand, and Tindal thinks he knows what the fundamental rule was, as I shall show.

Finally, if all this is true, then it follows that in matters of religion

[6] AOL, pp. 84-88

and morality, we have made no progress, that in fact, because of our attempts to clarify original truths, we have succeeded only in muddying the waters, and we would accordingly be better off returning to the original sources for another look, guiding this look by the principles of simplicity, the belief in man's universal power to understand God's commands, and the distrust of complex explanations and dogmas.

Professor Lovejoy points out, acutely in my opinion, that if one substitutes "poetry" or "art in general" for "religion and morality" in all of these cases, one has learned a lot about neo-classical aesthetics. Certainly he has learned the Deists' view of these matters. I would only add one thing to this general commentary: so far as I have been able to discover, the generally sceptical and simplistic view of art, morals and religion held by the Deists does not extend to their opinions of mathematics and science.

Central to all these points was the determination to search for the truth in morals and religion without hindrance by already established opinion or dogma. For this, inquiry and examination conducted according to "self-evident" principles, or if these are not applicable, "most probable" arguments, is essential. Superstition, education, prejudice, opinions, ignorance, tyranny – all of these must be overcome for this inquiry to proceed. The results of such an inquiry will contribute to the happiness of man, and contrary to the popular belief that ignorance is bliss, the Deists believed that "the discouragers of inquiry are (Mankind's) greatest enemies, by hindering them from trying, and keeping them in the dark, as to what is happiness, and the way to it."[7] In some Deists' opinions, the man who performed precisely these obstructionist functions was the civil magistrate, though most of them, being good Protestants, believed that if the magistrate had an equal or superior in the effort to hide the truth, he was the Pope of Rome.[8] In sum:

All *comfort* and *satisfaction* of *mind* and all *confidence* towards God, founded on the belief of opinions received from education, or from municipal laws, or from the mere authority of men, or from any other method, but that of an impartial examination, is irrational, fanatical, and anti-christian.[9]

It is difficult for us to understand all this furor over what seems or-

[7] Collins, Anthony, *The Scheme of Literal Prophecy Considered*, London, (1727) p. 426 (SLP)
[8] SLP, p. 426
[9] SLP, p. 426

dinary and commonplace to us. But goodness knows, the Deists had a cause! It is amply illustrated by these remarks by an adversary:

The *Pulpit* ought to do by the *Gospel*, as *Westminster Hall* does by the *Law*; which is, to determine by Authority, Prescription, and Presidents, what is Law; and not to examine the Right which the first Legislator had to institute it, and make it such.

I am so fully convinced of this being the proper Office of a Divine, that for my own Part, when any of these cavilling Genius's, who have a mind to hamper us Sticklers for Christianity, talk of *Enquiry*, I always answer, *Mystery;* when they ask for *Proof*, I cry, *Faith*; if they raise *Doubts*, I quote *Authority*; and whenever they mention *Reason*, I bid them consult *Tradition*.[10]

The Deists were often victims of guilt by association, because they were influenced by, often well-read in, the writings of Hobbes, Spinoza, and Locke, though the latter was considered to be a more respectable figure than the former two. But the Deists were more influenced by the *attitudes* of Hobbes and Spinoza than by their theories. Spinoza they admired mostly for his calm patience in the face of constant persecution, and Hobbes for his dispassionate, if mistaken, investigation into the political foundations of human societies. They did not share Hobbes' views in religion, or what they thought were his views, for Hobbes was wrongly interpreted as an atheist in the 17th century, and for the most part, the Deists were convinced believers in God. Furthermore, the Deists were often, though not always, politically radical, and Hobbes was a thoroughgoing conservative and absolutist.[11] And in Spinoza's case, I find that even when their views were much influenced by him, as in the case of John Toland's *Letters to Serena*, the influence seems not to have extended to their moral and religious beliefs. Indeed, if we are to take Lovejoy as an authority, Spinoza should have been among the most suspect of men as the systemizer *par excellence* of ethics in his time, and in fact, the complexity of his system was often used against the traditional theology by the Deists.[12]

2. SOME INDIVIDUAL DEISTS

At this point, I am going to investigate some of the thoughts of three

[10] HR, pp. 12-13
[11] COL, pp. 31-32
[12] COL, p. 37

of the most prominent Deists on those matters which Berkeley discussed. The first of these men is Anthony Collins. He was educated at Cambridge, and was an acquaintance, indeed a friend of John Locke. Locke left him a small bequest in his will, and Collins was greatly influenced by Locke's trust in reason and fact. The two corresponded frequently. Collins could see no distinction between the meanings of the phrases "above reason" and "contrary to reason". As one result, he was opposed to the theory that we could know God and truths about God analogically, at least if "analogically" meant what Peter Browne and others meant by it. This point will become important in the next chapter, because in the quarrel between Berkeley and Peter Browne, it seems to me that Berkeley comes out on Collins's side. In his view of free thought, Collins was the archetype of his age:

By Free-Thinking then I mean, The Use of the Understanding, in endeavouring to find out the Meaning of any Proposition whatsoever, in considering the nature of the Evidence for or against it, and in judging of it according to the seeming Force or Weakness of the Evidence.[13]

He thought that without free thought we could not know that God existed and that he was good, wise, powerful, etc. Furthermore, he thought that only free men could realize that God can only require us to use our reason on the materials he has provided.[14] Intermediary priests are not sufficient for this undertaking, because there are some matters that cannot be handled by a deputy, such as an issue in which what I must do is to *believe* something to be true myself, on the basis of knowledge. In such cases, of which religion is obviously one, I must convince myself and believe myself, and thus, I must study and know myself.[15] In order to accomplish these ends, I must, in the case of the Christian religion, study the scriptures, which are a body of testimony supporting certain truths. But testimony cannot be taken simply upon authority; it must meet certain tests before it is acceptable, because it is naturally possible for one man or many men to testify falsely. Thus, the persons who testify must be credible, and the things they testify about must be too. A credible person is one who a) has the means of information, b) is capable of understanding what he is informed of, and c) is honest and disinterested. This raises no great problems, with the possible exception that persons meeting the third criterion may be rarer

[13] Collins, Anthony, *A Discourse of Free-Thinking*, London (1713)) p. 5 (DFT)
[14] DFT, p. 37
[15] DFT, pp. 108-109

than we think. The thing related is credible when a) the words used to relate it stand for known ideas or ones which we can form, b) the words must signify those ideas which they have normally signified in the language of which they are a part, or which the informer says he intends them to signify, or which the informer or relator defines them to signify. Accordingly, whatever is told to us upon testimony must be reasonable, that is, we must be able to apprehend and understand it. For this reason, observations contrary to our perception are not allowed, for example, that five and five are eleven and that the parts are not equal to the whole.[16] This may seem simpleminded, but it is nonetheless important, for

whatever exists which falls not within the compass of our ideas, is nothing to us, nor can we talk or think about it. So much as we perceive of a thing by the mediation of ideas, so much we comprehend, and is agreeable to our reason; and what we do not perceive by the mediation of ideas, may . . . be called *above reason*, as a thing unknown to us, but not as an object of the mind about which we may employ our faculties: and 'tis to things as objects of the mind, that the distinction of above and contrary to reason is apply'd.[17]

If these claims are true about the sources of knowledge, then knowledge of the scriptures presupposes a knowledge of the laws of nature, because those things of which we can have ideas are the things which fall under natural law, and since we are concerned with the moral laws given in scripture, which must be universal and uniform, what we must first do is to ascertain what the laws of nature are, and then see if they admit of "any limitation or no" in any given cases.[18]

One of the conclusions that Collins' study of natural law led him to believe was that determinism was true. However, his determinism is of a strange and unusual sort in the end, akin to Spinoza's view, in that it finds true freedom in the awareness that the limits of human action are determined by the universal plan of God. As he says:

. . . *when I affirm* necessity; *I contend only for what is call'd* moral necessity, *meaning thereby*, that man, who is an intelligent and sensible being, is determin'd by his reason and his senses; *and I deny man to be subject to such necessity, as is in clocks, watches, and such other beings, which for want of* sensation *and* intelligence *are subject to an* absolute, physical, *or* mechanical necessity.[19]

Man is a necessary agent if his behavior is caused, because causes are

[16] Collins, Anthony, *A Vindication of the Divine Attributes*, London, (1710), pp. 6-11 (VD)
[17] VD, p. 22
[18] DFT, p. 12
[19] Collins, Anthony, *A Philosophical Inquiry Concerning Human Liberty*, London (1717) p. iii (PIC)

either necessary causes or no causes at all. If causes are necessary, then every act must have been what it was, and it follows that we cannot act otherwise than we do and have.[20] We are free in the sense that the causes of our moral actions are our own deliberations, rather than some outward impediments, but to say this is not to say that our judgments and actions are not necessary, for everything has a cause, and if causes are necessary then determinism is true.[21]

To support his contentions, he argues on two fronts, namely that the soul is passive, not active, and is thus determined by what it perceives; and secondly, he argues from the meaning of "cause" and the nature of God's creation, showing by a series of *reductio ad absurdams* that unacceptable conclusions follow if we assume that causation is not necessary.

He thinks that the soul is passive in reflection because reflection is the result of past sensations affecting the soul. "Reflection", he says, "is in reality no other than consciousness; which, when 'tis exercized about material objects, is termed sensation; and when on ideas, reflection."[22] If causes are necessary, then the soul is determined in its reflecting by objects and ideas. Similarly, the soul is passive in reasoning and judging, for in the formulation of propositions and the determination of the relations between the ideas of propositions, it is determined by past sensations and reflections, in that the mind or soul cannot assent to the truth of a proposition if the ideas do not correspond, and whether they do or not has nothing to do with the soul.[23] Further, any action following upon a judgment must be determined by that judgment as its cause, just as the perception of objects is the "unavoidable result of the object's affecting the soul," again provided that causes are necessary.[24] This covers every activity of the mind, thinks Collins, for he sees only three of these: (1) perception of ideas, (2) judging of propositions, and (3) doing as we will. But some philosophers have seen a difference between the first two and the last sort of activity, which difference is manifested in the questions "Whether we are at liberty to will, or not to will?", and "Whether we are at liberty to will one or the other of two or more objects?"[25]

The answer to the first question is negative, because:

---

[20] PIC, p. 11
[21] PIC, p. 14
[22] Collins, Anthony, *A Dissertation on Liberty and Necessity*, London (1724), p. 4 (DLN)
[23] DLN, p. 6
[24] DLN, p. 16
[25] PIC, pp. 31 and 37

. . . let an action in a man's power be proposed to him as presently to be done, as for example, to walk; the will to walk, or not to walk, exists immediately.[24]

The answer to the second question is either negative, or that the question is absurd. This is because Collins agrees with Locke when the latter says:

The question, whether a man be at liberty to will which of the two he pleases, motion or rest; carries the absurdity of it . . . manifestly in itself . . . For to ask, whether a man be at liberty to will either motion or rest, speaking or silence, which he pleases? is to ask, whether a man can will what he wills, or be pleased with what he is pleased with? A question that needs no answer.[27]

But if the question be interpreted as to whether or not one can will one of two things when the circumstances are equal, the answer is that no choice at all "can be made under an equality of circumstances" if causes are necessary, for the obvious reason that at one and the same time, two necessary causes cannot produce different effects through the same agent.[28]

Then Collins argues that determinism must be true if two other self-evident claims are true, namely that the universe has a beginning, and that it is not ruled by chance. As he says:

II. A second reason to prove Man a necessary Agent is, because all his actions have a beginning. For whatever has a beginning must have a cause; and every cause is a necessary cause.

If any thing can have a beginning which has no cause, then nothing can produce something. And if nothing can produce something, then the world might have had a beginning without a cause; which is, not only an absurdity commonly charged on Atheists, but is a real absurdity in itself.

Besides, if a cause be not a necessary cause it is no cause at all. For if causes are not necessary causes; then causes are not suited to or are indifferent to effects; and the *Epicurean System* of chance is rendered possible; and this orderly world might have been produced by a disorderly or fortuitous concourse of Atoms: or, which is all one, by no cause at all.[29]

And it is for these reasons that Collins believed the doctrine of free-will to promote atheism.

His handling of one objection against his theory of necessary causation is particularly interesting. The objection is that if he is right, then "2 + 2 = 6" and "Julius Caesar did not die in the Senate" are equally

[26] PIC, pp. 31 and 37
[27] Locke, *Essay*, I.2, C.21, sec. 25
[28] PIC, p. 52
[29] PIC, pp. 57-58

impossible propositions. But we can conceive of Caeser's being murdered elsewhere, though we cannot conceive of the first proposition being true. Thus, causation is not necessary. Collins's reply is that the two are indeed equally false, and that it is as impossible for Caesar to have died elsewhere than for two and two to equal six. Those who hold the opposite, he says, implicitly suppose something that is not justified:

For whoever does conceive his death possible any where else, supposes other circumstances preceding his death than did precede his death.[30]

In short, for Collins it boils down to the question of whether the first cause in the chain was necessary, and if it was, then all the subsequent effects must occur.

Certain people also objected to the theory on the grounds that it makes God the author of evil. Collins's answer to this is an affirmation. Evil as well as good must come from God, as everything must, for if it did not, God could not be perfect. If we could act in ways contrary to the ways we do act, that is, independently of God, then God is not all powerful. But we must understand so-called "evil" within the context of the whole, and not from the viewpoint of a given end or perspective. His final position on determinism is succinctly stated this way:

The Doctrine of the *Necessity of Human Actions* is unattended with all the Absurdities that of *Free Will* labours under, since it is intended to prove no more than what every unprejudiced Man without Argument will assent to. That each Being *Acts* the Part which his Creator brought him on the Stage to perform. What Contradiction more irreconcileable, than that any thing should resist his Will, for whose *Good Pleasure*, and by whose *Power* alone 'twas Created, and in whom All things Live, Move and have their Being, and who is well pleas'd with the Works of his Hands.[31]

But after all of this, Collins comes to a weird conclusion, which if he means it literally, seems either trivially true to me, or makes "power" a very strange notion indeed:

I take man to have a truly valuable liberty . . . He has a power to do as he wills, or pleases.[32]

Mathew Tindal wrote what has been called the "culminating point" of the Deist writings, *Christianity as Old as Creation.* He was educated at Oxford, and was for a time a Roman Catholic, but later rebelled against it. His *Rights of the Christian Church* had the distinction of being

[30] PIC, pp. 104-105
[31] DLN, pp. 22-23
[32] PIC, p. 113

ordered burned by the public hangman in the House of Commons because of high-church antipathy to it. Though a Deist and thus an advocate of the use of reason, his toleration for religious diversity was
limited. He rejected atheism, and the right of the atheist to speak out,
since he thought that atheism was destructive of conscience and that
therefore they could not claim toleration because of conscientious belief.[33] He believed that the Christian religion in fact required men to
conduct an "impartial search" into their religious beliefs, and that the
apostles themselves had urged men to "judge for themselves, to prove
all things."[34] Without trust in our senses and the efficacy of reason, we
are led into absurdities, like those of the Papists, "who will not allow
the senses to be judged in the case of transubstantiation, tho' a matter
directly under their cognizance". Reason and reason alone must be
the judge of whether or not our senses are deceived, and "if no texts
ought to be admitted as a proof in a matter contrary to sense, they
ought, certainly, as little to be admitted in any point contrary to
reason."[35] Thus, revelation must be consistent with the testimony of
the senses and reason, for if it is not and we suppose it to be the will of
God, we will thereby undermine proofs for the existence of God, which
are based upon such testimony.[36]

The sources of knowledge are our ideas, either of sensation or reflection, which provides the basis for our awareness of what happens in
the real world and in ourselves. There are no other sources.[37] It
follows that if we know anything, it comes from either the external or
the internal source, and Tindal thought that this was the sole important
difference between revealed and natural religion. Revealed religion
differs not in substance from natural, but rather in the mode of its
communication, being from the internal source rather than the external. Further, the knowledge of our religion, if it comes from God, must
be the same whether revealed or natural, and it must be unchanging,
for if God gave a religion to man, then it was perfect then, and must be
now, if God is perfect.[38]

With these principles, Tindal sets out in *Christianity as Old as Creation*
to show that: God has given us "an universal law", a "Law of Nature,
or Reason"; that this law is unchanging, perfect, and unchangeable;

[33] COL, p. 35
[34] Tindal, M., *Christianity as Old as the Creation*, London (1730) p. 2 (COC)
[35] COC, p. 179
[36] COC, p. 179
[37] COC, p. 181
[38] COC, p. 3

and that it is the subject of both revelation and natural religion.[39] He believes that there is a "natural light", a "clear and distinct light, that enlightens all men; and which, the moment they attend to it, makes them perceive those eternal truths, which are the foundation of all our knowledge."[40] The natural light of reason enables us to demonstrate that a perfect God exists, and that creatures can neither add to nor detract from his happiness, so that God could have no other motive in providing men with laws to live by than their own good.

If then, a Being infinitely happy in himself, cou'd not command his Creatures any Thing for his own Good; nor an All-wise Being Things to no End or Purpose; nor an All-good Being any Thing but for their Good; it unavoidably follows, nothing can be a Part of the Divine Law, but what tends to promote the common Interest, and mutual Happiness of his rational Creatures; and every Thing that does so must be a Part of it.[41]

This end is discoverable from the "volume of nature" and from a study of ourselves and our relations with others. God has endowed each man with a nature which makes him desire his own good, and since this is a manifestation of God's will, we should do everything to promote our personal well-being. Observation teaches that indulgence of the senses, "irregular passions", "unfriendly affections" and "excess of sensual delights" do not conduce to health of body and mind, and are thus contrary to our well-being and the will of God. Our true interests are therefore served by moderation, which "will conduce most to the exercize of his reason, the health of his body, and the pleasure of his senses, taken and considered together."[42] This much we learn from a study of ourselves. But in examining the relations between ourselves and others, we also find that we cannot subsist alone, "that men can't live without society and mutual assistance; and that God has endowed them with reason, speech, and other faculties, evidently fitted to enable them to assist each other in all matters of life." Men, however, find themselves in many different kinds of circumstances, and in order to serve the common good, we cannot be left to make moral decisions on the basis of the variant particular circumstances. As Tindal says:

In short, considering the Variety of Circumstances Men are under, and these continually changing, as well as being for the most Part unforeseen; 'tis impossible to have Rules laid down by any *External* Revelation for

[39] COC, p. 8
[40] COC, p. 11
[41] COC, p. 14
[42] COC, pp. 16-17

every *particular Case*; and therefore, *there must be some standing Rule*, discoverable by the *Light of Nature*, to direct us in all such Cases.[43]

The moral law read in the "Book of Nature . . . in characters legible by the whole world" is unchangeable. It is this unchangeableness which allows us to distinguish between what is "fit" and "unfit" with regard to morality. And here an evident affinity to Shaftesbury makes itself felt, though at the same time it is interesting to note that Tindal, like Berkeley, places the judgment of fitness in the mind and not the moral sense:

. . . a mind that's attentive can as easily distinguish fit from unfit, as the eye beauty from deformity, or the ear harmony from discord.[44]

Ultimately, Tindal's final court of appeal in moral matters is to this sense of fitness or unfitness, or the realization of it, which he calls "conscience". As he says:

. . . the only Tribunal God has erected here on Earth (distinct from that he has mediately appointed by Men for their mutual Defence) is every Man's own Conscience; which, as it can't but tell him, that God is the Author of all Things, so it must inform him, that whatever he finds himself oblig'd to do by the Circumstances he is in, he is oblig'd by God himself; who has disposed Things in that Order, and plac'd him in those Circumstances.[45]

All of this is discoverable from an examination of the internal and external sources of our knowledge, without appeal to blind faith and obedience. Since this is so, and since we know what the "internal marks of truth are" which validate God's laws, it is in fact contradictory to claim allegiance to the scriptures on the basis of faith alone:

How can we maintain, that the Scripture carries with it all those internal Marks of Truth, which are inseparable from God's Laws; and at the same Time affirm, it requires an implicit Faith, and blind Obedience to all its Dictates? if it does so, how could we have examin'd whether it had those internal Marks? Or how can we say, we can't know without the Scripture, what are the internal Marks of Truth; and at the same Time suppose, we must by our Reason know what are those Marks, before we can tell whether they are to be found in the Scripture?[46]

Tindal thought that "'tis the view with which an action is done, that makes it moral". The same action, done at one time from honesty and

[43] COC, p. 18
[44] COC, pp. 30-31
[45] COC, p. 106
[46] COC, p. 193

at another from a fear of the law, has two different moral values.[47] Of
course, honest differences of opinion over rights and duties sometimes
arise, and for settling clashes such as these, we need magistrates. Here
again, Tindal's limited toleration comes to the fore, because he thinks
that given that religion is in the public interest, and that atheists and
"those who make the notion (of God) useless" by denying God's benevolence or personal interest in us are acting against the public weal,
then the magistrates have the power to punish such disidents, and in so
acting they are obeying the moral law. The magistrates are, in fact,
over the churches, for the latter are quite capable of inculcating doctrines antipathetic to the general well-being, and thus for Tindal the
church does not or should not, constitute an independent power in the
state.[48]

The next and last Deist I am am going to consider in any detail is
John Toland. He was raised as a Roman Catholic, but before he was
16 he had become a protestant. He may have been illegitimate, and he
had a reputation for being indiscrete and tactless, which nonetheless did
not prevent his holding various diplomatic employments and being involved in several intrigues of state. He received a Master of Arts degree
from the University of Edinburgh, and he was also educated at Glas-
gow, Leyden, and Oxford. Dr. Molyneux, Shaftesbury, Locke and the
Queen of Prussia, Sophie Charlotte, were among his friends or acquaint-
ances at one time or another, and he was greatly influenced by Locke
and Spinoza. His *Letters to Serena* were to Sophie Charlotte. Upon the
publication of his *Christianity not Mysterious*, he became instantly infamous, and was ferociously attacked from all quarters, especially by
Bishop Peter Browne, of whom I shall have more to say in the next
chapter. This attack rendered him penniless, and when the furor
reached the point where the book was burned by the grand jury of
Middlesex, he was forced to flee the country, in actual danger of his
life. As one result, he was accused of trying to found his own religious
sect. Being a Deist was not always easy!

Like the other Deists, Toland believed in the primacy of reason over
all else. But more than the others, he was influenced by Spinoza. This is
shown in the second and third of his "axioms" (the first being the
primacy of reason) as they are given by Profesor Heineman: the second
axiom is "All things in the world are one, and one is All in all things".[49]

[47] COC, p. 367
[48] Tindal, M., *The Rights of the Christian Church*, London (1706) pp. 9-11 (RCC)
[49] Heineman, F. H., "John Toland and the Age of Enlightenment", *The Review of English Studies*, vol XX, no. 78, April (1944), p. 145 (H)

Within the one universe, there are an infinite number of other worlds, and motion is relative to the movements of the parts of the whole, while the whole itself does not move. This claim, almost always found in pantheists of the Spinozistic school, is emphasized and personalized in the third axiom, "The Universe is essentially Intellect and Motion", which on the one hand differentiates him from Spinoza because the latter of course held the universe to be essentially intellect and extension, and on the other hand separates him from some of the other Deists, for it leads to his avowal of the immanence of God, who is the soul and moving principle of the universe.[50] The fifth axiom is that "Freedom consists in following reason, that is the law of nature," which hints that he was of the same sort of determinist as was Collins, granting the differences in their metaphysics.

But Toland's most important theories concerned the nature of evidence and the foundations of possible knowledge, and they are to be found for the most part in *Christianity not Mysterious*. Toland was quite blunt about the role of reason *vis à vis* faith in theology:

... we hold that *Reason* is the only Foundation of all Certitude; and that nothing reveal'd, whether as to its *Manner* or *Existence*, is more exempted from its Disquisitions, than the ordinary Phenomena of Nature. Wherefore, we likewise maintain, according to the Title of this Discourse, that *there is nothing in the Gospel contrary to Reason, nor above it; and that no Christian Doctrine can be properly call'd a Mystery.*[51]

The foundations of knowledge are our ideas, by which he meant "the immediate object of the mind when it thinks, or any thought that the mind employs about any thing", and these thoughts or ideas may be representational, for example, the idea of a tree, or they may be some sensation such as heat or cold, smells or tastes, or they may be "meerly intellectual or abstracted thought", for example, the ideas of God, spirits, thinking in general, etc.[52] If we have no ideas of something, then we cannot think about it, much less know it. Further, if we know it only indirectly, through "intermediary ideas", if we cannot show their "constant and necessary agreement or disagreement" with the ideas we seek to know, our knowledge can only be probable. For example, we have an idea of what "inhabited" means and of what "moon" means, but no intermediate idea by which we can connect the two, and thus even if it seemed likely that the moon was inhabited,

[50] H. p. 145
[51] Toland, John, *Christianity Not Mysterious*, London (1720), p. 6 (CNM)
[52] CNM, p. 11

we could never conclude that it certainly was. Toland is concerned to point out that he has no intention of speaking about probable knowledge and in fact, he claims that he "banish(es) all hypotheses from my philosophy". He is concerned to speak about propositions expressing ideas between which there is an evident connection, and only of this kind.[53]

Before this can be done though, it is necessary to take preliminary steps to avoid a prominent confusion. We must distinguish between the "means of information" and the "ground of persuasion". The ground of persuasion is the rule according to which we judge truth, and the means of information are either experience or authority. Experience may be either external (e.g., ideas of sensible objects) or internal (ideas of our mental operations). Authority may be either human or divine, the former also sometimes being called moral certitude.[54] Divine authority is "the manifestation of Truth by Truth itself to whom it is impossible to lie." In short, unless it comes to us by sense or mental experience, or by human or divine revelation, nothing is knowable. But we cannot simply take everything presented to us without examination and on trust. Thus, the rule of truth, the ground of persuasion which justifies our acceptance of a given proposition, is evidence, which consists in "the exact conformity of our ideas or thoughts with their objects, or the things we think upon. For as we have only ideas in us, and not the things themselves, 'tis by those we must form a judgement of these."[55] Ideas being representative, "their evidence naturally consists in the property they have of truly representing their objects."[56] I believe that my idea of a rose is "evident" because it gives me a "true" representation of the flower. The way I know it is true is this:

... because the Rose must contain all the Properties which its Idea exhibits, either *really*, as the Bulk and Form, or *occasionally*, as the Colour, Taste and Smell. And I cannot doubt of this, because the Properties must belong to the exemplary Cause, or to Nothing, or be the Figments of my own Brain: But *Nothing can have no Properties*: and I *cannot make one single Idea at my Pleasure, nor avoid receiving Ideas when Objects work on my Senses*: Therefore I conclude the Properties of the Rose are not the Creatures of my Fancy, but belong to the exemplary Cause, that is, the Object.[57]

[53] CNM, p. 15
[54] CNM, p. 16
[55] CNM, p. 18
[56] CNM, p. 19
[57] CNM, p. 20

In the case of ideas of my own mental operations, these ideas are as certain and unquestionable as is the fact that we exist, and in an obvious Cartesian allusion, he notes that even in doubting our ideas of self, we reaffirm our existence, for "I doubt if I am" entails the positive affirmation of this claim.[58] He does not seem to notice however that we may have *mistaken* concepts of our mental acts, even though they are undoubtedly related to our mental processes in some ways.

One of the major points which Toland is anxious to derive from all of this analysis is that revelation is not a ground of persuasion, but a means of information. Thus, it must meet the test of truth, that is, the rules of evidence, before it can be accepted.[59] What is revealed, by anyone, must therefore be intelligible, and possible. Unintelligible relations are simply that, and cannot be the object of knowledge because in order to believe, deny, approve or affirm any proposition, it must first be intelligible.[60] Since this is so, there can be no mysteries if that means something unintelligible, but true. There may, of course, be mysteries in the sense of a proposition so obscured by other factors that it is not clearly understood, and that is the common acceptation of the term. But if one means "inconceivable" by "mysterious", then there can be no such thing. Toland then says that he will demonstrate that all the "mysteries" of the new testament are mysteries in the first sense, which is the import of the title of his book.

Toland is not saying that we must know the objects of theological truths directly, or that our ideas of these objects must be complete. Indeed, he thinks that we never know the real essence of anything, supernatural or not, but only the nominal essence, and since this is no objection to the knowledge claims we make about the natural world, it is ineffective as an objection to claims of theological knowledge.[61] We have clear ideas of the soul, but we do not know the constitution of that principle of thought, even though our understanding of loving, willing, hoping etc. is surely as clear as our knowledge of bodies.[62] The problem in "solving" mysteries is to clarify the metaphorical and analogical terminology in which they are couched, but it is possible to know *a priori*, as he now thinks he has shown, that under all the metaphors there must lie an intelligible proposition subject to the tests of truth. This even extends to miracles.

[58] CNM, p. 20
[59] CNM, p. 39
[60] CNM, p. 42
[61] CNM, pp. 79-82
[62] CNM, p. 85

No *Miracle* then is contrary to Reason, for the Action must be intelligible, and the Performance of it appear most easy to the *Author of Nature*, who may command all its Principles at his Pleasure. Therefore all those *Miracles* are fictitious, wherein there occur any Contradictions, as that *Christ* was born without opening any Passage out of the *Virgin's* Body; that a Head spoke some Days after it was sever'd from the Body, and the Tongue cut out.[63]

After all this, what has become of faith? In Toland s opinion, there is no such thing if we mean blind faith. In another of his clear-cut statements, he concludes the subject in this way:

. . . some will be apt to say, *Faith* is no longer *Faith* but *Knowledg*. I answer, that if *Knowledg* be taken for a present and imediate View of things, I have no where affirm'd any thing like it, but the contrary in many Places. But if by *Knowledg* be meant understanding what is believ'd, then I stand by it that *Faith* is *Knowledg*.[64]

In spite of his Spinozistic metaphysics then, Toland presents, with Tindal and Collins, a fairly uniform attack on the theory of Christian mysteries, and there is no doubt he would agree with the other two men in holding that natural religion must be identical with revealed, but for the modes of presentation of information. In the cases of all three men, their theological and philosophical requirements for truth seem to be based securely upon the Lockean concept of the correspondence of ideas, and all of them seem to be representationalists in spite of Toland s differing metaphysics. They all seem to have roughly the same classifications of the possible sources of knowledge, and the same tests for truth. In addition, they all share the idea of an active physical cause, though Collins is the strongest of the three in defining a cause as a necessary cause, and inferring determinism from that claim. They were all aware of the central role of metaphorical language in theology, and uniformly insistent upon the central role of reason, though they had varying opinions of the relation between morals and religion All of these characteristics, especially in so far as they are founded in the metaphysical, epistemological and ontological presuppositions of the Deists, will become important in the next chapter, when I consider Berkeley's criticisms of them and the import of these criticisms for his own moral philosophy and my claims about it.

[63] CNM, p. 146
[64] CNM, p. 139

CHAPTER IX

PETER BROWNE, BERKELEY, AND THE DEISTS

Among the best known critics of the Deists was Bishop Peter Browne. He became famous for his attack on Toland's *Christianity not Mysterious*, and he was primarily responsible for the persecution of its author. Interestingly enough, Browne also went to some lengths to criticize Berkeley over the latter's arguments against Browne's theory of analogical argument. The analysis of Berkeley's arguments against Browne and Browne's criticisms of him is interesting, for aside from the inherently intriguing question of analogical argument, the study reveals that Berkeley, in spite of his disagreements with the Deists, held certain principles which leave him rather more on their side than on Browne's over certain key questions. On some issues of course, Berkeley is in major disagreement with the Deists, and these areas of contention are informative for my purposes, because they show how moral and theological principles are for Berkeley deeply embedded in the fabric of his ontology and epistemology. First, I shall discuss Peter Browne, his criticisms of the Deists, and of Berkeley. Then I shall discuss Berkeley's examination of Browne, and his criticisms of the Deists.

1. PETER BROWNE AND ANALOGICAL ARGUMENTS

Peter Browne became the bishop of Cork and Ross in 1710, 13 years after he had written *A Letter in Answer to a Book entitled Christianity not Mysterious*. His two major works were *Things Divine and Supernatural*, in which he attacked Berkeley, and *The Procedure, Extent, and Limits of Human Understanding*. His view of analogy was greatly influenced by Archbishop William King's sermon on predestination, which was published under the tedious title *Divine Predestination and Foreknowledge, Consistent with the Freedom of Man's Will*. The central propositions he was concerned to prove were that there is no direct knowledge of the real nature of the divine attributes, but that in spite of this, we can have knowledge of them which is based upon analogical apprehension of what is revealed. Browne died in 1735.

His major argument against the Deists centered on their fairly frequent assertion that religious truths, or some of them, could only be understood in terms of "figure and metaphor," and their inference (or Browne's) that if this is true, then such claims can have "nothing of reality and solid truth at the bottom." Browne claimed that the Deists thus rejected all use of analogy in religion, and that for them moral principles are only acceptable if "deducible only from the light of reason . . . without the help of . . . Revelation." Thus, he thought that they rejected as sufficient grounds for knowledge everything but "*direct* and *immediate* objects of sense and reason." In Browne's opinion, this theory rested upon a basic misunderstanding of the nature of mysteries. In every mystery, according to him, there is something we do understand, and something we do not, and it is a mystery in respect to both of these. It is a mystery with regard to what we do know or understand, because we could never have come to know the meaning of it "by those powers of knowledge which we are now endu'd with", without aid from revelation. For example, we could presumably never discover unassisted that we will, if we are good Christians, be "chang'd into the likeness of Christ."[2] It is "this part of the mystery" which obliges us in conscience to believe it as an article of faith. The mystery is also mysterious in respect to that which we do not understand, for in fact in some of these cases we *cannot* understand the mystery fully; for example, although we know *that* we will be changed into the likeness of Christ, "it is impossible for us in this life to have any notion of the manner of that change."[3]

In order to understand our knowledge of theological matters, it is essential, thinks Browne, to distinguish among a number of different forms of predication and argument. Among these are Divine Metaphor, Human Metaphor, Divine Analogy, and Human Analogy. In the case of Divine Metaphor, we substitute our direct ideas of sensation and the words expressing them for terms of which we can have no knowledge when they pertain to God or his attributes. For example, we express our belief in the comprehensive wisdom of God by saying

---

[1] Browne, P., *The Procedure, Extent, and Limits of Human Understanding*, London, (1728), p. 38 (PEL)

[2] Browne, P., *A Letter in Answer to a book entitled Christianity Not Mysterious*, Dublin (1697) p. 14 (BL)

[3] BL, p. 15

that his "eyes are in every place", and everyone is familiar with allusions to the "hand of God". The distinguishing feature of Divine Metaphor is that there is no "correspondent reality or resemblance between the things compared."[4] Both human and divine metaphor share this characteristic, that is, they are not based upon the "real natures" of the things compared, but are rather arbitrary and invented. They also agree in that "neither of them are absolutely necessary to a true and real knowledge of the things designed to be expressed or conceived by the substituted ideas", and in that they both presuppose a prior knowledge of what is compared.

They would both be intirely useless, were not those things known otherwise more *immediately* and *directly*, or at least more *exactly before*, after another manner.[5]

Here, however, Browne seems to beg the question in the case of divine metaphor, because the question at issue is whether we *can* know the divine attributes. An example of human metaphor is the illustration of a man's anger by the roughness of the sea.

The two kinds of metaphor differ in these respects: in the case of human metaphor, what is expressed may be as immediately known as the substituted ideas used to illustrate it, whereas in divine metaphor, although the substituted ideas may be directly known, indeed, must be, the ideas supposedly illustrated by them may not be conceived by any direct and immediate idea, conception, or notion.[6]

The fundamental difference between metaphorical comparisons or arguments and those based upon analogy is this: analogy consists in using ideas or conceptions of things directly or immediately known to represent, or in substitution for other things, "whereof we can have no direct or proper idea, or immediate conception or notion at all". But, in these cases there must be "some resemblance, or correspondent reality and proportion" between the idea used to represent, and the thing represented. When the analogy concerns supernatural things, it is called Divine Analogy, as when we use our concept of human wisdom to represent "an inconceivable but correspondent perfection of the Divine Nature." Human Analogy is used to illustrate things of this world, for example, considering animal instinct by analogy with the rational faculty in men.[7] It is worth considering Browne's own summary of the difference between metaphor and analogy:

[4] PEL, p. 106
[5] PEL, p. 106
[6] PEL, p. 107
[7] PEL, p. 107

To sum up the Difference then between Divine Metaphor and Divine Analogy in full. Metaphor expresses only an *Imaginary* Resemblance Correspondency; Analogy conveys the Conception of a *Correspondent Reality* or *Resemblance*. Metaphor is rather an *Allusion*, than a real *Substitution* of Ideas; Analogy a proper Substitution of Notions and Conceptions. Metaphor at best is but the using a very remote and foreign Idea to express something *Already* supposed to be more exactly known; Analogy conveys something correspondent and answerable, which could be *No otherwise* usefully and realy known without it. Metaphor is mostly in Words, and is a Figure of *Speech*; Analogy a *Similis Ratio* or Proportion of *Things*, and an excellent and necessary Method or Means of *Reason* and *Knowledge*. Metaphor uses Ideas of Sensation to express immaterial and heavenly Objects, to which they can bear *No Real* Resemblance or Proportion; Analogy substitutes the Operations of our *Soul*, and Notions mostly formed out of them, to represent Divine Things to which they bear a *Real* tho' *Unknown* Correspondency and Proportion. In short, Metaphor has No real Foundation in the *Nature* of the Things compared; Analogy is founded in the *Very Nature* of the Things on both Sides of the Comparison: And the Correspondency or Resemblance is certainly *Real*, tho' we don't know the exact *Nature*, or *Manner*, or *Degree* of it; at least we may safely presume this from the Truth and Veracity of God, who has thus made his Revelations to Mankind under the Analogical Conceptions and Language of this World.[8]

When scripture makes use of the objects of human knowledge to characterize divine properties having no resemblance to them, we are using a "sort of type(s) and figures(s) of things" whose real nature remains closed to us.[9] This does not mean that what is revealed in a mystery is inconceivable in principle, because mysteries are from God. But *we* may not be able to conceive them in this life "because of the frail and limited condition of our understandings in this life."[10] If a mystery is clearly revealed to us, then we may understand it; but there are four things to be revealed concerning anything we do not know, and we must distinguish between them. They are the existence, essence, and properties of the thing, and the relations it has to other things and ourselves. We can know that a thing exists without knowing its properties or its essence, and in connection with heavenly things, it is precisely the essence and properties of which we are ignorant. Before the time of Christ, according to Browne, we were ignorant of all four factors, but now we know the existence of heavenly things, and their relations to us. It is because the essence and properties of supernatural things remain unknown that we must conceive of them by analogy, but this should

[8] PEL, pp. 141-142
[9] BL, pp. 48-49
[10] BL, p. 101

not seem strange says Browne, because it is the same with material things – we know that they exist, but we are ignorant of their essence. In addition, we have no ideas of mental occurrences or beings, yet we know that they exist.[11] Thus, Browne held the distinction between nominal and real essence, and it is fundamental to his treatment of analogy. For Berkeley, of course, this distinction is without foundation in the case of natural objects and minds. Browne is at pains to point out that although God and his attributes, and other supernatural facts, may thus be known by analogy, and although there is a true resemblance foundational to these analogies, as for example between the power and wisdom of God and our own intellectual capacities, this does *not* mean that we should conceive God's attributes in the same way we conceive our own. For example, we should not conceive of God's power as a power to "change things", even infinitely, if we mean this in the literal sense, nor is his thought simply "infinite thinking". If we did this, we would be in fact concluding that the terms expressing God's attributes are *literally* applicable to ourselves, and vice versa, because we would be assuming that the difference between God and men is one of *degree*, albeit an infinite degree. This is without foundation – God and men are different in kind, and had the Deists realized this, and understood the proper use of analogy, Browne thinks they would have understood that there may be mysteries in religion, revealed in the scriptures, and conceivable in principle, though not wholly conceived by us in fact.[12]

2. BROWNE AND BERKELEY

Browne took considerable pains to attack Berkeley at length in the second part of *Things Divine and Supernatural*. I am going to discuss this attack and Berkeley's disagreements with Browne, before examining Berkeley's relations to the Deists, because it seems to me that if Berkeley is to be consistent with his own principles, manifested in the criticisms of Browne, then he must hold a theory of the place of reason in theological matters that is very similar if not identical to that of the Deists. And if this is true, then Berkeley's own theological definism in moral philosophy is in considerable danger from his own principles. Before going into this however, I wish to show an amazing similarity of views between Berkeley and Browne over the question of abstract

[11] BL, pp. 137-139
[12] PEL, pp. 84-85

general ideas. This is important not only for the speculator in questions of historical philosophy, but because Browne evidently did not realize that Berkeley's remarks upon the subject were part of his attack on the idea-correspondence theory of truth, and the thesis of it which said that all significant words must stand for ideas. From Browne's own remarks on the matter, it seems astonishing that he had not read Berkeley's account closely enough to see that this was the case, but evidently he did not, for many of his criticisms of *Alciphron* turn on just this point, namely, that all words must stand for ideas if they are to be significant. In addition, Browne seems to have failed to see that he was criticizing himself as well when he said this, for as we have seen, he also claimed that we have no ideas of our own minds or those of others, yet he claimed that sentences about them were true or false. I think it worthwhile to quote at length from Browne and leave it to the reader to consult the almost identical passages in Berkeley. *Alciphron* appeared before Browne's book did.

. . . we do not form specific or universal Ideas, or Notions, by collecting all the Powers and Qualities observed in the Particulars of every kind; and then putting them together to make up one Idea or Notion to stand for them all, and which is supposed to be formed by *Abstracting* from all the *Individuals*. But what is quite the reverse, all our specific or universal Ideas and Conceptions are formed thus; the Mind substitutes the Idea or Conception it has already obtained of some one Individual, to stand for and represent all the Individuals of the same Kind, As for instance, when I would form an *Universal* Notion of *Mankind*, I do not first collect all the Powers and Qualities I observe common to all particular Men, and then put them together into one abstract Notion of Mankind, to include all the Individuals: But on the quite contrary, having obtained the clearest *Complex* Notion I can of one individual Man, the Intellect makes that a Representative of all the Men in the World; and thus renders it *General* in its *Signification*. . .[13]

Later on in the same book, he pursues the topic still further:

Another Act of the pure Intellect in relation to the Ideas of Sensation commonly reduced to this head of Judgment is said to be *Abstraction*, which is usually distinguished into two Sorts, and both of them equaly groundless.
1. The first is a *Logical* Abstraction in order to form *General* Ideas; which is thought to be performed by withdrawing the Mind intirely from all the *Individuals*, and then forming one single Idea which shall represent the *Whole* Kind of Species at once; as when we remove our Thoughts intirely from all the Individuals of *Men*, and frame to our selves one general Idea distinct from them all to represent the whole Race . . . Thus the *General abstract Idea of Man*, shall not be of black or white, short or tall, thick or

[13] PEL, p. 123

210 PETER BROWNE, BERKELEY, AND THE DEISTS

slender Man; but shall be *All* these and *None* of them at the *Same* time: The general abstract Idea of a Triangle shall be neither of an *Equilateral*, nor *Equicrural*, nor *Scalenum*; neither *Oblique* nor *Rectangle*, but all and none of these at once. . .
When we say *Mankind*, it expresseth no one *Distinct, Abstract, General* Idea which stands in the Mind for all the Individuals at once; but it signifies the Idea of *One Individual*, which is no otherwise made general, than by our conceiving all the rest of the same Kind *By* that one; so that in truth it is the single Idea of any one Individual which is made to stand for and represent the whole Species. There is no such thing in Nature as any *Universal* realy *Existing*, either to strike upon our Senses, or to be an Object of our Reason; and Consequently there can be no such general abstract Idea in Mind.[14]

The parallel passages in Berkeley, some of them almost identical, are as follows: *First Draft of the Introduction to the Principles of Human Knowledge*, vol. II, Jessop and Luce, pages 123-132; *Introduction to the Principles of Human Knowledge*, sections 9, 10, 12, 13, 15; *Alciphron, or the Minute Philosopher*, Dialogue VII, sections 5-7, in the first and second editions only. In Jessop and Luce, these sections may be found in volume III, Appendix I, pages 331-335.

It seems strange that a man who held to the then standard Lockean view of material substance did not realize the consequences for this theory if the above views are true.

I have already discussed Berkeley's view of arguments from analogy in theology in the fifth chapter. These are the remarks with which Browne disagrees. Berkeley does not think that analogy is what Browne thinks it is, –

metaphore nous laissant étrangers à la chose, – *but rather* selon le sens mathematique, similitude de proportions, en l'èspace, entre nos facultes finies et les facultes infinies.[15]

Proper analogy occurs when we attribute properties to God proportionably. As Berkeley says,

. . . from natural motions, independent of man's will, may be inferred both power and wisdom incomparably greater than that of the human soul . . .[16]

Remembering that "motion" here must be given its Berkeleyan interpretation, the other operative word seems to be "incomparably." This is not the problem of God's existence: that inference is a necessary

[14] PEL, pp. 186-187
[14] PEL, pp. 186-187
[15] Gueroult, M., "Dieu et la grammaire de la nature selon George Berkeley," *Revue de de théologie et de philosophie*, 3 (1953) p. 163
[16] Alc. IV, 4

one from the principle that every passive idea must have a cause, and the truth that no human mind or minds causes them all. Ideas in the world are not signs of God, as one author thinks,[17] because ideas are only signs for other ideas; but because of the necessary relation between cause and effect, they provide grounds for inference to God. Since I know that the nature of the divine cause must be mental or spiritual, there is only one way that I *can* conceive of this cause, namely by analogy with the only mind I know, my own. This is not a metaphorical analogy (eg. the finger of God) for Berkeley, but an analogy in which properties are predicated of God in a proportion of infinitude when compared with man. Thus, we *can* conceive God's attributes, but "without any of that alloy (imperfection) which is found in creatures", and if this is true, then it follows that Browne and others are wrong when they say that men can no more have notions of God's attributes that blind men can of colors. Berkeley thinks that if this were true, all syllogisms brought to prove the being of a God, or any of his attributes, would be four-termed.[18]

But at the same time, Berkeley believed in the necessity for revelation.[19] Part of the reason for his insistence on this was his conviction that the belief in God was not "natural" in the deistic sense, and that therefore revealed and natural religion were not identical. Moreover, what we know through reason and revelation is the effect of God's will, and although our ideas of what God wills may be clear, our idea or notion of what he is is not, and at times Berkeley speaks as though he is very sceptical about having any notion of God at all: I have "some sort of an active thinking image of the deity", but "God is a being of transcendent and unlimited perfections; his nature is therefore incomprehensible to finite spirits."[20] And in at least two other places he is even more pessimistic about understanding mysteries; in *Commentaries* #720, he notes that involved in the holy mysteries are "propositions about things . . . that are altogether above our knowledge out of our reach", and in the 584th entry he notes that ". . .to demonstrate or reason anything about the Trinity is absurd here an implicit Faith becomes us." It would therefore seem that Berkeley finds himself in a dilemma. On the one hand, through his theory of analogy, he admits that we cannot reason about that of which we have no idea or notion,

---

[17] Gueroult, M., "Le Dieu de Berkeley", *Revue de métaphysique et de la morale*, 58 (1953) p. 9
[18] Alc. IV, 22
[19] SE, X, pp. 129-133
[20] DHP, pp. 232-234

but he thinks there (Alciphron IV) that we *can* have a notion of God, or at least of his attributes, and he sometimes equates the two, as when he characterizes arguments about God's existence and his attributes as about "the same thing".[21] But on the other hand, he seems to say that "infinite" and "transcendent" mean what they say, and that we cannot reason about the mysteries. The question is, where does the role of reason come to an end? It seems to me that if Berkeley were to be consistent, he would have to say that although we can know *that* God exists, we can know nothing else about him demonstrably, and also that probable arguments about his attributes are only as good as Berkeley's theory of analogy, which he himself seems to doubt.

Thus, I agree that some of Browne's criticisms of Berkeley are well done, as when he notes that if Berkeley is right, then God's attributes are nothing but "infinite human perfections,"[22] and when he argues that if there is such a thing as an infinite difference in degree, as Berkeley says, then God becomes nothing but a perfect man.[23] Yet if this is not true, then as Browne says, God must be a being different in kind, and he must be "altogether incomprehensible as (he) is in (him)self."[24] Furthermore, I think he is correct when he says that the very concept of a proportion or a ratio between something finite and something infinite borders on the contradictory,[25] at least if we are speaking of things rather than numbers, and perhaps even in the latter case.

But Browne does not see the implications of his own case, as Berkeley did. He remains convinced that we can know God by analogy, using his theory of analogy, but it seems to me that his theory comes close to being self-contradictory itself, as when he asserts that we can know that there is a real ground of resemblance between God and man, yet in the same breath asserts that God's real nature is incomprehensible. Thus he says:

But the Resemblance and Correspondency which is the Ground of Analogy, is not *Imaginary* and *Arbitrary*; but founded in the very *Nature* of the things compared; as when in human Analogy we say, what *Reason* is to Man, that natural *Instinct* is to Brutes. And accordingly when we attribute Knowledge and Wisdom and Goodness to God, we do it by Divine *Analogy*; because it can be undoubtedly proved that there are Perfections in him *Correspondent* and *Similar* to those Properties or Qualities of an human Mind: Which we are under a *Necessity* of applying or transferring to God Analo-

---

[21] Alc. IV, 22
[22] Browne, P., *Things Divine and Supernatural*, London (1733), p. 384 (DS)
[23] DS, p. 407
[24] DS, p. 407
[25] DS, p. 451

gically, for want of any *Direct* or *Immediate* or (in this Author's Language) *Formal* Ideas or Conceptions of those divine Perfections; which are totaly imperceptible and incomprehensible to us, as to their *Real Nature* and *Kind*.[24]

Certainly this *is* a contradictory view if Berkeley's conviction that the real essences of minds cannot be separated from their attributes is true. Furthermore, for this reason, his argument against Berkeley's "four-term syllogism" criticism also seems to me to be unsound.[27] One of Browne's examples of a syllogism he thinks valid, and that Berkeley would no doubt criticize, is this:

If no Being could make itself; then there must have been an eternal Being. But no Being could make itself. Therefore . . .[28]

He argues that this is valid because "being" is taken "in the same *general* acceptation" in both premises, "as including all kinds of beings whatever". But he seems to fail to see that in that event, the argument can equally well prove that the eternal being was a man *or* a God, and that to save it, a premise or premises to the effect that the beings in the major and minor are different in kind would have to be added, thus bringing Berkeley's criticism into force.

Furthermore, Browne does not see the point of Berkeley's acute analysis of sentences and terms which may, at given times, be used as ruling principles without ideas. As he says:

he expresly maintains this dangerous Position directly destructive of all Religion; *That Words may be vital, active, ruling Principles; tho' they have no clear and destinct, or determinate Idea or Conception annexed to them*; Nay, *Tho'* in some Instances *It is as impossible to affix any such Idea to them*, as if they were altogether inarticulate.[29]

Yet ironically, Browne himself would have to agree with Berkeley here, at least in the case of notions of minds and abstract general ideas, which is, again, what Berkeley was attacking. Browne clearly saw the consequences of a purely emotive theory of ethical language:

Men may be affected indeed by affixing to the Word or Signs very *General* and *Indeterminate* and *Obscure*; or very *Mistaken* and *False* Ideas and Conceptions; or such as are very *Different* from those affixed to them by him who uttered or wrote them: But where they have *None* annexed to them or excited by them, they are downright Nonsense; and of no real Influence, Use,

---

[26] DS, pp. 449-450
[27] DS, pp. 482-483
[28] DS, pp. 482-483
[29] DS, p. 377

or *Signification*. But if it were true, as this Author asserts, that Words without any Ideas or Conceptions belonging to them could realy affect and move us; such Emotions would be merely *Mechanical*: At best Men must be affected as mere Animals only;[30]

But the very criticism shows that he was not familiar with, or ignored, many of Berkeley's remarks about the place of reason in ethics, and about the necessity for our being *able* to "cash" our ethical words in ideas or notions, whether literally or metaphorically. He accuses Berkeley of saying that "grace" is significant, "tho, it hath no idea, nor . . . conception, nor complex notion annexed to it,"[31] yet Berkeley is not clear on this point, and his denial is not as specific as Browne makes it appear. I have already discussed the possibility that grace is a relation for Berkeley, and that consequently we either have a notion of it, and not an idea, or we know it metaphorically.

Ultimately then, the Browne-Berkeley controversy points up the uncertainty of Berkeley's own thoughts on the matter of our knowing God and his attributes, as opposed to knowing *that* God exists, and suggests that his acceptance of implicit blind faith in some instances might be understood as an unavoidable conclusion of his own reasoning. This, of course, does not improve Berkeley's standing as a theologian, though it does his philosophical reputation, and it leaves his theological definism, especially those parts of it which rest on probable arguments about God's attributes, on a very shaky footing from the viewpoint of reasoned justification. I think that the soundness of his other arguments relevant to this subject though, especially his unique argument for God's existence, must be judged on independent grounds, namely, upon whether or not Berkeley's immaterialism is sound.

Certainly the general integration of Berkeley's moral philosophy with his ontology and epistemology also plays a role in his arguments with Browne. He would, for example, have argued against any first cause argument which posited motion as a datum in the relationships between natural signs, and he certainly disagreed with the nominal-real essence distinction in the realms of both body and mind, arguing that both of these principles imply the material substance theory, which Browne accepted. Berkeley of course, believed that this theory led to scepticism and atheism, and his stated purpose in the preface and introduction to the *Principles* is to refute both. Thus, the epistemological studies in the beginning of that book, and which extend throughout his

[30] DS, p. 536
[31] DS, p. 536

works from the *Commentaries* through the *Principles* to *Siris*, cannot be divorced from his moral and theological goals, for that was their purpose – the establishment of theism and the defense of Christianity as essential to the morality of men. The relevance of the relations between his moral philosophy and the rest of his system becomes more evident in his criticisms of the Deists.

3. BERKELEY VERSUS THE DEISTS

I think that the simplest way to study Berkeley's disagreements with the Deists is to list the positions commonly held by many Deists, and then show why Berkeley disagreed with these claims, and what we can learn about his moral philosophy from the criticisms. Commonly then, though not in every case, the Deists held the following beliefs:

1. For every word, there must be a corresponding idea, if the word is to be significant.

2. Natural and revealed religion are essentially identical, so that what is taught in the scriptures and the "Book of Nature" must be the same.

3. Blind faith is irrational and unjustified, since to be true, the scriptures must meet the requirements, internal and external, of truth, in which case faith is unnecessary.

4. Our ideas are representative, and the intuitive knowledge of their correspondence with the real is the ultimate test of the truth of a proposition, or, in the case of propositions affirming a connection between two or more ideas, both of which themselves correspond to their causes, the test involves in addition an intuitive awareness of the relation between the ideas themselves.

5. Not knowing the essence of God is no bar to theological knowledge, since we don't know the real essence of physical objects either.

6. Probability is not a sufficient ground for theological knowledge claims.

7. Faith is knowledge.

8. Maxims inculcated by education are suspect.

In addition to these general claims, the following specific ones by particular Deists were criticized by Berkeley:

Anthony Collins held: 1. The soul is passive in perception, thought and willing; 2. all causes are necessary causes, and there are necessary causes in the natural world which act upon us. 3. Free-will is not necessary to explain the origin of moral evil, and in fact God is the source of good as well as evil.

John Toland, more explicitly than the others, affirmed a theory of active material substance, though the others more or less agreed with the Lockean version of the substance theory, while Toland was influenced by Spinoza.

Mathew Tindal argued that God was not an arbitrary being, and that therefore we could know that his will was constant and immutable. But in all other respects in his actual writings in normative ethics, he is in remarkable agreement with Berkeley, and the reader may verify this by looking again at chapter eight.

I have already examined Berkeley's replies to many of these remarks. Thus, chapter six deals with his rebuttal of the first point, and argues persuasively for the complexity of the uses of language in ethics, while maintaining Berkeley's position as a cognitivist. It remains here only to emphasize that Berkeley's analysis of the uses of language in ethics cannot be divorced from his epistemology nor from his ontology, for he believed that even in the case of signs which do stand for ideas, the ideas themselves were not representative of anything, and the truth of the propositions containing the signs did not depend upon a correspondance between the signs and the ideas, as in the "Melampus is an animal" example.

His reply to the second point is related to what he says in the first dialogue of *Alciphron* about the meaning of the word "natural". For the Deists, natural knowledge must be universal, original, and the same in all nations and climes.[32] But as Berkeley notes, the knowledge of God does not meet these requirements, though we can learn about God's wishes from nature, as well as about some characteristics of his being. Since natural and revealed religion are therefore dissimilar, we do not know their truths in the same *way*, and revelation is necessary even if theoretically the truths so revealed are in principle knowable by the light of reason alone. This is probably why Berkeley was willing to admit at least verbal demonstration in natural religion, but not in the case of such matters as the Trinity, because we may have ideas and notions corresponding to the terms of propositions about natural religion, but not about the subjects of mysteries such as the Trinity, except in an incomplete and metaphorical way.[33] What is natural for Berkeley is the Language of the Author of Nature, though of course it

---

[32] Alc. I, 14
[33] PC, 584, 586, 719-123, and Jessop's remarks on these entries.

is "original" with God, not man. The point here is that the natural language is the foundation for probable arguments about God's attributes, which arguments provide sufficient grounds for faith. But that probability is irrelevant when we are concerned with such matters as the Trinity and other mysteries. Even here however, one must keep in mind Berkeley's own scepticism about the possibility of extensive theological knowledge.

The third and fourth points should be taken together, because the correspondence of ideas to reality is one of the Deists' tests for truth, and obviously Berkeley would reject it, because for him ideas *are* reality. Perceiving the "connexion or disagreement between ideas"[34] could mean only one of two things for Berkeley. Either it refers to the knowledge of sign-to-thing-signified relationships, or it is the recognition that one idea is of the same sort as another. In either case, correspondence with something that is *not* an idea is not involved, and for Berkeley, is impossible, for ideas only resemble other ideas. The scriptures do not need to meet this test, any more than any other body of propositions does, and the justification for the redundancy of faith which is based upon the claim that they must meet it therefore fails. Moreover in the case of spiritual entities, of which God is one, we have no ideas in any event, just notions. For this reason, some of the truths of scripture are not irrational, but *non*-rational, and if faith is concerned with the non-rational, it is unjustifiable to accuse it of being irrational for failing to meet the tests of rational arguments. Furthermore, the representative theory of perception, upon which the idea-correspondence theory is based, is itself based upon the material substance theory, and if the latter theory is mistaken, then the other two are as well.

The falsity of the material substance theory is also relevant to the fifth claim, for although Berkeley sometimes seems to agree that we do not know the essence of God, he would certainly disagree with the claim that this is no bar to our knowledge of truths about him because the same is true of our knowledge of objects. Berkeley holds that we *do* know the essence of objects, and repudiates the nominal-real essence distinction because it rests on the material substance theory, and the mistaken distinction between primary and secondary qualities. Moreover, I have given some reasons in the last few chapters to believe that he would also repudiate the claim that some sort of nominal-real essence distinction is applicable to mental entities, for such a claim seems enmeshed in the confusion that a mind is some "thing" separate morf

[34] Alc. VII, 3; Locke, *Essay*, IV, i, 2

the activities of willing, loving, hating etc. which Berkeley clearly believes to be false if it involves a reification of minds. For Berkeley, I
believe that the assertion that we do not know the essence of God boils
down to the claim that we know little of his attributes, and that what
we do know of them is based upon analogical arguments.

This brings me to the sixth and seventh points, which are crucial for
Berkeley, for the only *demonstrative* knowledge we have in theological
matters for Berkeley is the knowledge *that* God exists, and if there is no
probable knowledge, then that is all we can know. His position here is
unequivocal:

Let any Man shew me a Demonstration not verbal that does not depend
either on some false principle or at best on some principle of Nature which
is ye effect of God's will and we know not how soon it may be changed.[35]

The relevance of this claim to the question of probable knowledge is
this: if demonstration is not merely verbal, and it is possible to demonstrate about natural things, religiously material or not, then two
other principles must be true: a) causes must be necessary and active in
the real world, and/or b) God must act uniformly, and we must know
that he does. But according to Berkeley, there are no causes at all in the
natural world, where the phrase "natural world" refers to the world of
sense, and one can confirm this by an examination of presented data,
which contain no motion. If there are no causes in this world, then
there are no necessary causes. But if it be replied that the *mental* causes
of ideas are necessary, then two other rebuttals are used. The first is
Berkeley's arguments against determinism in any form, which I have
already discussed in chapter three, and in the event that the claim be
that God is the necessary causal agent, Berkeley's reply is that this is
inconsistent with the omnipotence of God, and that even if it were true,
we could not know it, and thus demonstrations based upon this assumption are in fact only probable arguments. For Berkeley, therefore,
probable arguments in theology are sufficient for the excellent reason
that they are the best we can do. The pragmatic Berkeley was not
above adopting the Pascal-James wager in the face of the uncertainty
in which we live about the future, temporal and eternal:

Whatever effect brutal passion may have on some or thoughtlessness &
stupidity on others yet I believe there are none amongst us that do not at
least think it as probable the Gospel may be true as false. Sure I am no man
can say he has two to one odds on the contrary side. But if life & immortality

---

[35] PC, 734

are at stake we should play our part with fear & trembling tho 'twere an hundred to one but we are cheated in the end. Nay if there be any the least prospect of our winning so noble a prize. & that there is some: none, the beastliest libertine or most besotted Atheist, can deny.[36]

Of course, this theory of probability, when extended to theological propositions, depends upon Berkeley's view of analogy, and as I have shown, he himself has doubts about that. But leaving the difficulties for the moment, he thinks that if there is as much reason to suppose that the benefits of grace derive from God, as there is to suppose that the benefits of natural laws derive from God, then we should trust the one as much as we do the other.[37] And Berkeley did think that this analogy between the benefits of grace and those of nature had some foundation, but the foundation seems to presuppose his other arguments for utilitarianism and the immortality of the soul. As he says:

There is some analogy between the methods of grace and the ordinary course of nature. Providence hath made provision for our welbeing both in this life and in that which is to come: but a supine indolence and neglect on our part will equally deprive us of both these advantages.

As in the one case if we neglect to sow the corn and to spin the flax and wool; we are left to perish with cold and hunger: so in the other if we neglect to perform our part by faith and good works, notwithstanding all the schemes of providence to save us we shall be irrecoverably lost.[38]

Though this is not a good argument, it is clear that Berkeley's reply to the sixth point would be that if probability is not a sufficient ground for faith, then nothing is, and his reply to the seventh would be that if faith is knowledge then it must be probable knowledge. But of course, he did not think that faith was knowledge. And it is clear that the difficulties with the theory of analogical argument, upon which probable arguments from the natural language rest, all remain.[39] Finally, his instrumentalist view of "truth" must be kept in mind.

The eighth point is one of Berkeley's favorite targets. He thinks that liberty and truth are not in themselves of cardinal value, but only as means to a further end, human happiness, and that the free-thinkers use these valuable means on occasion to destroy precisely that end. Further, they in fact use liberty and truth to promote just the opposite beliefs, as is seen from their arguments in favor of determinism.[40]

[36] SE, I, p. 12
[37] Alc. VI, 31
[38] SE, VI, p. 91
[39] For an interesting summary of these, see *NSBP*, Chapter VIII, pp. 108-109
[40] SE, IX, p. 215

Secondly, it proves nothing about the truth or falsity of a proposition to show that it was taught to children when they were not old enough to understand its justification.[41] Such a belief would indeed entail certain absurd conclusions in other fields:

Certainly, if a notion may be concluded false because it was early imbibed, or because it is with most men an object of belief rather than of knowledge, one may by the same reasoning conclude several propositions of Euclid to be false. A simple apprehension of conclusions as taken in themselves, without the deductions of science, is what falls to the share of mankind in general.[42]

Practically speaking, even if these notions are not fully understood by the bulk of society, the cessation of instruction in them is simply asking society to create "so many monsters, utterly unfit for human society."[43] Finally, in so far as such theological and moral truths are based upon probable knowledge, all his criticisms of the Deists' claims for demonstrative knowledge in these matters would also come to bear.

So far as the particular theories mentioned in connection with particular Deists are concerned, it is possible to consider all of Collins' maxims together, because Berkeley's criticisms of them are all closely related. Berkeley's final position on the psychology of the mind is to be found in the 712th, 713th, and 714th entries in the *Commentaries*. There he notes that the soul is active, perceiving, willing, and judging, but that the will and the understanding are not separate entities, being rather simply aspects, activities, of the same substance, where we are to take such words as "substance" with the same attitude of wariness as Berkeley recommends for the word "thing" when used in the context of the analysis of mind. We are reminded that acts of will differ only in their effects,[44] and that because of the inactive nature of ideas, effects can cause nothing, whether an effect in my mind, or an effect in the natural chain of things. Thus, the will, which is free and spontaneous, cannot be determined by causal agents in the natural world,[45] and one mind can effect another only with the concurrence of God. Morality consists in willing, and our moral conduct is not determined by the non-existent causes of nature, nor by my ideas of moral actions, because there are no such ideas. Nor is it determined by indifference, as Locke had believed.[46] Sin consists in "the internal deviation of the

[41] D. p. 203
[42] D. p. 205
[43] D. p. 204
[44] PC, 854
[45] PC, 611-669
[46] PC, 158, 159, 160, and Correspondence with Johnson.

will from the laws of reason and religion,"[47] and thus God is not the author of evil. Without free will therefore, it *is* impossible to explain the origin of evil, as opposed to Collins' view. All of these arguments of course depend ultimately upon Berkeley's arguments against determinism, which are directly aimed against Collins. Those arguments in turn depend upon the principles of analysis first broached systematically in the *Principles*, and thus one of the two great principles of morality which Berkeley enunciated, Free-will, depends upon these fundamental epistemological and ontological axioms. The first four chapters also show, I think, that the support for the second great principle, the being of God, also depends upon these axioms. Thus, Berkeley's moral philosophy cannot be divorced from his systematic treatment of other philosophical topics.

Berkeley's major disagreement with John Toland, in addition to those held by Toland as well as the other Deists which I have examined, would have concerned the issue of material substance and a substance which, in Toland's view, was indistinguishable from intellect. Berkeley's replies to this assertion would be similar to the ones he used against Locke and the material-substance theorists of the Aristotelian tradition; there is no evidence for some sort of "general" mind, only for particular ones; there are no grounds for an inference to it based upon our sense-knowledge, and none based upon grounds of reason; the natural world is passive, but mind is active; it has no explanatory power; even if it were true, we could not know that it was. Thus, it is useless. If the theory is false, then so is the determinism entailed by it.

He would have disagreed with Mathew Tindal over the latter's substance theory. Moreover, since Tindal's major thesis was that natural and revealed religion are identical, but for the means by which they are communicated to us, Berkeley's criticisms of this theory would also apply to him, as would his criticisms of the representative theory of perception, the theory that the world of nature contains active necessary causes, and the criticisms of determinism and scepticism. His defense of God's freedom would apply to Tindal's claim that God is not an arbitrary being, and that we can be sure that the causes in nature must be as they are, that is, necessary.

Yet in spite of all these fundamental differences between Berkeley and Tindal, the similarity in the actual statements of their normative theories, both utilitarian in tone, is really remarkable, and Berkeley is

[47] DHP, p. 237

much closer to him in this respect than to any other figure among his contemporaries.

Certainly it is now clear that the criticisms Berkeley offers of the various Deists, and of Mandeville and Shaftesbury, are both essential to a knowledge of his moral philosophy, normative and meta-ethical, and that those criticisms are part and parcel of his non-ethical philosophy. Perhaps it is a mistake to use the word "non-ethical", for Berkeley was through and through a theist, and as I have repeated many times already, his purpose in writing philosophy in the first place was to establish Christian theism, which he thought inseparable from morals. In the conclusion, I shall try to tie all these threads together.

CHAPTER X

CONCLUSION

During the course of the research for this book, I was often asked by friends just what I was working on. When I told them that I was studying the moral philosophy of George Berkeley, the standard reaction was an expression of surprise that Berkeley had a moral philosophy at all. Throughout the previous chapters I have tried to show that he indeed did have such a philosophy, and often I have mentioned the sort of evidence I believe would be sufficient to prove this claim. That sort of evidence is simple: if Berkeley discussed the range of problems thought to constitute moral philosophy, and if his conclusions together form a series of possible answers to the questions raised by these problems, then it would seem that he had a moral philosophy. In this brief concluding chapter, I should like to outline what problems are thought to constitute moral philosophy, and to summarize Berkeley's answers to the questions raised.

I. MORAL PHILOSOPHY

Moral philosophy in the Western Tradition is at least as old as Socrates, and one would think that in the centuries that have since passed, most of the problems he raised would have been solved. Alas, such is not the case. We are still wondering what "good" means, and how we can justify our moral principles. Indeed, we are still wondering about just what those moral principles are. But at least that period of Greek ethics beginning with Socrates and ending with Aristotle outlined some of the difficulties involved in the study of moral behavior, moral rules, and moral justification. In addition to the problem of the meaning of "good", the issue of the relation between private and public good was raised, achieving as one result the magnificent analysis of the political community presented in both the *Republic* of Plato and the *Nicomachean Ethics* of Aristotle. Both Plato and Aristotle, as well as Socrates, also discussed the question of whether or not pleasure was the only intrinsic good, and at least Socrates and Aristotle attempted to discover that fundamental ethical principle from which all others could be derived. All three of these men also realized the essential *practical* nature of ethics; they believed that the study of ethics should teach men how to *act*, and not just make them aware of the intricacies of the problems associated with moral philosophy. It was for this reason that they concentrated in that peculiar Greek way upon the *functions* proper to men and the arts and skills necessary to fulfill those functions. Probably because of this emphasis upon end-serving activity, they also realized the difference between that which is valuable as a means to something else, and that which is valuable in and for itself. Finally, Aristotle in particular realized that there were problems with the logic of moral reasoning, and he set out to solve them in his discussions of the "practical syllogism".

By the end of the first centuries of what is formally considered as the western philosophical tradition, the basic problems of moral philosophy had therefore already been outlined: the meanings of moral terms, the structure of moral reasoning, the search for first principles, the nature of public and private good and their relations, the justification of principles, the relation of moral reasoning to activity, etc. Subsequent history has refined the approaches to the problems, and defined the issues themselves in more detail, but with few exceptions it has not greatly expanded the list of types of problems *per se*.

One of the exceptions, however, was introduced with the spread of Christianity, and the attempts to justify it philosophically. The addition was the claim that God's will is the source of ethical standards, and the complementary effort to justify the view that what human reason discovers as the set of ethical standards is, under the proper conditions, identical with that which God wills. With the advent of this type of theory, theology became the "Queen of the sciences", the means whereby philosophy could be related to revealed religious truth, which in turn became the touchstone against which philosophical truths were tested. Ethics became the study of the codes of conduct which, if followed, would lead to eternal happiness in the hereafter, provided that the moral agent was a faithful believer. In the eyes of Paul and Augustine this world became valuable only as a means for ultimate communion with God and the saints.

Augustine, as everyone knows, was primarily influenced by the philosophical tradition of the Neo-platonists, particularly as exemplified in the philosophy of Plotinus, with its overtones of mysticism and transcendentalism. With the increasing availability in Europe of some of the works of Aristotle, thanks to the work of the Arabic and Jewish translators, a new influence, a profound one, was felt in Christian ethics, theology and philosophy. It received its most careful defense and formulation in the writings of Thomas Acquinas, and its crowning jewel was the concept of moral natural law. Acquinas did not invent the concept, for it is present in the writings of Aristotle, and the idea that nature is rational is to be found in the Stoics as well, particularly in their identification of human reason with the Logos. What Acquinas did do was to perform a synthesis of Christianity with Aristotelianism, especially emphasizing the teleological view of the natural world. According to this theory,

... the promptings of informed reason and moral conscience represent an inherent tendency in the nature of man, and conformity to this nature fulfills both the cosmic plan of the Creator and the direct commands of God revealed in the Scriptures. Natural law is the divine law as discovered by reason, and therefore then precepts of the church and the Bible, and scientific knowledge of the universal needs and tendencies of man, provide complementary rather than competing standards of ethical knowledge.[1]

This theory is obviously objective, for according to it, the truth of moral judgments may be established independently of any maker of such judgments, and it does not depend upon any particular epoch or culture. It is also clearly theological, for it places the source of moral obligation in God's will, and as a consequence, normative ethics became merely the attempt to discover what it is that God wills, followed by the encouragement to do it. In practice, ethics became coextensive with what the church said was right, meet, fitting and just. What we would now call meta-ethics became the attempt to resolve such problems as the seeming incompatibility of free will with predestination as necessitated by God's foreknowledge.

For several centuries after Acquinas, this view of morality prevailed, and outside of modern philosophical circles, it is not a grievous exageration to say that it still does. But within philosophy, the first large crack in the wall came with the advent of Thomas Hobbes' *Leviathan*. If Hobbes was right, then atheists could be moral men, and convention is

---

[1] *The Encyclopedia of Philosophy*, Paul Edwards, editor, The Macmillan Company and the Free Press, New York (1967), volume three, "Ethics, History of", and "Ethics, Problems of", pp. 81-113, and 117-133, respectively.

the source of morality. It was mistakenly supposed by Hobbes' critics that he was an atheist, perhaps because his philosophy entails that there is no moral objective order in the universe, and that determinism is true. Moreover, the phrase "natural law" loses its theological and teleological connotations, and becomes merely a name for the expedient agreements men make for their own self-preservation. The source of moral obligation hence passes from God to the hands of a sovereign given his power by men for their own selfish interests, and all moral imperatives become maxims of prudence.

The reaction to Hobbes was immediate and violent, and Berkeley must be considered within the tradition of this reaction. Some thinkers argued that moral principles are self-evident, having the same certainty and immutability as the laws of mathematics. Both Henry More and Ralph Cudworth, as well as several other Cambridge Platonists, held this view. Still others, such as Richard Cumberland, attempted to defend a version of the older natural law theory, and to show how all moral laws are derivable from one, or a few, basic principles which are such natural laws. In Cumberland's case, the fundamental principle or natural law was that all actions ought to promote the general good, which is an obvious forerunner of the utility principle later made famous by Bentham and Mill. But in spite of the rather rabid defense which was the reaction to Hobbes' supposed antireligious bias, some permanent trends had been established, the most important of which was the future emphasis upon reason rather than faith, clarity rather than mystery, and debate rather than acquiescence. This new attitude toward ethics and religion as a proper field for inquiry and argument found its most famous manifestation in the Age of Enlightenment in the 17th and 18th centuries, and in the British Isles, the Deists were the embodiment of the spirit of the age.

George Berkeley was both a part of this age and this spirit, and in some respects, an opponent of it. As a Christian clergyman, he was an apologist for the role of faith and the relevance of religious mysteries, and as such he stood opposed to the attitude of the majority of freethinkers. But as an heir of the Renaissance and the Protestant revolt, and as a man acutely aware of the importance of the rise of science, he was committed to the defense of belief by reason and opposed to the dogmatic tradition of continental theology. We must therefore also consider his views in the light of this basic tension, as well as in the context of his historical time.

2. DID BERKELEY HAVE A MORAL PHILOSOPHY?

I do not pretend that I have adequately traced the history of moral philosophy in the first section, nor even that I have set out all of the problems with which the subject deals. My intention was merely to set Berkeley within the tradition of moral philosophers by indicating in a general way the trends of thought relevant to ethics which led from Socrates to Berkeley's contemporaries. But some may say that this is putting the cart before the horse, since I ought to show that Berkeley said something about the relevant issues before placing him in a tradition. What then were those relevant issues? They were then largely what they are today, as I hinted when I said that the problems of moral philosophy had been outlined for the most part by the end of the Greek period. What is right, and what is wrong? For what should we blame and praise moral agents? What is worthwhile or valuable in itself, as opposed to that which is valuable only as a means? What is the source of moral obligation? Are moral judgments objectively justifiable? If they are, how do we justify them, that is, how do we make moral decisions? How may we solve apparent conflicts in our ethical judgments? What is the nature of the relation between moral rules? What are the definitions of moral terms such as "good", "right", etc.? How do we *know* what is right and what is wrong, what is good and what is bad? What does it mean to say that moral judgments are true, or false? Is there a difference between private and public good? If there are moral rules, are there basic moral principles, and if so, what are they and how do we discover them? Is man free?

One could of course continue to add to this list, mainly by specifying issues involved in the attempts to solve these problems in more detail. But surely a philosopher who proposed answers to all or most of these problems must be admitted into the class of moral philosophers, especially if his contentions form a systematic approach, and more especially if his views on these subjects are logically related to those parts of his general philosophy already acknowledged to constitute a system.

George Berkeley begins by telling us that the two great principles of morality are the "Being of a God and the Freedom of Man." His arguments supporting both of these principles are alike rooted in his ontology and epistemology: there are no efficient causes in the natural world, and the only active things are minds. Those things in the natural world which we are accustomed to believe are related as cause to effect are in reality related as signs are to what they signify. Everything has a cause however, and causes must be active. Hence, only minds are causes, and if the natural world is caused, its cause must be a mind. No human mind can be the cause of all that exists, and so there is a cosmic mind – God. *Esse est Percipi* for all things but minds, and it is *percipere* for them. These conclusions are reached as a result of an empirical and logical analysis of the possible components of our knowledge, and they also provide the foundation for the second of the two basic principles, the freedom of man. The antithesis of the doctrine of free will is determinism, which tells us that all of our actions are caused, either by forces in the physical world, or by our previous judgments. But if Berkeley is correct, there are no physical causes, and the argument that we cannot be free because our judgments, and hence our moral actions, are determined by previous judgments ends in an infinite regress. Our immediate experience of our own mental lives further assures us that we are free to act spontaneously for that which we desire.

We act for that which we believe to be in our own interests, and hence:

Self-love being a principle of all others the most universal, and the most deeply engraven in our hearts, it is natural for us to regard things as they are fitted to augment or impair our own happiness; and accordingly we denominate them good or evil. Our judgement is ever employed in distinguishing between these two, and it is the whole business of our lives to endeavour, by a proper application of our faculties, to procure the one and avoid the other.[2]

Yet, just exactly what those things are which augment our happiness is not immediately evident, for "experience informs us that present good is afterwards oft attended with a greater evil". To understand what *true* happiness is, and hence to understand what those things are that are *truly* denominated "good" and "evil", we must attend the book of nature, of which God is the author. Nature is really a language, and this is proven by comparing the properties of artificial languages with those of the natural world. When this is done, it becomes evident that the relations between signs and what they signify in nature are identical with the relations between words and other artificial signs and what they signify. So also is the ground of our expectations and our inferences the same in both cases. And because this is so, then since we can infer some of the properties of human agents from their language, for example, their moral properties and some of the ends for

---

[2] PO, 5

which they act, we ought to be able to infer some of the properties of
the author of the natural language from what is "said" in that language. If one does this, then one will discover that God is good, wise,
provident, benevolent, and that he enables us to best serve our own
happiness by following the laws of nature. Rational agents act for
ends, for purposes, and God's purpose is our happiness; not the happiness of one individual or group of individuals, but the happiness of
the most people, in all times and in all places. If happiness is what is
good, then what is right is action leading to it, and hence to discover
what is right we need only discover the kind of conduct which leads to
happiness. Happiness, in the temporal world, is bodily and mental
health, and moderate conduct, governed by reason, is the sort of
action which leads to these states. Hence, it is right conduct. If we
follow the laws of nature which are moral laws, we will discover that
some pleasures are valuable only as means, and others as ends in themselves.[3] We will see that there is a scale of pleasures, ascending in
value from the pleasures of the sense, through those of imagination, to
those of intellect; we will notice a difference between "fantastical"
and "natural" pleasures, the latter alone being rational; we will see
that to achieve the maximum individual happiness, the maximum
social or public happiness must be served first, because in the moral as
in the natural world, the happiness of the whole depends upon that of
its parts, and *vice versa*.[4] Hence, Berkeley in effect argues against both
egoistic hedonism and also against any hedonistic doctrine that would
claim sensual pleasure to be the *summum bonum*.

There are different kinds of moral rules, namely, the positive and the
negative sort. The former allow a role for circumstances in the making
of moral decisions, such as postponing positive action until advantageous times. The latter allow no exceptions whatsoever, and in any case
of conflict between the two sorts of rules, the negative always takes
precedence over the positive. Any kind of moral rule, positive or negative, must be based upon the sort of regularity in the natural language which may be used for the voluntary direction of rational agents.
It is because the instinct for self-preservation is not a regularity of this
sort, but rather merely a universally occurring phenomenon, that it is
not a moral natural law. One can also tell that it is not such a law by
considering that if it were, then we should be permitted to do anything
whatsoever to preserve our own lives, which is absurd because it would

[3] TV, 127-130
[4] TVVE, 42; Price, pp. 33-46

conflict with the principle that the general happiness for all times and places is the moral end of man, and the desire of God.

If it is true that God desires the general happiness of mankind as the moral end and so informs us through the natural language, then in what way does he enjoin us to make moral decisions? There are two ways he could do this: either by making judgments in each particular case as to whether or not a particular action would serve the general good, or by observing certain rules known to have a general tendency to accomplish this end. The first way is impractical for many reasons. Any man could justify any action simply by saying that he believed it would serve the general good at the time he made his decision; it is difficult, perhaps impossible, to calculate the consequences of any particular action for the long run; making decisions in this way would result in a chaos of conflicting moral judgments, and this would violate the utility principle itself; and such decisions, were they possible, would simply take up too much time to be of practical use in everyday affairs. For all of these reasons, the second method for making moral decisions must be the one God enjoins upon us, if he desires the general happiness: to act according to rules known to be justified in the long run by the principle that action in accordance with them serves the general well-being. It follows that we ought to justify our particular moral decisions simply by reference to rules which are themselves justified by the utility principle, without calculating the effects of our actions in each case. "Our practice must always be shaped by the rule", the rule itself having been "framed with respect to the good of mankind."[5]

Moral responsibility presupposes free will, and hence, as I have noted, determinism must be wrong. But the reasons which tell us that determinism is mistaken also have consequences for Berkeley's moral philosophy, the most notable of which is that moral acts are all of them mental acts, distinguishable from the observer's viewpoint only by their effects in the world of perception. Consequences therefore provide us with the criteria for judging an agent's motive, and guilt consists only in the will. A virtuous man is one who wills in a certain way, as it were, and right acts are those acts of will such that they are intended to produce consequences in accordance with the moral law. Because there are no necessary connections in the natural world, and because the production of consequences by a mind in that world is dependent upon the all-powerful will of God, it is possible for us to misjudge a

[5] PO, 31

man's intentions if the consequences he intended do not follow upon his act of will.

Because death and deterioration are phenomena which occur in the natural world subject to natural law, and because the soul is a logically different sort of entity than that found in the world of nature, the soul is naturally immortal. Our interests are therefore not coextensive with the duration of our bodies, and if we are to act reasonably, we must serve our long term well-being. Hence, eternal, not temporal happiness is the ultimate moral end. Moral dessert arises solely from obedience to God's moral laws in the temporal order, but the justice of God presupposes that such dessert will not go unrewarded. This is why rewards and punishments, both here and in the hereafter, are efficacious in promoting our happiness, given that we act for our own interests, as we do.

Ultimately then, goodness is that happiness which we will have in eternal life. We do not know exactly what this happiness is, since the happiness we are acquainted with is that of this life, bodily and mental health. But it is not necessary that we be directly acquainted with it in order to know that it is desirable, any more than it is necessary for a man promised a good thing by a trustworthy person upon the performance of some task to have a distinct idea of that good thing present to his mind before he can believe that it is in his interests to do the job. Language has many uses in addition to the communication of ideas, and among these are the exciting to action or passion, the raising of emotion, etc. To say this however is not to say that non-cognitivism is true for Berkeley, for it is not. There is moral knowledge. It is only because of a mistaken theory of meaning and truth that one might become convinced that moral judgments are neither true nor false, a theory of truth which also led to the mistaken theory of abstract general ideas, and which encouraged atheism and scepticism. Given that this theory is mistaken, these other beliefs based upon it do not follow.

There is more than one kind of evidence that the general wellbeing for all times and places is the moral end desired by God. Our instincts to social cooperation testify to this fact, as does the analogy between these instincts and the forces of attraction and repulsion which preserves the very structure of the universe. These instincts, this "natural conscience", lead us in the direction of right conduct. But they are not, as some have claimed, even for Berkeley, sufficient for claiming that a given course of action is right or wrong. They suggest, but they do not enable us to infer. For knowledge, reason is always required, and conscience is not absolute in the sense that it permits transgression of the moral law.

All of this, and much more, was actually stated by George Berkeley. In addition, much may be drawn from what he said in the way of inferences, and together, what was said and what may be inferred surely constitute a series of answers to most of the questions which I have suggested as the subject matter of moral philosophy. It also seems evident to me that all of his thoughts on moral philosophy are systematically related to his general ontology and epistemology, for they all are derivable from his dualistic theory of the components of reality, his thesis that causality in the natural world is really a relation between signs and what they signify, and his analysis of mind. There is clear proof that he attempted to make some of his arguments about morals and theology consistent with his general philosophy, as we saw when we discussed his theory of how the account of creation in Genesis could be true. Together, these facts imply not only that he had a moral philosophy, but that it may, without exageration, be called a *system* of moral philosophy.

3. SOME GENERAL CRITICISMS

Throughout this book, I have emphasized the exposition of Berkeley's views rather than my criticisms of it. I do not intend at this point to undertake any detailed evaluation of his theory, but I should like to finish the book with a few general comments about some of its inadequacies.

"Inadequacies" is exactly the right word, for most of the "mistakes" in what he says are not so much overt errors as they are essential subjects left undiscussed, problems realized but not solved, or implications following from his premises which he would not want to accept. For some of these inadequacies he can be blamed no more than is any author of whom we say "I wish he had finished his work", for after all, Berkeley did not complete the second part of the *Principles*, and we know not what he might have contributed toward the resolution of such issues as the problem of the nature of the resemblance between our ideas and God's Ideas. Nonetheless, the problems are there.

The first of them concerns his argument from analogy, used to show that nature is a divine language. As with all arguments from analogy, it depends upon a comparison between resembling properties. The trouble is, there certainly seem to be many more *dis*similarities between artificial languages and the natural world than there are resemblances. It is not necessary to list these dissimilarities here, for anyone may see them for himself. The most important relevant dissimilarities seem to me to concern the functions which artificial languages serve, and which nature does not, and I think these are the most important dissimilarities because Berkeley's definition of nature as a language depends upon the central contention that the scope and variety of the natural language is as wide, if not wider, than that of normal languages. But does nature express emotion? Do the signs in nature *describe* what they signify? Are there names in the natural language? Are there natural meta-languages? But if nature is not really a language, then the ontological foundation of Berkeley's moral philosophy will not stand examination. This is because his argument that God has morally relevant properties depends upon this premise, as do many of the properties of natural moral laws.

Not unrelated to this difficulty is the problem of the relation between God's Ideas and what we perceive. God causes the natural world which we perceive as the world of ideas of sense. The existence of this world consists in God's (or some mind's) perceiving it. Yet the perception of God, Berkeley admits, is not the perception of man. There is no "sensory" in God, and though he knows pain, he does not suffer it. Hence what it means to say that God knows, or perceives, is not what it means to say the same thing of human minds. How then do we justify the claim that the objects of our knowledge of the natural world are the objects of God's perception? In order to justify this view, which it is essential to do if we are to take natural laws as indicative of God's desires for us, and as evidence that he has certain properties or attributes, we must claim at the least that there is a relation of resemblance between our ideas and God's. At times, as in the philosophical correspondence with Johnson, Berkeley realizes this problem, and goes so far as to refer to the Ideas in the mind of God as "archetypes" of our ideas.[6] Yet in the same place he objects to the theory that there are archetypes or universals existing independently of any perception of them, and nowhere does he give an analysis of how Ideas and ideas may resemble one another if there are no universals.

There is also the problem of meaning and truth in Berkeley's overall philosophical system. Words such as "cognitivist" and "emotivist" were obviously unknown to Berkeley, but the issue of whether or not

---

[6] S., 289; *Philosophical Correspondence with Johnson*, p. 274; DHP, p. 254; *Philosophical Correspondence with Johnson*, p. 292

he was an objectivist may still be raised legitimately, as may the question of the nature of truth, if he claims that moral judgments are either true or false. I have argued that he is a cognitivist and an objectivist, and I have argued that his theory of truth is largely pragmatic or instrumentalist in character. But Berkeley is not clear enough about these matters. Even in the *Principles of Human Knowledge*, and the other major *loci* of his attack on abstract general ideas, he does not directly raise the issue of what it means to say that a sentence is true. Usually, his remarks are couched in terms of the *function* of the sentence, as in the cases of Melampus and the die, and in his remarks about mathematics. Without an adequate theory of meaning and truth of course, his moral philosophy, as with his epistemology and ontology, is incomplete and inadequate.

I discussed the problem of arguments from analogy in Berkeley's philosophy in the ninth chapter, and there I mentioned Berkeley's own reservation about the possibility of our knowing God or his attributes, and his scepticism about using arguments from analogy to prove conclusions about supernatural things. There Berkeley points out how many syllogisms brought to prove something about God commit the fallacy of equivocation, resulting, in a syllogism, in the fallacy of four terms. Yet Berkeley may himself be involved in just this sort of fallacy in his "necessary" argument for the existence of God. In the fourth chapter, I argued that this inference depended, in Berkeley's eyes, upon the definitions of minds and ideas, and given that no idea exists unperceived, then it would be a contradiction to assert that there is an object unperceived by human minds, which exists, and which is not perceived by any other mind. I certainly think that this is indeed what Berkeley thought, but I do not think that his argument is valid. The reason is simple: if one argues from the premises that 1. the *esse* of ideas is *percipi* and 2. there are some ideas not perceived at all times by human minds, to the conclusion that there must be a cosmic mind that perceives them at least when no human minds do, then clearly "perceives" must mean the same thing in the conclusion as it does in the premises. But by Berkeley's own admission, it does not. Hence, the argument is invalid.

Secondly, this "necessary" argument rests upon an implicit but unexpressed analogy, which is that God's mind (or simply, God) stands to ideas as do human minds. But I have already given reasons why one might doubt this, and indeed some evidence for believing that Berkeley doubted it too. Now if the necessary argument therefore fails, and if, for the reasons I have given in connection with the criticisms of the "language of nature" thesis, the probable argument is also inadequate, then Berkeley has failed in his attempt to justify one of the two basic principles of morality in his system, the being of a God. He has also failed of course, for the same reasons, to accomplish the purposes for which he indulged in the entire philosophical enterprise – the refutation of scepticism and the defense of theism – for his arguments against the former depend upon his justification of the latter.

In addition to these remarks, one might point out that certain difficulties obtain against any theory which maintains, as does Berkeley's, that the objective criterion of moral value is what God commands us to do. Such theories must hold one of three possible positions. They must argue that what makes an action right is the fact that God commands it, or that the rightness of the action itself is what makes God command us to do it or act in accordance with a rule enjoining this sort of conduct, or, finally, they must claim that the fact that God commands it, and the fact that the action is right, are identical, in short, that "X (an action) is right" and "X (an action) is commanded by God" are identical in meaning. Berkeley's position is closest to the last of these positions. For him, good is that which is present to the mind of God, which happens (contingently) to be the general happiness of the most men for all places and times, and what is right is that which leads to this end. What courses of conduct lead to the general happiness is also contingent upon the will of God, and we learn what these are through our study of the natural language, which teaches us that if we follow certain moral rules, which have a general tendency to achieve the general well-being, we will serve the good.

But each of these three sorts of theory has a particular difficulty associated with it. The first theory implies that God could command whatever he wished to command, for example, genocide, and this would surely make God immoral. It will not do to argue that God would not wish this because he is good, for this would beg the question. The second theory leaves God's omnipotence subject to question, for it makes what is right or wrong independent of God's will, a position which Berkeley would not accept. The third position implies that an atheist could not possibly be a moral man, for to deny God exists, and hence to deny that he wills anything, is to deny that there is goodness. Berkeley, I think, would have held the latter position, though strangely, for a bishop of the times, he never says that an atheist cannot act morally. Of course, it is clear that a philosopher-theologian who held the third position need *not* argue against the atheist this way, for the most he need maintain is that the atheist, though acting in accordance with the moral laws of God, and intending to achieve the good, is simply in error about the source of moral obligation. Unless one equates error with evil, which Berkeley does not do, he is not then obliged to argue that the atheist is immoral, though he might wish to claim that he is ammoral or non-moral. Nonetheless, even this position is suspect for obvious reasons, and in Berkeley's particular case, the arguments against his case for the existence and goodness of God add fuel to the fire.

In addition to these criticisms, I have argued, principally in the fourth section of chapter four, that Berkeley's solution to the problems of natural evil is inadequate and may be refuted by the criticisms of Hume, and I there stated that I thought his defense of the efficacy of reward and punishment, especially when considered in the context of an eternal life, was unjustified. It is questionable whether any crime a man could commit, no matter how heinous, is deserving of *eternal torture*, and there seems to be no *prima facie* evidence which indicates that because suffering and right conduct sometimes (too often!) go together here, all will be requited in the hereafter. For all of these reasons, and many which for lack of space must remain unexamined, it is clear to me that the moral philosophy, the ontology and the epistemology of George Berkeley are inadequate.

What then is the value in considering it in the first place? One answer to this riddle, or rather, to this conceptually mistaken question, might be the one I often give to those students who question the value of a philosophical technique which destroys theories, but which does not provide the true answers to the questions the mistaken theory sought to answer. The reply is that it is surely as much an advance in knowledge to learn that a convincing theory is mistaken as it is to learn that another theory is at least partially correct. One is then spared the necessity of making the same mistakes, though alas, they seem to be made again and again. But more importantly, there is a style, an aura, an ineffable quality, about a system of philosophy which is well done, even if mistaken, that one does not find in mediocre works. If anyone has that quality, then George Berkeley has. It is not simply his philosophical system, and the acuteness of his arguments against such people as John Locke, the Deists, and Shaftesbury, which is attractive: it is also his command of that marvelous tool, the English language. It is not without reason that the *Dictionary of National Biography* classifies his *Three Dialogues Between Hylas and Philonous* as the greatest example of writing in the dialogue form after Plato. In Berkeley's case, this is a fortunate bonus, for as we all know, he is in addition an innovator, a devastating critic, and a forerunner of modern analytic techniques. Of such a mind, the effort involved in investigating everything he ever said, and the implications of it, is certainly deserving.

This book has been an attempt to expose George Berkeley's thoughts about the subjects which constitute moral philosophy.

BIBLIOGRAPHY

THE MORAL PHILOSOPHY OF GEORGE BERKELEY

NOTE: The reader will notice a series of capital letters after almost all of the entries in the bibliography. These letters are the short form for the entry to which reference is made in all footnotes, but for the first reference to the work. No abbreviations are given for the works of Berkeley, since these are given in the Preface.

I – BOOKS

Albee, Ernest, *A History of English Utilitarianism*, George Allen and Unwin, London (1901), chapter 4. – HEU

Armstrong, D. M., *Berkeley's Theory of Vision*, Melbourne University Press, Victoria (1960).

Berkeley, George, "Draft Introduction to the Principles of Human Knowledge", MS #3, the "Chapman" MS, Trinity College Library, Dublin. Jessop refers to it as "MS.D.5.17" in his bibliography, listed below.

Berkeley, George Monck, Literary Relics, London (1789) – MON

Blount, Charles, *The Oracles of Reason*, London (1693) – OR

Bracken, Harry M., The Early Reception of Berkeley's Immaterialism, Martinus Nijhoff, The Hague (1965) – ERI

Browne, Peter, *A Letter in Answer to a Book entitled Christianity Not Mysterious*, Dublin (1697) – BL

— *Things Divine and Supernatural*, London (1733) – DS

— *The Procedure, Extent, and Limits of Human Understanding*, London (1728) – PEL

Catalogue of Manuscripts, Books and Berkeleiana exhibited in the Library of Trinity College, Dublin, on the occasion of the Commemoration of the Bicentenary of the Death of George Berkeley, July 7-12, 1953.

Collins, Anthony, *A Discourse of Free-Thinking*, London (1713) – DFT

— *A Discourse of the Grounds and Reasons of the Christian Religion*, London (1724) – DCR

— *A Dissertation on Liberty and Necessity*, London (1724) – DLN

— *A Philosophical Inquiry Concerning Human Liberty*, London (1717) – PIC

— *A Vindication of the Divine Attributes*, London (1710) – VD

— *The Scheme of Literal Prophecy Considered*, London (1727) – SLP

Fowler, Thomas, *Shaftesbury and Hutcheson*, London (1882) – STF

Fraser, A. C., *The Philosophy of Theism*, Edinburgh (1896) – PT

Gildon, C., *Miscellaneous Works of Charles Blount*, London (1695) – MW

Hervey, Lord John, *Some Remarks on the Minute Philosopher*, London, (1732) – HR

Jessop, T. E., *A Bibliography of George Berkeley*, Oxford University Press, London (1934).

— *George Berkeley*, London: Longmans, Green (published for the British Council) (1959).

—, and Luce, A. A. *The Works of George Berkeley, Bishop of Cloyne*, Thomas Nelson and Sons Ltd., London (1949), nine volumes. A lasting contribution to scholarship, and deservedly the definitive edition of Berkeley's works.

King, William, *De Origine Mali*, (Law's translation) London (1732); two volumes – DOM

— *Divine Predestination and Foreknowledge, Consistent with the Freedom of Man's Will*, Dublin (1709) – PFC

Locke, John, *An Essay Concerning Human Understanding*, London (1690) – E

Lovejoy, A. O., *Essays in the History of Ideas*, Johns Hopkins, Baltimore (1948) – AOL

Lovejoy, A. O., *The Great Chain of Being*, Harvard University Press, Cambridge (1936) – GCB

Luce, A. A., *Berkeley and Malebranche: A Study in the Origins of Berkeley's Thought*, Oxford University Press, New York (1934)

— *Berkeley's Immaterialism*, Nelson, Edinburgh (1946)

— *The Life of George Berkeley*, Bishop of Cloyne, Nelson, Edinburgh (1949)

— *Sense without Matter, or Direct Perception*, Nelson, Edinburgh (1954)

Mackintosh, Sir James, *Miscellaneous Works*, Edinburgh (1846).

Mandeville, Bernard de, *A Letter to Dion*, contained in *Vice and Luxury, Public Mischiefs*: or, *Remarks on a Book Entitled The Fable of the Bees*, by John Dennis, London (1724) RFB. Also in this volume: "Some Remarks on the Minute Philosopher", by an anonymous author. – LD

— *The Fable of the Bees, or Private Vices, Public Benefits*, London (1714). – FB

Phillips, G., *Remarks Upon Two Pamphlets*, etc., London (1730) – R

Richards, I. A., and Ogden, C. K., *The Meaning of Meaning*, Harcourt Brace and Co., New York (1923), – TMM

Sillem, Edward A., *George Berkeley and the Proofs for the Existence Of God*, Longmans, Green and Co., London (1957) – PEG

Steinkraus, W. E. (editor), *New Studies in Berkeley's Philosophy*, Holt, Reinhart and Winston, New York (1966) – NSBP

Stroll, Avrum P., *The Emotive Theory of Ethics*, Berkeley and Los Angeles, University of California Press (1954) – ETE

Shaftesbury, Third Earl of (Anthony Ashley Cooper), *Characteristics of Men, Manners, Opinions, Times*, London (1737-1738) – CH. See also the modern edition edited by J. M. Robertson, with introduction by Stanley Grean, The Bobbs-Merrill Co., Inc., The Library of Liberal Arts, New York, (1964). The first edition of the *Characteristics* was published in 1711.

Tindal, Mathew, *Christianity as Old as the Creation*, London (1730) – COC

— *The Rights of the Christian Church*, London (1706) – RCC

Toland, Junius Janus (John), *A Collection of Several Pieces*, London (1726), two volumes – CS
— *Christianity Not Mysterious*, London (1702). In the same volume: *The Life and Writings of John Toland*, by a friend, London. (1722) – CNM
— *Letters to Serena*, London (1704) – LTS
Turbayne, Colin Murray, *The Myth of Metaphor*, Yale University Press, New Haven (1962) – MM
— editions of Berkeley's *The Principles of Human Knowledge*, *Three Dialogues Between Hylas and Philonous*, and *Works on Vision*, all with the Bobbs-Merrill Co., The Library of Liberal Arts, Indianapolis and New York, Published in 1957, 1965, and 1963 respectively. There is no clearer exposition of Berkeley's language of nature metaphor than in the introductions to these works, and in Turbayne's *The Myth of Metaphor*.
Woolston, Thomas, *A Series of Pamphlets*, London (1727-1830)

ARTICLES

Aiken, H. D., "The Fate of Philosophy in the Twentieth Century", *The Kenyon Review*, Spring, (1962). – FP
Ardley, J. W. R., "Berkeley's Philosophy of Nature", *The University of Aukland Bulletin*, 63, (1962)
Broad, Charlie Dunbar, "Berkeley's Theory of Morals", *Revue Internationale de Philosophie*, (1953) – BBTM
Colie, R., "Spinoza and the Early English Deists", *Journal of the History of Ideas*, XX, (1959) – COL
Conroy, Graham P., "Berkeley on Moral Demonstration", *Journal of the History of Ideas*, Vol. XXII, no. 2, (1961) – BMD
Denard, V. W., "Berkeley's Theological Utilitarianism", *Actes du XIe congrès internationale de philosophie*, 13, (1953) – BTU
Gueroult, M., "Dieu et la grammaire de la nature selon George Berkeley", *Revue de théologie et de philosophie*, 3, (1953) – GN
— "Le Dieu de Berkeley", *Revue de métaphysique et de la morale*, 58, (1953) – LDB
Heinemann, F. H., "John Toland and the Age of Enlightenment", *The Review of English Studies*, vol. XX, no. 78, April, (1944). – H
Johnston, G. A., "The Development of Berkeley's Ethical Theory", *Philosophical Review*, New York, vol. 24, np. 369, pp. 419-430. – DB
Jessop, T. E., "Berkeley and the Contemporary Physics", *Revue Internationale de Philosophie*, 7, (1953)
— "Malebranche and Berkeley", *Revue Internationale de Philosophie*, 1, 1, (1947).
— Review of: E. A. Sillem, "Berkeley and the Proofs for the Existence of God," *Journal of Theological Studies*, 9, (1958).
Luce, A. A., "Berkeley and the Proofs for the Existence of God", *Theology Journal*, (1957), pp. 780-784 – BPE
— "Berkeley's Existence in the Mind", *Mind*, 50, (1941).
— "Developments within Berkeley's Commonplace Book", *Mind*, 49, (1940)
— "The Unity of Berkeley's Philosophy", *Mind*, 46, (1937)

Leroy, Andre-Louis, "La Pensée religieuse de Berkeley et sa philosophie", *Revue philosophique de la France et de l'étrangère*, 62 (1947) – PRB

Mabbot, J. D., "The Place of God in Berkeley's Philosophy", *Journal of Philosophical Studies*, London, vol. 6, pp. 18-29. – PGB

Olscamp, Paul J., "Wittgenstein's Refutation of Scepticism", *Philosophy and Phenomenological Research*, vol. XXVI, no. 2, (December, 1965)

— "The Philosophical Importance of C. M. Turbayne's 'The Myth of Metaphor' ", *International Philosophical Quarterly*, vol. VI. no. 1, (March, 1966)

— "Some Suggestions about the Moral Philosophy of George Berkeley", *Journal of the History of Philosophy*, April, (1968)

Orange, H. W., "Berkeley as a Moral Philosopher", *Mind*, vol. 15 (old series) pp. 514-523. – BM

Popper, K. R., "A note on Berkeley as Precursor of Mach", *British Journal of the Philosophy of Science*, 4, (1953-54)

Turbayne, Colin Murray, and Ware, Robert, "A Bibliography of George Berkeley, 1933-1962", *The Journal of Philosophy*, vol. LX, no. 4, February, (1963). – BIB

Turbayne, Colin Murray, "Berkeley's Two Concepts of Mind", *Philosophy and Phenomenological Research*, 20, (1959-1960)

— "The Influence of Berkeley's Science on his Metaphysics", *Philosophy and Phenonenological Research*, 16, (1955-1956)

— "Kant's Refutation of Dogmatic Idealism", *Philosophical Quarterly*, 5, 20, (July, 1955)